Activity-Based Models for Cost Management Systems

Activity-Based Models for Cost Management Systems

Ronald J. Lewis

Q

QUORUM BOOKS
Westport, Connecticut • London

Library of Congress Cataloging-in-Publication Data

Lewis, Ronald J.
Activity-based models for cost management systems / Ronald J. Lewis.
p. cm.
Includes bibliographical references and index.
ISBN 0–89930–965–8 (alk. paper)
1. Cost control. 2. Cost accounting. I. Title.
TS165.L48 1995
658.15'52—dc20 94–37876

British Library Cataloguing in Publication Data is available.

Library of Congress Catalog Card Number: 94–37876
ISBN: 0–89930–965–8

First published in 1995

Quorum Books, 88 Post Road West, Westport, CT 06881
An imprint of Greenwood Publishing Group, Inc.

Printed in the United States of America

The paper used in this book complies with the Permanent Paper Standard issued by the National Information Standards Organization (Z39.48–1984).

10 9 8 7 6 5 4

Contents

Exhibits and Tables

EXHIBITS

TABLES

I

Management Accounting Concepts and Systems

1

Concepts and Terminology

This chapter introduces and explains the traditional cost concepts and defines the terms used in American industry by workers and managers in production, engineering, marketing, and accounting activities. The changes brought about by the global competitive market and the technological impact of computers have made it necessary to learn not only traditional terminology but new cost concepts and terms as well. The following chapter will discuss the new developments in managerial accounting brought about by the expansion of domestic industries into a global market environment.

THE ENVIRONMENT

Three major categories of businesses are discussed: manufacturing, merchandising, and service industries. The manufacturing company combines and consumes economic resources to produce a finished product. Merchandising firms, such as wholesalers and retailers, provide the middleman function of getting the manufactured product to the consumer. Service industries provide services instead of manufacturing a product.

Even though there are major differences in the functions performed by manufacturers and by merchandising or service firms, the terms and concepts of managerial accounting apply equally well to all industries. Only the methods and format of presentation may differ. Examples of the industrial groups include:

1. Manufacturers
    a. Mining
    b. Industrial goods
    c. Consumer goods
    d. Construction
2. Marketing
    a. Wholesalers
    b. Retailers

   c. Brokers
   d. Warehousing and transportation
3. Service Industries
   a. Recreation and personal care industries
   b. Health care: hospitals, nursing homes, clinics
   c. Information systems: computers, word processing
   d. Government agencies: federal, state, local

There are important implications to a change in our priorities on managerial accounting. The production-line manufacturing industries are ideal for a highly structured, standardized cost accounting systems approach. The service and marketing industries are not. They require an emphasis on decision-making techniques that are flexible and timely.

Marketing Activities

Marketing includes demand-creating and demand-servicing activities. The demand-creating activities are called promotional and include advertising and selling functions. The demand-servicing activities are called logistics or physical distribution and include all physical movement functions from the production line to the ultimate consumer.

Contemporary cost systems have not yet satisfied the informational requirements of the marketing profession. Marketing managers are continually asking for accounting expense classifications that will augment their decision-making capability. There will continue to be a growing demand for managerial accounting techniques in the field of marketing.

Government Agencies

The role of the federal government has grown enormously since World War II. As evidenced by our taxes, all government agencies, including those at the state and local levels, have become more influential in our lives. There have been occasional attempts at restraint by conservatives, but none has been successful in reversing this long-term trend.

Government agencies are primarily service providers, however, as consumers of military hardware they have been actively involved in cost accounting standards. The Cost Accounting Standards Board established in 1970 and expiring in 1980 was involved in establishing standards for government contracts. A law passed and signed by President Reagan late in 1988 restored the Cost Accounting Standards Board in the executive branch with the exclusive authority to "make, promulgate, amend, and rescind cost accounting standards and interpretations thereof designed to achieve uniformity and consistency in the cost accounting standards governing measurement, assignment, and allocation of costs to contracts with the United States." There is and will continue to be a need for managerial accounting procedures and techniques by government agencies.

Service Industries

The changes taking place in American industry suggest that there may be more emphasis on service industries. These may be the growth industries for the next decade. Emphasis will be on decision making and flexibility rather than rigid systems of cost accumulation. Microcomputers will play an important role in providing immediate information to service industries. The techniques used in managerial cost accounting to analyze and interpret this information will be required to facilitate this shift in our nation's resources.

COST TERMINOLOGY

In managerial accounting, emphasis is not on the measurement, timing, and recording of costs, but on the interpretation and analysis of cost data for decision making. The result is that a wide range of descriptive adjectives has developed in managerial accounting to allow for more precision in the interpretation of the data. Each adjective used with cost gives it a more precise meaning.

In financial accounting, *cost* has been defined as a sacrifice of resources incurred for a future benefit or objective. The resources that are sacrificed are in the form of cash or a cash equivalent, such as payment in kind, or the incurrence of a liability. A future benefit refers to assets such as inventory, machinery, equipment, property, and intangibles. The expenditure for a future benefit (asset) that lasts only during the current period is a cost that is expensed. For example, the cost of office supplies used in the current fiscal period is classified as an expense because it does not have benefits that carry over to future fiscal periods.

A *cost objective* is an activity or product for which the total or unit cost is to be determined. A cost objective may be the product manufactured or the service performed, or it may be a department, a process, or a function, all of which are referred to as *cost centers*. The cost center is the smallest unit for which costs are accumulated for reporting and analytical purposes.

In the next section the cost terms that are used throughout the book are examined. Some of them are defined and explained in this chapter, whereas other terms are described as they occur in the subject matter in later chapters. Following is a summary of the more widely used cost terms separated into groups that have a common connotation:

A. Actual versus estimated costs
   1. Historical (acquisition)
   2. Replacement (current)
   3. Opportunity
   4. Budgeted
B. Traceability to a cost objective
   1. Direct versus indirect
   2. Joint (common)
   3. Controllable versus noncontrollable

C. Variability with respect to an activity base
   1. Variable versus fixed
   2. Mixed (semivariable)

D. Identification as a product cost or an expense
   1. Product versus period
   2. Unexpired versus expired
   3. Prime
   4. Conversion
   5. Nonmanufacturing (administrative and marketing expenses)

E. Relevance to a management decision
   1. Differential (incremental)
   2. Sunk

F. Cost systems with respect to the production process
   1. Job-order
   2. Process

G. Cost systems with respect to the absorption of costs into production
   1. Actual
   2. Normal
   3. Standard
   4. Absorption (full)
   5. Variable (direct)
   6. Activity-based

Actual or Estimated Costs

Historical costs are the actual monetary or monetary equivalent costs that are recorded in the financial records at the time of acquisition. Thus, historical costs are also called *acquisition* or *actual* costs. Generally accepted accounting principles (GAAP) support the general principle of historical costs, but have allowed notable exceptions, such as the valuation of marketable securities, inventories, and long-term investments at other than historical cost.

Replacement costs are the current costs of replacing an asset. They are based on estimates and may be recorded in the financial records only as an exception to the historical cost principle. The reporting of replacement or current costs is required by GAAP for specified public corporations.

Opportunity costs are the benefits of alternatives that must be sacrificed or foregone. Where more than two alternatives are possible, the benefit of the next best alternative is the opportunity cost. The alternative refers to an investment of limited economic resources such as production facilities, machinery, equipment, or vehicles. It may also refer to systems, such as computational or word processing systems, or channels of distribution.

The *cost benefit* refers to the monetary value attributed to an alternative. It is most likely an estimate based on an assumption of future revenues or reduced future expenditures. For example, a building may be used (1) to store product A at an estimated cost savings of $10,000 per year; (2) to assemble product B, which will yield an estimated $18,000 in annual net revenues; or (3) to lease to an outside party for $1,200 per month, less $200 per month in estimated lessor expenses. Note that these monetary values are estimates because they are based on future events. The cost to store product A may be based on the expected future cost, or it may be based merely on an allocation of costs, which is itself an estimate.

The *sacrificed benefit* refers to the next best opportunity that must be given up in order to take advantage of the most beneficial alternative. In the preceding example, the warehouse may be used for only one of the three alternatives at the same time. Each of the other two must be foregone, and the sacrifice must be bona fide. The foregoing of a desired opportunity that is not likely to occur is not a bona fide opportunity cost.

The most beneficial alternative is to assemble product B at a net benefit of $18,000 per year. The opportunity cost is to lease the building to an outside party at a net benefit of $12,000 per year ($1,200 - $200) times 12 months.

Budgeted costs are estimated costs that are used in planning future operations. A budget may be a complete system or one part of a system of estimated costs and expenses.

Traceability to a Cost Objective

Direct versus Indirect Costs

The directness of a cost is the basis for identifying its traceability to a cost objective. The cost objective is a product, a department, a process, or a function, each of which can be referred to as a cost center. A *direct* cost can also be referred to as a *separable* cost, as opposed to a common or joint cost.

Using the product as the cost objective, direct labor and direct materials are the only costs that are direct. They are directly associated or traceable to the product itself. All other factory costs are indirectly related to the product. An indirect product cost may, however, be a direct cost in regard to some other cost objective in or out of the factory. For example, the wages of direct labor in Production Department A are a direct cost in regard to the product, whereas, the salary of the supervisor of Production Department A is an indirect cost in regard to the product. But, the supervisor's salary is a direct cost in regard to Production Department A. Materials handling labor is also an indirect cost to the product, but is a direct cost in regard to the warehouse or storage function.

Joint Costs (Also Called Common Costs)

Some basic ingredients, such as wheat and crude oil, can be formed into a variety of final products. Wheat is used in making flour, bread, and pastries, and crude oil is further processed into gasoline, kerosene, or plastics. Those costs that are incurred for the basic ingredients which may be further processed, are called joint costs. Joint costs can also include direct labor and factory overhead.

Controllable versus Noncontrollable

Controllability is the authority of a specific manager to either incur or avoid incurring a cost. The manager who controls a cost or a group of costs is responsible for them; the higher up in the management hierarchy, the broader is the range of responsibility. A cost must be traceable to the cost center, which is under the jurisdiction of the specific manager, in order for it to be controlled.

Variability with Respect to an Activity Base

Variable, Fixed and Mixed Costs

Total production costs are generally observed to fluctuate with changes in volume. *Total variable* costs are those that vary directly and in proportion with volume changes. *Total fixed* costs do not change at all in response to volume increases or decreases. *Mixed* costs are made up of both variable and fixed costs. This aspect of costs, their variability (behavior), is such an important characteristic that it merits special attention. A chapter is devoted to a comprehensive treatment of cost variability.

Identification as a Product Cost or an Expense

Product Costs and Period Costs

Costs that are incurred for the purpose of manufacturing a product and that are embodied in the ending inventories of direct materials, work in process, and finished goods are referred to as *product costs*. Product costs are also called *inventoriable costs*. Nonmanufacturing costs that are incurred during a given fiscal period are called *period costs*. Period costs are *expenses*. Examples of period costs are marketing and administrative expenditures that are incurred during the given fiscal period. Office equipment is an asset which becomes an expense in the form of depreciation. A portion of the original cost of the equipment is charged against the revenue of each accounting period as depreciation expense. Other expenses are salary and wages of sales and office personnel, and supplies, utilities, and various other items that are used in administrative or sales offices. Whether they are paid for directly in cash or accruals, they are expenses related to the accounting period, not to the product.

Expired and Unexpired Costs

Unexpired costs are assets; they are product costs that are still contained in the manufacturer's inventories or other assets. As the inventories are sold, the unexpired costs (assets) become expired costs (expenses); that is, they are matched to the revenues of the period as cost of goods sold.

Expired costs can also refer to other assets purchased in prior periods or in the current period. For example, prepaid insurance is an asset (unexpired cost); as time passes a proportionate share of the insurance cost is expensed (expired cost).

Prime Costs

Prime costs include both direct material and direct labor, but exclude factory overhead. The significance of isolating the total direct product costs is that they are the major inputs to the product. They are normally a preponderant portion of the total costs of production.

Conversion Costs

Conversion costs include direct labor and factory overhead. Direct materials are not included in conversion costs. The significance of the term conversion is that it represents the costs of transforming direct materials into units of the finished product. As with prime costs, the conversion costs are a significant portion of total production costs. In those industries where raw materials are relatively inexpensive, and where factory overhead is extensive to accommodate the requirements of the labor force, the conversion costs may exceed prime costs.

Nonmanufacturing Costs

The nonmanufacturing activities in the manufacturing firm include

1. Marketing Activities
    a. Promotional
    b. Physical distribution
2. Administrative Activities (not in the factory)
    a. Executive offices
    b. Accounting, legal, and financial
    c. Engineering and research
    d. Maintenance, security, and housekeeping
    e. Personnel and human resources

The descriptive titles of these activities vary among companies and this list is not all-inclusive. Expenditures for these activities are period costs; that is, they are charged to the current period as expenses. Marketing expenses arise from promotional activities such as selling and advertising and from logistical or physical movement of the product. Administrative expenses include all other nonfactory activities from the president's office to the janitorial services.

Relevance to a Management Decision

Differential Costs (Revenues)

In the process of selection among alternatives there are categories of costs or revenues that are common to both alternatives. Differential costs (revenues) are measured by the difference in the costs (revenues) between the alternatives. Costs that are unique to only one of two possible alternatives are always differential costs. For example, where only one alternative requires an expensive installation, the entire cost is differential. Differential costs (revenues) are also referred to as *incremental costs* (revenues). Incremental costs (revenues) refer specifically to increases in costs (revenues), but for practical purposes, it is appropriate to consider the terms differential and incremental as synonymous.

Sunk Costs

A *sunk cost* is one that has already been incurred, or for which the decision pertaining to its incurrence is absolutely irrevocable. A building purchased ten years ago at a cost of $80,000 and one-half depreciated, has a book value of $40,000. It is presently not in use, but is being considered for the production of a new product line. The original cost (historical cost) of $80,000, the current book value of $40,000, and the depreciation of $4,000 per year are sunk costs. None of these costs is relevant to the decision to produce a line of products.

The reason that the recorded and book values and the depreciation amounts are sunk costs is that they have already been incurred. Depreciation represents the conversion of the capital expenditure into periodic expenses to be charged against revenues. They are not inherently relevant to future decisions. As tax deductible business expenses, however, depreciation may become relevant. The tax effects of depreciation will be considered in capital budgeting decisions.

Although sunk costs are normally considered to have already been incurred, there is another category of costs that should be considered as sunk costs for practical purposes. Those costs that have not yet been incurred, but have been irrevocably and irreversibly committed by management, have the practical characteristics of sunk costs.

For example, a contractual commitment for a future expenditure that involves compliance with a law, the violation of which would result in jail terms for corporate officers, should be considered a sunk cost. Even though it has not already been incurred, the cost commitment is irrevocable and irreversible in a practical business sense.

Perhaps a more graphic example would be the costs of bringing the manned spaceship back to earth after it has been launched. Based on the traditional definition, the costs of the personnel and scientific equipment to bring the spaceship back to earth have not yet been incurred and are thus not sunk costs. It is doubtful, however, that anyone would argue that the commitment to bring the crew back is not irrevocable and irreversible and that these costs are in essence, *sunk*.

Cost Systems with Respect to the Production Process

Job-order costing systems are used by companies whose products or batches of products are treated as individual jobs. *Process* costing systems are used by companies with homogeneous products such as crude oil, chemicals, and grains. Both job-order and process costing systems serve to develop unit costs of production, but because of the inherent differences in the physical characteristics of the products the two methods differ.

Cost Systems with Respect to Absorption of Costs into Production

Actual costing systems absorb actual direct material, actual direct labor, and actual factory overhead into production costs. *Normal* costing systems absorb actual direct materials and actual direct labor, but absorb estimated factory overhead into production costs.

Standard costing systems, widely used by manufacturing companies, absorb standard direct materials, standard direct labor and standard factory overhead into production costs. Standard costs are estimated costs that may have a close relationship with budgeted costs.

Absorption (Full) Costing

GAAP, the formal statement of generally accepted accounting principles, requires that the valuation of inventories by manufacturing firms for external reporting include the full cost, that is, direct materials, direct labor and total factory overhead. This system of product costing is called ***absorption costing or full-absorption costing***. GAAP also requires that for external reporting ***actual*** costs be used except where the estimated costs are not materially different from actual costs.

Direct (Variable) Costing

Direct costing differs from full-absorption costing only in regard to one category of costs, ***fixed factory overhead***. Direct costing includes direct materials, direct labor, and variable overhead in the product costs. Fixed factory overhead is charged directly to the accounting period. Ending inventory, therefore, never includes any fixed overhead. This system of costing has not been approved for external reporting purposes by GAAP, but may be used for internal purposes.

Activity-Based Costing

The purpose of activity-based costing (ABC) systems is to focus on the causes behind indirect costs. It is primarily a system of allocation. Activities rather than traditional departments are emphasized in order to isolate the cost drivers, which are the factors most likely to cause or contribute to the incurrence of costs. ABC systems are designed to be complementary with the technological changes in the factories due to enhanced global competition.

ACCOUNTING STATEMENTS AND COST CLASSIFICATIONS

Presented here are cost classifications and definitions of terms found in the balance sheet and the income statement. The illustrations reveal the inherent differences in accounting for merchandising and manufacturing firms. Government agencies and service industries have unique characteristics that are not included in the illustrations.

Balance Sheet

The merchandising firm has only one inventory account, which represents the merchandise it buys and sells in a finished form. It normally performs none of the manufacturing functions. (In economics, the manufacturing process is called the "creation of form utility." Some wholesalers and retailers may perform assembly functions on a limited basis.)

The manufacturing company has additional inventory accounts such as factory supplies, raw materials, and work-in-process. Its finished goods inventory account is equivalent to the merchandise inventory account of the merchandising firm, which represents only the completed product or products. Other differences in the balance sheet account of the merchandising firm, as compared with the manufacturer are now discussed.

Property, Plant, and Equipment

The manufacturing company has production machinery and vehicles that can be identified separately on the balance sheet. In addition, there are factory buildings, such as assembly plants, warehouses, and other specialized production facilities that are not needed by merchandising firms. These buildings can be shown separately on the balance sheet of the manufacturer.

Intangibles

The retailer or wholesaler is more likely to have a franchise, such as the right to market branded products or to use a nationally advertised name, for example, Simmons Beautyrest mattress or Holiday Inn. Manufacturers are more likely to hold patents, particularly on their manufacturing processes and on the products they manufacture. There are many other possible differences in the merchandise firm and the manufacturer that could be reflected in the balance sheet, however, there are none that merit special attention at this time.

Balance Sheet
December 31, 19X5

Merchandising Firm Assets		Manufacturing Firm Assets	
Cash	$ 200	Cash	$ 200
Accounts receivable	500	Accounts receivable	500
Office supplies	70	Office supplies	70
		Factory supplies	120

		Materials Inventory	130
		Work-in-process Inv.	200
Merchandise inventory	600	*Finished goods* Inv.	150
Prepaid expenses	30	Prepaid expenses	30
Total current assets	$ 1,400	Total current assets	$1,400
PP&E: Equipment	800	PP&E: Equipment	800
		Factory machinery	120
Buildings	500	*Factory buildings*	380
Land	300	Land	300
Total PP&E	$ 1,600	Total PP&E	$ 1,600
Intangibles	80	Intangibles	80
Franchises	120	*Patents*	120
Total Assets	$ 3,200	Total Assets	$ 3,200

Income Statement

The major difference in the income statements of the merchandising firm and the manufacturer is that the purchases account is replaced by the cost of goods manufactured account. Cost of goods manufactured is a summary account on the income statement of the manufacturer and must be supported by a cost of goods manufactured statement. Examples of the formats of the cost of goods manufactured statement and of the income statement follow.

Manufacturing Company
Cost of Goods Manufactured Statement
Period Ended December 31, 19X5

Direct materials and supplies used in production	$ 800	
Direct labor	470	
Factory overhead	500	
Current cost of production		$ 1,770
Add: Beginning work-in-process inventory		430

Deduct: Ending work-in-process inventory		(470)
Cost of goods manufactured		$ 1,730

Comparative Income Statements
Period Ended December 31, 19X5

Merchandising Firm		Manufacturing Firm	
Sales	$ 2,500	Sales	$ 2,500
Cost of Goods Sold:		Cost of Goods Sold:	
Beginning inventory	$ 550	*Beginning finished goods inventory*	$ 120
Add: Purchases	1,750	*Add: Cost of goods mfd.*	1,730
Merchandise available	$ 2,300	Merchandise available	$ 1,850
Less: Ending inventory	600	*Less: Ending finished goods inventory*	150
Cost of goods sold	$ 1,700	Cost of goods sold	$ 1,700
Gross margin	$ 800	Gross margin	$ 800
Expenses:		Expenses:	
Administrative	320	Administrative	320
Marketing	180	Marketing	180
Total expenses	$ 500	Total expenses	$500
Net income	$ 300	Net income	$ 300

Manufacturing Inputs

Direct Materials

A manufacturing firm purchases materials that are consumed in the production process. An inventory of raw materials is kept in a storeroom (or storerooms) along with other necessary supplies. The materials that when consumed become part of the product itself are called *direct materials*. Supplies, lubricants, abrasives, and all other materials that are used in the factory, but that do not become part of the product itself are called *indirect materials*. Indirect materials are classified as *factory overhead*.

Direct Labor

In a manufacturing plant there is a division of labor in accordance with the functions performed. *Direct labor* includes only those production workers who perform operations directly on the product itself. Others, such as foremen, supervisors, and plant engineers, who provide services to keep the factory in operation but do not work directly on the product are called *indirect labor*. Indirect labor is classified as factory overhead.

It is the function performed that determines whether the cost is direct or indirect. The same worker may perform both direct and indirect labor functions. For example, a factory worker may work on the assembly line in the morning and be reassigned to a repair crew in the afternoon. Although union contracts may not allow such dual roles, there are numerous nonunion shops that do. Thus, the morning hours multiplied by the hourly wage rate would be charged as direct labor, whereas the afternoon hours multiplied by the hourly rate would be classified as factory overhead.

However, the benefits of recording such a precise distinction between direct and indirect labor may not justify the cost. Common sense and judgment by the controller dictate the extent of precision used in classifying and recording manufacturing costs.

Cost of Goods Sold

Exhibit 1-1 illustrates the flow of all costs of production into the ending inventory accounts or into cost of goods sold. The production process begins with raw materials (or semimanufactured materials), which laborers transform into a finished product. In this process, the laborers use machinery, materials, supplies, electricity, and other support costs that are classified as factory overhead. The total of all these costs are accumulated in inventory accounts until the finished product is sold. At that point the costs that are accounted for in the *units sold* are shown on the income statement as *cost of goods sold* and are matched against the revenues of the current accounting period in the process of determining net income. The costs accounted for in the ending inventories of finished goods, work-in-process and raw materials are shown in the balance sheet as assets.

Exhibit 1-1
Accounting Model--Cost of Goods Sold

Direct Materials *plus* Direct Labor *plus* Factory Overhead	*equals*	Total Manufacturing Costs
Total Manufacturing Costs *plus* Beginning Work-in-Process Inventory *minus* Ending Work-in-Process Inventory	*equals*	Cost of Goods Manufactured
Cost of Goods Manufactured *plus* Begin. Finished Goods Inventory *minus* Ending Finished Goods Inventory	*equals*	Cost of Goods Sold

Cost of Goods Manufactured

The manufacturing company incurs both costs of manufacturing the product and expenses of operating the business. These are, for convenience, classified as product (factory) costs, administrative expenses, and marketing expenses. To illustrate the way in which these expenditures are treated in the accounting statements, Exhibit 1-2 shows the costs incurred by a manufacturing company for the month of June, 19x5.

Exhibit 1-2
Summary of Manufacturing Costs, Month Ended June 30, 19X5

Inventory Accounts	Beginning Balance	Ending Balance
Materials	$ 1,000	$ 1,100
Work in Process	3,000	2,800
Finished Goods	4,000	4,600

Costs Incurred	Factory	Administrative Expense	Marketing Expense
Direct materials purchased	$ 4,000		
Direct labor	7,900		
Indirect labor	1,600		
Indirect materials	1,400		
Rental of space	1,000	400	300
Power and fuel	800	200	250
Insurance	700	200	200
Depreciation of equipment	500	150	
Supplies	400	150	150
Maintenance and security	200	100	100

In Exhibit 1-2, the costs incurred are separated into factory, administrative, and marketing. Incurrence at the factory implies, for classification purposes, that the expenditure was made for the manufacturing of the product. Incurrence elsewhere indicates that the expenditure will be classified as an expense and will appear on the income statement only.

Exhibit 1-3 shows a detailed cost of goods manufactured statement. All of the costs included in the statement are incurred at the factory. Note that only costs listed in the factory column from Exhibit 1-2 are used to determine the current costs of manufacturing (also referred to as the total manufacturing costs or total factory costs). In addition, the beginning and ending balances of direct materials and work-in-process are needed to determine the amount for direct materials used and the amount for cost of goods manufactured, respectively.

Exhibit 1-3
Cost of Goods Manufactured Statement:
Month Ended June 30, 19X5

Direct materials in beginning inventory	$ 1,000	
Direct materials purchased	4,000	
Direct materials available	$ 5,000	
Less direct materials in ending inventory	(1,100)	
Direct materials used		$ 3,900

Direct labor		7,900
Factory overhead:		
Indirect labor	$1,600	
Indirect materials	1,400	
Rental of space	1,000	
Power and fuel	800	
Factory insurance	700	
Depreciation of equipment	500	
Factory supplies	400	
Maintenance and security	200	
Total factory overhead		6,600
Current costs of manufacturing		$18,400
Add: Work-in-process in beginning inventory		3,000
Subtract: Work-in-process in ending inventory		(2,800)
Cost of goods manufactured		$18,600

Some common factory overhead accounts are included to indicate the nature of the costs that are classified as overhead. A large corporation may have several dozen factory overhead accounts, so this list is not exhaustive. Also, the overhead costs shown are assumed to be actual costs. In later chapters, modifications are made to the treatment of overhead.

When it is observed that all factory costs other than direct materials and direct labor are overhead, it is easy to understand how important and extensive they are. Indirect materials and supplies, indirect labor, supervision, insurance, rent of facilities, depreciation of equipment, leasing of equipment, fuel for heating and cooling, electric power, maintenance, security, housekeeping, landscaping, and an almost endless number of items constitute the costs of operating a manufacturing complex.

In addition to the factory costs there are administrative and marketing expenses. Exhibit 1-4 shows an income statement including some of the more common expenses that are incurred by functions that are not directly related to the factory. Administrative expenses are those traditionally incurred in the executive offices, such as the expenses of the president and of the legal staff; in addition, they include the expenses of the accounting and finance offices, and of engineering and research. If administrative offices occupy the same building as the factory, they must bear their proportionate share of the costs of operating the building and equipment.

Exhibit 1-4
Income Statement
Month Ended June 30, 19X5

Sales			$30,000
Beginning finished goods inventory		$4,000	
Add: Cost of goods manufactured		18,600*	
Goods available for sale		$22,600	
Subtract: Ending finished goods inv		4,600	
Cost of goods sold			18,000
Gross margin			$12,000
Admin. expenses: Executive salaries	$2,000		
Accounting and finance	1,600		
Rent of buildings	400		
Power and fuel	200		
Depreciation of equipment	150		
Insurance and Supplies	250		
Maintenance and security	100		
Total administrative expenses:		$ 4,700	
Marketing exp: Sales commissions	$1,000		
Advertising	800		
Rent of buildings	300		
Power and fuel	250		
Insurance and Supplies	350		
Maintenance and security	100		
Total marketing expenses		$2,800	
Total expenses			7,500
Net income			$4,500

*From cost of goods manufactured statement (Exhibit 1-3).

SUMMARY

Before studying the analytical tools of the management accountant, it is necessary to understand the concepts and know the terms used professionally. This chapter has presented the basic differences between merchandising and manufacturing companies, the categories of costs incurred by and the statements prepared by manufacturers.

The main purpose of this chapter has been to present the traditional concepts and terminology that have been used by several generations of accounting, administrative, and operating personnel, and to define and explain the cost terms that are used throughout the book. Familiarity with the precise definitions of cost terms, such as those used to identify the characteristics of traceability and variability, is an absolute necessity,

Chapter 1 also describes the formats and cost classifications of the balance sheet, the income statement, and the cost of goods manufactured statement, and emphasizes the differences between statements prepared by manufacturing firms and marketing firms.

The emergence of world class competition in American industry has made it impossible to remain static. New concepts of both production processes and of cost analysis techniques have been developed along with new terminology. Total cost management, activity-based costing, and activity-based management are innovative concepts that have emerged in the last decade to answer the demands of global competition. The activity-based costing systems and methods will be examined and described in subsequent chapters.

2

Job-Order Costing for Manufacturing

COSTING SYSTEMS

The subject of costing systems was introduced in Chapter 1. The discussion of cost concepts and terminology pointed out the many variations of the word *cost* and also of *cost systems*. The systems were described as follows:

Cost Systems with Respect to the Production Process	
1. Job-order costing	2. Process costing

Cost Systems with Respect to the Absorption of Costs into Production	
Costing Systems	Costing Approaches
1. Actual	4. Absorption (full)
2. Normal	5. Variable (direct)
3. Standard	6. Activity-based

The subject of this chapter, *job-order costing*, was defined in Chapter 1 as a costing system used by companies whose products, or batches of products, are treated as individual jobs. These companies receive requests for bids from customers that include detailed specifications regarding the product. The specifications are used as a basis for estimating the total cost of completing the job and submitting a bid to the customer. The job shop that receives the order, usually the lowest bidder, begins to work on the job in accordance with the time schedule requested by the customer.

With respect to absorbing costs into production, this chapter uses a *normal costing system*, in which direct material and direct labor are charged to production at *actual*, and factory overhead is assigned to production at an *estimated* (predetermined) rate. This chapter also follows the *absorption* costing approach, which includes all production costs (full costing). The selection of particular costing systems and approaches for adoption is made to assist management in directing the company toward its goals and objectives. Defining the systems being used is like announcing the rules of the game to the managers.

Industries that use a job-order costing system include production machinery and tools, construction, aircraft, industrial equipment, and vehicles. For example, the automobile industry, which is concentrated in the lower Michigan area, is surrounded by numerous tool and die shops. They manufacture production tools, templates, and dies almost exclusively for special orders placed by General Motors, Ford, and Chrysler. The order calls for only one (or a small number of exact units) of a specialized tool that has a relatively large unit cost. This describes a situation that is suited for a job-order costing system. The object of this system is to isolate and record the total costs of each individual job.

Process costing, not included in this chapter, is another cost system with respect to the production process. Industries that have homogeneous products such as grains, chemicals, oil, cement, and other building materials are most likely to use process costing.

JOB-ORDER COSTING

In a job-order system, the major cost components must be traced to the individual job where possible. Raw materials used in the job can be directly traced and recorded on cost records which must be kept accurately and systematically. Similarly, direct labor can be traced to each job. Factory overhead, however, is made up of indirect costs that by definition, are not traceable to a given product or job. We examine each of these three cost components to see how a job-order costing system works in order (1) to present the customer with a reasonable and competitive price quotation, (2) to record the total production costs to be matched against the revenues of the period, and (3) to assist managers in making decisions.

Direct Materials

In Chapter 1, the materials that are part of the product, those at the beginning of the process or those added later, are referred to as direct materials. Direct materials must be traceable to the product. They are requisitioned from the materials storeroom, stores, or whatever name given to the area in which all factory materials and supplies are placed for convenient withdrawal. A *materials requisition* should include the date, a description, item number, quantity, unit cost, and extension. Materials requisitions are usually consecutively numbered and provide for the job number charged and the signature of the requisitioner. Materials requisitions for a specific job are charged to that job by recording the amount of the materials to a *job cost record*, as shown in Exhibit 2-1.

Exhibit 2-1
Illustration of Job-Order Cost Record:
Washmont Manufacturing Company

Job No. 102										
Date begun	Jan. 4, 19X1					Description: Seat TA-500				
Date completed	Jan. 31, 19X1					Batch size: 100				
Direct Material			Direct Labor				Overhead Applied			
Date	Ref	Amount	Date	Ref	Hrs	Amount	Date	Ref	Amt.	
1-4	123	$1,500	1-4	024	200	$3,200	1-31	J-1	$2,500	
1-8	127	2,200	1-16	135	50	800				
		1,300	1-18	167	50	800				
			1-22	231	100	1,600				
			1-31	256	100	1,600				
		$5,000				$8,000			$2,500	
Applied to Job:			Total DLH		500		Total amount		$15,500	

Cost Flow for Material

The company purchases materials and places them in the storeroom. Materials are requisitioned out of the storeroom for a specific job, (DM) or for general factory use (indirect material or supplies). The direct material is recorded to the job cost record of the specific job. Indirect material and supplies requisitioned are recorded as factory overhead (FO).

Cost Flow for Labor

Time cards are used to record the hours worked by factory workers who are paid hourly. The time card is primarily used as a payroll record. In a job-order costing system, it must also be used to record hours spend on each separate job. Total hours paid to the employee must be reconciled with the total time recorded to the jobs. Any difference may be attributed to idle time or general factory overhead.

Cost Flow for Overhead

Other factory salaried and hourly workers, such as maintenance, plant engineering, supervision, and security employees are recorded as factory overhead.

Factory overhead consists of indirect material, indirect labor, and all other operating costs incurred in the factory, such as, factory utilities, insurance, and depreciation. *Actual* factory overhead incurred is recorded in the factory overhead account, but *applied* overhead is recorded to the jobs in process. The discussion that follows explains the system of determining and recording applied overhead.

Applied Overhead and Predetermined Rates

In a job-order costing system, the customer frequently requests bids from more than one supplier. A bid, or total cost estimate of the job, must be submitted by the job shop, and the customer usually accepts the lowest bid that meets the specifications. If the manufacturer, or job shop, bids too high, the job may be lost; if the bid is too low, there will be less profit or even a loss.

It is not difficult to estimate the quantities of direct materials and direct labor to be used in a specific job, but it is very difficult to estimate the factory overhead. Overhead is not traceable to any specific job and, therefore, must be allocated. Allocation could be based on actual factory overhead incurred if there were an assurance that actual costs would be reasonably uniform each month. Instead, there are wide fluctuations in the timing of actual overhead costs. Some overhead is variable, rising and falling with production, and other overhead is fixed, remaining fairly constant each month. There are seasonal variations as well as other influences that cause actual overhead to fluctuate. The customers cannot wait until the end of the year for an accumulation of total actual overhead costs. It is necessary to estimate the total annual factory overhead and apportion it into units that can be charged directly to a specific job.

The method used is to apply overhead based on a *predetermined rate*. The predetermined rate is based on the total annual estimated factory overhead divided by an *activity base*. The traditional activity bases most frequently used in a factory are direct labor hours, direct labor dollars, and machine hours.

Based on Direct Labor Hours

$$\frac{\text{Predetermined rate per}}{\text{Direct labor hour}} = \frac{\text{Estimated annual factory overhead costs}}{\text{Estimated annual direct labor hours}}$$

The result is given as a dollar amount per hour, for example:

$$\frac{\text{Overhead costs}}{\text{Direct labor hours}} = \frac{\$150{,}000}{100{,}000} = \$1.50 \text{ per hour}$$

Based on Direct Labor Dollars

$$\text{Predetermined rate per Direct labor dollar} = \frac{\text{Estimated annual factory overhead costs}}{\text{Estimated annual direct labor dollars}}$$

The result is given in a percentage of direct labor dollars, for example:

$$\frac{\text{Overhead costs} = \$150{,}000}{\text{Direct labor cost} = \$100{,}000} = 150\% \text{ of direct labor } \$$$

Developing a Predetermined Rate

A *predetermined* or estimated overhead rate is preferred over an actual overhead rate for the following reasons:

1. Timing-the actual rate is not determinable in time to quote customer prices.
2. Inaccuracy-the wide fluctuations in the actual expenditures for overhead would cause commensurate fluctuations in the actual rate.

The following illustration describes how the predetermined rate is calculated and exposes the wide fluctuations that would result if an actual overhead rate were used. Exhibit 2-2 shows that the estimated annual overhead is $120,000, and the estimated annual direct labor hours are 24,000. In January, the actual overhead costs were $9,600 and in February, $9,200. Actual direct labor hours in January were 2,000 and in February, 1,000.

Exhibit 2-2
Factory Overhead Costs

	Actual data		Estimated
	January	February	Total Year
Factory overhead costs	$ 9,600	$ 9,200	$120,000
Direct labor hours	2,000	1,000	24,000
Factory overhead rate	$ 4.80	$ 9.20	$ 5.00

Exhibit 2-3 shows the results of using the estimated annualized rate as compared with the actual monthly rates.

Exhibit 2-3
Actual and Predetermined Rates

	Actual			Predetermined	
Month	Hours	Rate	Amount	Rate	Amount
January	2,000	$ 4.80	$ 9,600	$ 5.00	$10,000
February	1,000	9.20	9,200	5.00	5,000
Total			$18,800		$15,000

Note the following observations:

In January, the actual overhead rate of $4.80 is less than the predetermined (or estimated) rate of $5.00. Customers placing an order in January would receive a lower price quotation if it were based on the actual rate.

In February, the actual overhead rate of $9.20 is 84 percent higher than the predetermined rate of $5.00. Customers placing orders in February would be quoted a much higher price if the actual rate were used.

In regard to overhead costs charged to production for the period, the actual rates would result in $18,800 charged to jobs in process, whereas only $15,000 would be charged to the same jobs using a predetermined rate. The discrepancy is based solely on factors beyond the control of the customer. There is no reasonable basis for charging the customer more (or less) than average estimated costs over an annual period. In subsequent illustrations, a normal costing system will be used, in which the factory overhead rate is predetermined by dividing estimated annual factory overhead costs by estimated annual direct labor hours.

The difference of $3,800 ($18,800 minus $15,000) is called *underapplied* overhead. Where the applied (based on predetermined rate) $15,000 is less than the actual ($18,800) the difference is called underapplied, and conversely, where applied is greater than actual overhead the difference is called *overapplied*. There is no cause for alarm when either over- or underapplied overhead occurs on a monthly basis. It is expected, however, that the annual cumulative difference between actual and applied will be relatively small.

Normalized Predetermined Rates

In the preceding discussion, the predetermined rates were based on a one-year period to illustrate that an average rate based on reliable estimates of overhead costs is better than using an actual rate. Even an annual period may have some shortcomings as a base for calculating overhead rates. Economic cycles have the effect of causing sales and production to be lower than normal for two or three years and then swing into a high cycle. Using one annual period may result in a predetermined rate that is either higher or lower than normal. A *normalized* predetermined overhead rate is based on several years activity rather than one.

It is an average of the period of at least five years as shown in the table.

Predetermined Overhead Rate

Period	Annual	Normalized
19X1	$ 3.00	$ 5.00
19X2	$ 4.00	$ 5.00
19X3	$ 5.00	$ 5.00
19X4	$ 6.00	$ 5.00
19X5	$ 7.00	$ 5.00

Plantwide versus Departmental Overhead Rates

Manufacturing companies may have numerous production plants the sites of which are determined by the location of raw materials, by the market destination, or by other economic factors. Each plant has production costs that include factory overhead. In some small plants that perform only a few major operations, it may be expedient to develop an overhead rate based on one activity base, such as direct labor cost. This *plantwide overhead rate* used to apply factory overhead to all units of output is a single overhead rate based on one activity base. The following demonstration problem will illustrate the differences between plantwide and departmental overhead rates.

The Washmont Company has a plant in Denver, Colorado, that produces metal washers. The washers require only a few simple operations that are performed by three departments: cutting, stamping, and grinding. The company now uses one plantwide overhead rate based on direct labor cost. Budgeted monthly production costs are shown in Exhibit 2-4.

Exhibit 2-4
Washmont Company
Budgeted Monthly Production Costs

	Cutting Department	Stamping Department	Grinding Department	Total Factory
Direct materials	$20,000	$ 5,000	$ 0	$25,000
Direct labor cost	7,500	12,500	20,000	40,000
Factory overhead	10,000	25,000	15,000	50,000
Total costs	$37,500	$42,500	$35,000	$115,000

Units of washers				100,000
Direct labor hrs	1,000	1,000	2,000	4,000
Machine hours	1,250	500	250	2,000
Hourly labor rate	$7.50	$12.50	$10.00	$10.00

The plantwide overhead rate based on direct labor cost is determined as follows:

$$\frac{\text{Total factory overhead} = \$50{,}000}{\text{Direct labor cost} = \$40{,}000} = 125\% \text{ or } 1.25$$

During the month of May 19X5, the Washmont plant produced 106,000 washers with the *actual* cost data shown in Exhibit 2-5.

Exhibit 2-5
Washmont Company
Actual Production Data

	Cutting	Stamping	Grinding	Total
Direct materials	$16,000	$ 5,000	$ 5,000	$26,000
Direct labor cost	8,000	12,000	22,000	44,000
Factory overhead	11,000	22,000	16,000	49,000
Total	$35,000	$39,000	$43,000	$119,000

	Cutting	Stamping	Grinding	Total
Direct labor hours	1,100	900	2,200	4,200
Machine hours	1,300	400	400	2,100

The amount of factory overhead applied to the 106,000 washers produced in May 19X5 is calculated below using the plantwide overhead rate.

Direct labor incurred	$44,000
Times plantwide rate	1.25
Applied overhead	$55,000

Departmental Overhead Rates with One Base

An alternative method to the use of one plantwide rate is to use *separate rates* for each production department using *one base*, such as direct labor cost. The overhead rates for the three production departments at the Washmont Company using one base, direct labor cost, are calculated as follows:

Cutting Department

Factory overhead	=	$10,000	= 133.33%
Direct labor cost	=	$ 7,500	

Stamping Department

Factory overhead	=	$25,000	= 200%
Direct labor cost	=	$12,500	

Grinding Department

Factory overhead	=	$15,000	= 75%
Direct labor cost	=	$20,000	

Based on the actual costs for May 19X5 the amount of overhead applied to production using departmental rates would be calculated as shown in Exhibit 2-6.

Exhibit 2-6
Washmont Company
Applied Overhead Using Departmental Rates

	Cutting	Stamping	Grinding	Total
Actual direct labor cost	$ 8,000	$12,000	$22,000	
× departmental rate	1.3333	2.00	0.75	
Applied overhead	$10,667	$24,000	$16,500	$51,167

The overhead applied to the 106,000 washers produced in May amounts to $51,167 using departmental rates as compared with $55,000 using one plantwide rate. Although this difference may not appear to be significant, it amounts to 3.6

cents per washer or 7 percent of the applied overhead. In job-order shops, contracts are awarded through the process of submitting bids that are based on estimated production costs. The difference between the winning bidder and the closest losing bidder may be only 1 or 2 percent. The method of applying overhead may make the deciding difference in winning a contract. Each company must decide which method best serves its interests, neither grossly overestimating nor underestimating its average or normal production costs.

Departmental Overhead Rates with More than One Base

Production departments may be labor dominant, machine dominant, or may use a large amount of space. It may be beneficial to the company to examine the extent to which each production department is affected by direct labor, machines, space usage, or any other dominant factor that drives the costs of overhead upward.

Washmont Company's production manager proposes that the company consider departmental rates based on the most logical activity base for each of the three departments. The recommended bases are:

Cutting department	Machine hours (MH)
Stamping department	Direct labor cost (DLC)
Grinding department	Direct labor hours (DLH)

Calculation of Department Overhead Rates

Cutting Department

Factory overhead	=	\$10,000	=	\$8.00 per MH
Machine hours	=	1,250		

Stamping Department

Factory overhead	=	\$25,000	=	2.00 or 200% of DLC
Direct labor cost	=	\$12,500		

Grinding Department

Factory overhead	=	\$15,000	=	\$7.50 per DLH
Direct labor hours	=	2,000		

The amount of factory overhead applied to the 106,000 washers produced in the month of May 19X5, using the departmental rates, is calculated as follows:

Cutting department	1,300 MH × $8.00	=	$10,400
Stamping	$12,000 × 2.00	=	24,000
Grinding	2,200 DLH × $7.50	=	16,500
Total overhead applied			$50,900

The use of departmental rates more closely reflects the dominant factor in each department. The cutting department has a preponderance of the machine hours; the grinding department has a preponderance of the direct labor hours; and the stamping department has the highest labor cost on a per hour basis. With the use of departmental rates, a product that bypasses one of the departments would be assigned an amount of overhead that reflects the true costs of the departments it passes through.

Departmental Rates for Both Direct Labor and Factory Overhead

Job 480 was started and completed in May and requested 1,000 washers with special requirements. The actual data from the job order cost record shows:

Job 480	Cutting	Stamping	Grinding	Total
Direct materials	$2,200	$ 600		$2,800
Direct labor hours	100	100	200	400
Machine hours	140	40	30	210

Summary of costs for Job 480			
Direct materials			$ 2,800
Direct labor			
Cutting	100 DLH × $ 7.50	= $ 750	
Stamping	100 DLH × $12.50	= 1,250	
Grinding	200 DLH × $10.00	= 2,000	
Total direct labor			$ 4,000

Factory OH applied			
Cutting	140 MH × $ 8.00	= $ 1,120	
Stamping	$1,250 DLC × 200%	= 2,500	
Grinding	200 DLH × $ 7.50	= 1,500	
Total overhead			$ 5,120
Total cost of Job 480			$ 11,920

The total cost of production for Job 480 is $11,920. In order to charge the customer a fair price, the Washmont Company must add its marketing and administrative expenses and a profit to the production costs. It is customary to add a percentage to the estimated costs, called the *cost plus* system, when submitting a bid to the customer. Assuming that the Washmont Company adds 40 percent to its production costs, the price quoted would be $16,688 ($11,920 × 1.40).

3

Standard Costing

Profit motivated companies seek to reduce costs and expenses in the process of manufacturing and marketing their products or performing their service to the customer. In order to control costs there must be a precise notion of what a particular cost should be under normal conditions and in normal times. This basis for comparison is referred to as a standard.

A *standard cost* is a monetary value used as a basis for comparison; it is a norm. It is usually a unit cost; it may be called a standard cost per unit of input, such as direct labor, or per unit of output. In contrast, budgets are total costs. The budget system and the standard costing system may be interrelated if both are based on the same estimates. Large corporations that use standard costing usually base the production budget estimates on the standard costs.

There are three costing systems with respect to the absorption of costs into production that are described in this book: actual, normal and standard. The actual costing system was used in demonstrating the manufacturing statements in Chapter 1, the normal costing system was used in illustrating the job-order costing system in Chapter 2, and the standard costing system is described in this chapter. The basic characteristics of the three systems with respect to which costs are charged to production are shown in the table.

Costing System with Respect to Absorbing Costs into Production

Costs of	Actual System	Normal System	Standard System
Direct materials	Actual	Actual	Standard
Direct labor	Actual	Actual	Standard
Factory overhead	Actual	Estimated	Standard

It is important to distinguish between actual costs and an actual costing system. Actual costs are the same historical or acquisition costs that are recorded in accordance with the cost principle. An ***actual costing system*** is a costing system with respect to the absorption of costs into production that uses actual rather than estimated, budgeted, or standard costs.

A *normal costing system* differs from the actual costing system only in how factory overhead is charged to production. The normal system uses a predetermined or estimated rate for overhead but, like the actual system, uses actual costs for both direct material and direct labor.

A *standard costing system* is used by large manufacturing companies to more effectively control and monitor production costs. Standard costs are developed for direct material and labor as well as overhead, providing a basis for measuring the effectiveness of utilizing labor and the efficiency of processing material. The other two systems do not provide a basis for monitoring the direct material and labor against norms or standards. In this chapter the determination of standards, the system of standard costing, and models for analyzing the deviations, called variances, from standards are described.

SETTING STANDARD COSTS

The level of the standards in a standard cost system is an individual management decision for each company. Management sets standards at a level that will most effectively assist them in measuring the performance of company segments and controlling costs and expenses. The classification of these levels is as follows.

Ideal Standards

The highest level of standards is called an *ideal standard*. An ideal standard is 100 percent utilization of the theoretical capacity. There are no allowances for lost time or wasted materials. Ideal standards may discourage rather than encourage workers, so they are seldom adopted. There are situations where ideal standards are appropriate, such as in automated machining operations, and particularly where robots have replaced human labor.

Currently Attainable (Practical) Standards

A *currently attainable standard* is based on realistic estimates that allow for material spoilage, idle time, and other normal production interferences. Currently attainable standards allow for normal deviations, but not for abnormal or exceptional deviations (variances). They provide motivation for workers to achieve favorable results because they are reasonable. The standards referred to in this and the following chapters are assumed to be currently attainable.

Setting Standard Costs for Direct Material

Direct material standards are set by company policy. Standards may be communicated throughout the company by a cost accounting manual from the controller's office. For example, the Cost Accounting Manual of Clark Equipment Company states that standard costs include direct material, which is defined as follows:

1. Direct material is any material that becomes part of the finished product, by being attached thereto as purchased, or that, through the application of labor, has its properties changed and value added so as to result in a salable product.
2. Items of insignificant value that become part of the product may be treated as overhead.
3. Packaging materials and supplies that are of significant value, are measurable, and can be uniformly applied to the product may be considered direct.
4. Freight-in, which can be readily identified and measured as a separate value, may be incorporated in material costs.

The standard cost of direct material is defined by the company, as illustrated by the Clark Equipment Company's Cost Accounting Manual. A list of direct materials is determined by the company, which specifies the quantity and quality or grade of materials to be purchased. In addition, an allowance is made for normal waste or spoilage in determining the standard quantity per unit.

Prices are determined by estimating the normal delivered price per unit of material. Delivery terms and lot sizes must be specified to account for extra charges or discounts on quantity purchases. The standard price is multiplied by the standard quantity to calculate the standard cost.

Standard quantity	Standard price	Standard cost
3 pounds	× $2.50	= $7.50

Notice that the standard price is per pound, which is a unit of *input*; whereas the standard cost is per unit of *output*.

Setting Standards for Direct Labor

There are two widely used options for setting labor standards, *estimated* and *scientific*. The estimated option uses historical costs to estimate future costs. This practice is widely used where it is too costly or impractical to use time-study or scientifically measured labor standards. The scientific option is based on measurements of time to complete individual tasks. Engineered time and motion studies are usually preferred for those operations that are repetitive and are measurable. The Cost Accounting Manual of Clark Equipment Company states:

Engineered or Estimated Standards

Industrial engineering time standards are to be used in developing standard costs. Such standards are to be consistent with actual methods and processing relative to current production runs. Estimated time standards are acceptable for a new process or product. Management, however, should exert efforts to develop industrial engineering standards on a timely basis.

There are many factors that affect the price and use of direct labor. The illustrations in a textbook cannot capture and reflect the complexity of the real problems faced by large corporations. Direct labor is made up of skilled, semiskilled and unskilled workers, some in organized labor unions. Labor rates vary among different classes of labor. There are also large differences in rates due to location. Many companies pay substantially different wage rates for the same work done in two different locations. Automobile workers in Flint, Michigan, on the average are paid more than automobile workers in Kentucky and Tennessee.

In textbook illustrations, a single labor rate may be given; this rate may represent an average or composite rate for a single operation, one factory, or a small company with one major product. In large corporations, there are actually many labor operations to be analyzed depending on the number of different production processes in the factories. Measuring the quantity of direct labor is less of a problem. The quantity of direct and indirect labor is measured in hours. It is relatively easy to record hours worked on time cards and to assign hours or fractions of hours to specific jobs or departments in the factory.

Setting Standards for Overhead

Direct labor hours have become an important activity base for the allocation of indirect costs in a factory. Costs that are not directly traceable to the product must be allocated to the product in order to account for the full costs of production.

The most widely used activity bases are direct labor dollars and direct labor hours. Most of the reasons for the incurrence of overhead are related to direct labor, not direct material. Supervision, heat, light, food, health services, and liability and workmen's compensation insurance are all related to the use of direct labor. Both variable and fixed overhead are assumed to be applied on the basis of direct labor hours unless otherwise specified.

STANDARD COST VARIANCE ANALYSIS

Differences between actual costs and standard costs are called *variances*. There are price variances and quantity variances. Following is a summary of the variances included in this chapter.

Input	Price variance	Quantity variance
Direct material	Material price	Material quantity
Direct labor	Labor rate	Labor efficiency

Standard Cost Variance Models

Two models for analyzing and calculating the standard cost variances described in this chapter are the *analytical model* and the *working model*.

Analytical Model

The analytical model uses algebraic equations to calculate the two variances, price and quantity. With this model, it is necessary to form the equations that represent the differences in actual and standard prices and quantities. The notations used for actual and standard prices and quantities are

Actual price	=	P_a	Standard price	=	P_s
Actual quantity	=	Q_a	Standard quantity	=	Q_s

Price Variance

The *price variance* represents the difference (in dollars) in actual prices paid and standard prices that should have been paid for the actual quantity of material purchased. The equation that represents this variance is

$$(Q_a \times P_a) - (Q_a \times P_s) \text{ or } Q_a (P_a - P_s)$$

Quantity Variance

The *quantity variance* represents the dollar difference between the actual quantity used and the standard quantity that should have been used in production at the standard price. Quantities are measured in hours, pounds, kilograms, liters, board feet, and other measurements that apply to materials and labor used in production. The equation that represents the quantity variance is

$$(Q_a \times P_s) - (Q_s \times P_s) \text{ or } P_s (Q_a - Q_s)$$

The standard price is used instead of the actual price in order to isolate the quantity difference at normal or expected prices. In the model format given, a positive result represents an unfavorable variance and a negative result represents a favorable variance. There is no conceptual significance to the positive or negative aspects of the result.

Working Model

The working model is a diagrammatic representation of the analytical model. It is less demanding of conceptual understanding and is easy to implement and is accurate. Its great advantage is that the same general format applies to all cost variances. The left variance is always the price variance and the right is always the quantity variance. The *total variance* (also called a net variance) is the difference between the extreme left, actual times actual, and the extreme right, standard times standard. The total variance always equals the sum of the price and quantity variances. Unlike the price and quantity variances, the total variance does not separate price and quantity sources of the variations from standards. The working model and the rules that help in applying it are shown below. (Dollar signs are omitted in the working model.)

Q_a = Actual × P_a = Actual	Q_a = Actual × P_s = Standard	Q_s = Standard × P_s = Standard
Price Variance		Quantity Variance
Total Variance		

Rule 1. Any left total of quantity times price, that is greater than any right total, results in an unfavorable variance. **Rule 1a.** Any left total that is less than any right total is favorable, for example:

Q_a = 10	Q_a = 10	Q_s = 9
P_a = 5	P_s = 6	P_s = 6
50	60	54
10 Favorable Price Variance		6 Unfavorable Quantity Variance
4 Favorable Total Variance		

Rule 2. An unfavorable variance is always a debit to the variance account and a favorable variance is always a credit to the variance account.

Direct Material Variances

Direct material is purchased to satisfy the production requirements. The purchasing department has the responsibility to purchase both the quantity and quality that meet the needs and specifications of production, at the lowest price available. It is customary to hold the purchasing agent responsible for *material price variances* and to hold the production manager responsible for *material quantity variances.*

Direct Material Variance Model

Q_a = actual quantity used
Q_s = standard quantity allowed for actual units of output
P_a = actual price paid
P_s = standard price per unit of input

The purchasing agent of Cody Company buys 600 pounds of material X for $4,800. The standard price is $10.00 per pound. Actual production for the period is 250 units of product A. The standard quantity allowed for one unit of product A is 2. All 600 pounds of material X were used in producing the 250 units of product A. The working model for materials is illustrated below.

<table>
<tr><td colspan="2">Q_a = 600</td><td colspan="2">Q_a = 600</td><td colspan="2">Q_s = 500 (250 × 2)</td></tr>
<tr><td colspan="2">P_a = 8.00</td><td colspan="2">P_s = 10.00</td><td colspan="2">P_s = 10.00</td></tr>
<tr><td colspan="2">4,800</td><td colspan="2">6,000</td><td colspan="2">5,000</td></tr>
<tr><td colspan="3">1,200 Favorable
Material Price Variance</td><td colspan="3">1,000 Unfavorable
Material Quantity Variance</td></tr>
<tr><td colspan="6">200 Favorable
Total Material Variance</td></tr>
</table>

The working model shows that the material price variance is $1,200 favorable and the material quantity variance is $1,000 unfavorable. These variances isolate the sources, but do not explain why they occurred. Concerned managers must investigate the source and find the reasons for the variances. An unfavorable variance is not presumed to be bad, just in need of explanation. A favorable variance should not be considered good; it too requires an explanation.

Managers use the variances to assist them in isolating those areas that need attention. This policy allows them to focus on problem areas only, which is an efficient use of management time.

Material Purchase Price Variance

In the preceding working model example, the material price variance is isolated at the time the material is placed into use or production. In practice, the material price variance may be isolated when the material is purchased rather than used. If isolated at the time of purchase, the variance directs attention to the performance of the purchasing department instead of the production department. In this book the term *material purchase price variance* is used to describe isolation at the time of purchase and the term *material price variance* indicates isolation at the time of use.

The assumptions for calculating the material price variance are modified for the material purchase price variance as follows: Assume that the purchasing department purchases 1,000 pounds for $8,000 and that 600 pounds are placed into production.

Summary of Information

Standard data	Quantity in pounds	Price per pound	Total cost
Material X	2	$ 10	$ 20

Actual data

Purchased 1,000 pounds @ $8 = $8,000
Production 250 units using 600 pounds of material X

Working Model (two-level)

Q_a = 1,000	Q_a = 1,000
P_a = 8	P_s = 10
8,000	10,000
2,000 favorable Material Purchase Price Variance	

Q_a = 600	Q_s = 500
P_s = 10	P_s = 10
6,000	5,000
1,000 unfavorable Materials Quantity Variance	

The materials purchase price variance of $2,000 favorable represents the variance for all of the material purchased rather than just the amount used in production. This method allows for an immediate analysis of the total amount purchased by the purchasing department. There is no difference in the quantity variance; it is $1,000 unfavorable regardless of when the price variance is isolated.

Direct Labor Variances

Direct labor, unlike direct material, cannot be stored. It is consumed at the time of production and wasted if not used efficiently. The direct labor price variance is called a *labor rate variance* and the quantity variance is called a *labor efficiency variance*. Even though union contracts restrict the flexibility of both rates and usage of labor, there are still options left to management in the utilization of direct labor. The variance system allows for evaluation of production and departmental managers in their efficient application of direct labor in the manufacturing operation.

Direct Labor Variance Model

Q_a = actual DLH	P_a = actual rate paid per DLH
Q_s = standard DLH allowed for actual output	P_s = standard rate per DLH

Cody Company uses 650 direct labor hours in producing 250 units of Product A at a total cost of $7,150. The company standards are:

Direct labor hours	Rate	Cost
2.5	$ 12.00	$ 30.00

Using the working model for direct labor:

Q_a = 650	Q_a = 650	Q_s = 625 (2.5 × 250)
P_a = 11	P_s = 12	P_s = 12
7,150	7,800	7,500

650 favorable Labor Rate Variance	300 unfavorable Labor Efficiency Variance

350 favorable Total Labor Variance

PRODUCTION MIX AND YIELD VARIANCES

This chapter has described direct material and direct labor price and quantity variances. The analysis has been applied to only one material or one class of labor at a time. It is equally important to consider the effects of various mixtures of either direct materials or direct labor in the production process.

Most products require more than one material or labor input. Although products such as aspirin and artificial sweeteners have few ingredients, an automobile may have several thousand parts. For many ingredients or parts there are substitutes or alternative sources of supply. These substitutes may result in a change in the overall results of the process. For the mix and yield analysis of variances, it is assumed that there is substitutability of inputs.

Mix and Yield Variances for Direct Material

The *materials mix variance* measures the dollar effects of the substitution of nonstandard materials for the standard materials. The *materials yield variance* measures the effects of the quantities of nonstandard materials as compared with the standard quantities of the standard mix of materials on a given output. The materials mix and yield variances are derived from the materials quantity variance, as calculated from the working model, which is shown here.

Working Model for Materials Variances

Q_a =	Q_a =	Q_s =
P_a =	P_s =	P_s =
	Materials Price Variance	Materials Quantity Variance
		Mix and Yield Variances

Working Model for Mix and Yield Variances

Q_{at} =	Q_{at} =	Q_{st} =
P_{wa} =	P_{ws} =	P_{ws} =
	Mix Variance	Materials Quantity Variance
		Mix and Yield Variances

Where:

Q_{at} = Total of actual quantities.
Q_{st} = Total of standard quantities.
P_{wa} = Weighted average price based on *actual* total inputs.
P_{ws} = Weighted average price based on *standard* total inputs.

Illustration of Material Mix and Yield Variances

Standard Costs for 100 Packages			
Ingredient	Quantity	Price	Total
A	100 oz.	$ 2.00	$ 200
B	200 oz.	$ 1.20	$ 240
C	40 oz.	$ 3.00	$ 120
Total	340 oz.		$ 560

Actual Costs for 100 Packages			
Ingredient	Quantity	Price	Total
A	90 oz	$ 2.10	$ 189
B	220 oz	$ 1.00	$ 220
C	42 oz	$ 2.50	$ 105
Total	352 oz		$ 514

Working Model for Material Mix and Yield Variances

$Q_a \times P_s$		$Q_s \times P_s$	
A	90 oz × $2.00 = $180	A	100 oz × $2.00 = $200
B	220 oz × $1.20 = $264	B	200 oz × $1.20 = $240
C	42 oz × $3.00 = $126	C	40 oz × $3.00 = $120
Total	352 oz $570	Total	340 oz $560

Q_{at} = 352 oz	P_{wa} = \$570/352 oz = \$1.619
Q_{st} = 340 oz	P_{ws} = \$560/340 oz = \$1.647

Q_{at} = 352	Q_{at} = 352	Q_{st} = 340
P_{wa} = 1.619	P_{ws} = 1.647	P_{ws} = 1.647
570	580	560

10 favorable Materials Mix Variance	20 unfavorable Materials Yield Variance

Equation Method for Material Mix and Yield Variances

Mix Variance
$(P_{wa} - P_{ws})\ Q_{at}$
(1.619 - 1.647) 352 = 10 Fav.

Yield Variance
$(Q_{at} - Q_{st})\ P_{ws}$
(352 - 340) 1.647 = 20 Unf.

Analysis of Mix Variance (Rounded to whole dollars)

Material A	(90 - 100) × (\$2.00 - \$1.647)	= \$ 4 Fav.
Material B	(220 - 200) × (\$1.20 - \$1.647)	= \$ 9 Fav.
Material C	(42 - 40) × (\$3.00 - \$1.647)	= \$ 3 Unf.
Mix variance		\$10 Fav.

Observations

1. Less of Material A is used at a standard price, which is greater than the weighted average standard price (P_{ws}), resulting in a favorable effect.

2. More of Material B is used at a standard price, which is less than the weighted average standard price of \$1,647, resulting in a favorable effect.

3. More of Material C is used at a standard price greater than P_{ws}, resulting in an unfavorable effect.

4. The unfavorable yield variance was the result of a greater total input of materials being used to yield a given quantity of output.

Mix and Yield Variances for Direct Labor

The production process may require a specific class of direct labor for each operation. Skilled, semiskilled, and unskilled classes of labor demand different wage rates. Where it is necessary to substitute one class of direct labor for another, the mix and yield variance analysis can be applied.

Illustration of Mix and Yield Variance Analysis for Direct Labor

Standard Costs for 100 Units			
Skilled labor	50 hrs × $20.00	=	$1,000
Unskilled labor	100 hrs × $12.00	=	$1,200
Total standard costs			$2,200

Actual Costs for 100 Units			
Skilled labor	54 hrs × $21.00	=	$1,134
Unskilled labor	80 hrs × $11.00	=	$ 880
Total actual costs			$ 2,014

Working Model of Mix and Yield Variances for Direct Labor

	$Q_a \times P_s$		$Q_s \times P_s$	
Skilled	54 hrs × 20	= 1,080	50 hrs x 20	= 1,000
Unskilled	80 hrs × 1	= 960	100 hrs x 12	= 1,200
	134 hrs	2,040	150 hrs.	2,200
	160 favorable Labor Efficiency Variance			

Q_{at} = 134 hrs.	P_{wa} = 2,040/134 = $15.224
Q_{st} = 150 hrs.	P_{ws} = 2,200/150 = $14.667

Q_{at} = 134	Q_{at} = 134	Q_{st} = 150
P_{wa} = 15.224	P_{ws} = 14.667	P_{ws} = 14.667
2,040	1,965	2,200
75 unf. Labor Mix Variance	235 fav. Labor Yield Variance	

Equation Method for Labor Mix and Yield Variances

Mix Variance
$(P_{wa} - P_{ws})\, Q_{at}$
(15.224 - 14.667) 134 = 75 Unf.

Yield Variance
$(Q_{at} - Q_{st})\, P_{ws}$
(134 - 150) 14.667 = 235 Fav.

Analysis of Mix Variance for Direct Labor

Skilled labor	(54 - 50) × (20 - 14.7)	= $21 Unf.
Unskilled labor	(80 - 100) × (12 - 14.7)	= $54 Unf.
Total mix variance		$75 Unf.

Observations

1. More of the skilled labor was used, at a greater cost than the weighted average (P_{ws}) resulting in an unfavorable effect.

2. Less of the lower cost unskilled labor was used resulting in an unfavorable effect.

3. The favorable yield variance was the result of fewer total labor hours being used than the standard hours allowed to produce a given number of units.

4

Budgeting

DEFINITION OF BUDGETING

Budgeting is the process of preparing a written financial plan called the *budget*, which shows in detail the expected flow of resources into and out of the organization during a specified period of time. It is expressed in quantitative terms and is based primarily on financial data. The budget is a plan for a future period. It is based on estimates that should be realistic and reasonable.

A *master budget* is a comprehensive plan for the overall company prepared for a given time period, which is usually one year. The master budget may be formulated by summing the separate budgets from the divisions, branches or groups of the overall corporation; or it may be prepared in total and apportioned among the various groups of the company. It is usually prepared as a *static or fixed budget*, that is, based on only one expected sales level, which is the management's goal for that time period. The master budget may be divided into quarters or months on a prorata basis, and/or it may be sub-divided into the various organizational units of the overall company.

Activity-based budgeting is appropriate where Activity Based Costing/Activity Based Management (ABC/ABM) systems have been implemented. The budgeting process can be designed to include cost drivers, activities, activity centers, and business processes, rather than the traditional departments as cost centers. The emphasis in the ABC/ABM system is on tracing consumption of resources to activities, and activity costs to cost objectives. The two budgeting systems may coexist, but ABC/ABM budgeting will probably not replace the traditional system.

Budgeting Process Flow Chart

Operational Budget System

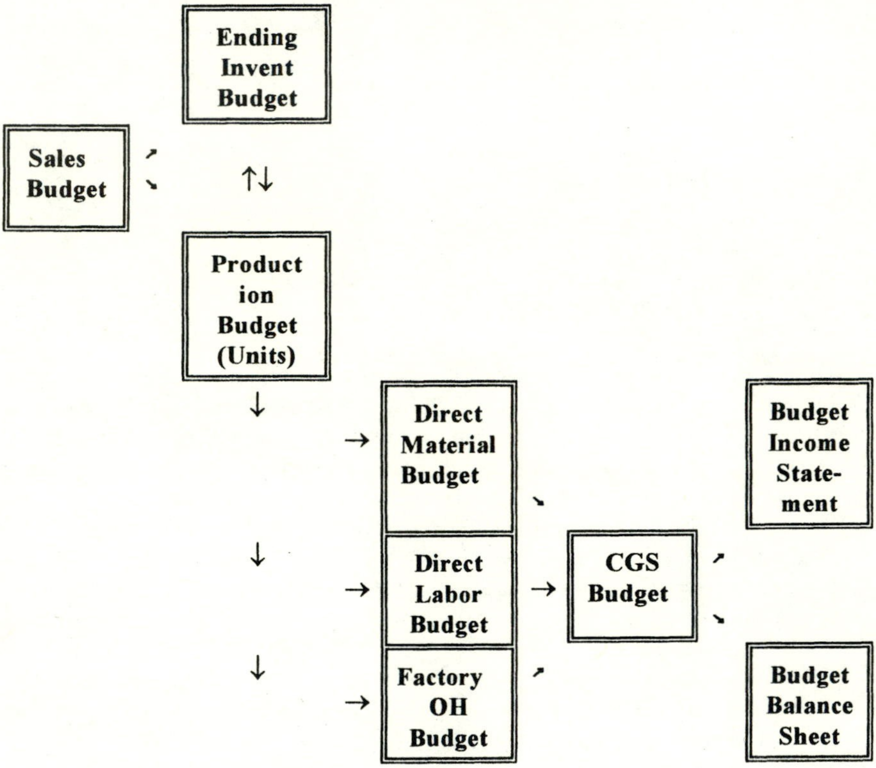

Financial Budget System

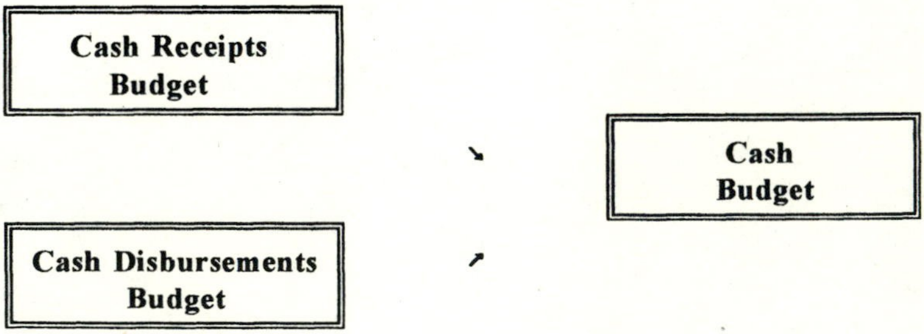

BUDGET AUTHORITY

The budget is the most widely used financial planning tool in the business world. It is also used by individuals in personal financial planning, by nonprofit charitable and educational organizations, and by government agencies. For most organizations, a budget is necessary for the following reasons.

1. The budget is a source of authority; it authorizes a budget head to spend up to a total amount without requesting further permission. The only restriction is that budget guidelines regarding the appropriateness of the expenditure must be followed.

2. The budget places a limit on the absolute maximum amount that can be spent. The top executives know that no more than the budgeted total amount can be spent without their special approval.

3. It assures management that its goals are more likely to be met. The budget represents the approved plan for meeting top management's objectives. There is no known better method to attain these objectives.

4. It establishes the number of units to be produced, the amount and types of material to be purchased, labor to be hired, inventory levels to be maintained, and numerous other details to be followed in achieving company objectives.

5. The budget coordinates the financial activities of the organization, large or small. In complex conglomerates, such as Beatrice and ITT, and in giant corporations, such as General Motors and IBM, coordination of the divergent activities to attain corporate goals and objectives would be virtually impossible without budgeting.

BUDGETING IN PUBLIC VERSUS PRIVATE ORGANIZATIONS

Private U.S. domestic corporations are motivated by short-term profit, which puts pressure on maximizing revenues and reducing costs and expenses each fiscal year. Budgeting is used universally in profit-motivated companies to plan and control both revenues and expenditures.

Charitable organizations, most colleges and universities, foundations, professional societies, and municipal, state, and federal governmental agencies operate on a nonprofit basis. The difference in revenues and expenditures is called surplus or deficit, rather than profit or loss. In contrast to a profit organization, the nonprofit organization should, at least theoretically, seek to balance the budget in preference to having a surplus.

Nonprofit organizations usually have to struggle to obtain revenues, but have little difficulty in spending. Thus, a budget is just as necessary in nonprofit as in profit companies. It serves to provide the same advantages itemized earlier for planning and control of expenditures.

A public organization, or government agency, is created by and primarily supported by the public. It is created directly or indirectly by legislation and supported by taxes. Public agencies are usually classified as city, county, state, or federal. City water departments, county road commissions, state universities and the Federal Department of Natural Resources are examples of public entities that must prepare budgets to ensure the stewardship of public funds.

Public organizations, notorious for their inefficiency, prepare budget requests based on the public needs. The public's needs habitually seem to exceed their ability to pay. The result is a budget deficit. Deficits are supported by borrowing or by passing legislature to raise taxes, or both. Deficits are a chronic problem in the federal budget and have resulted in enormous national debt.

The major problem in the public sector is the lack of motivation to reduce expenditures. The predominant pressure in public sector budgeting is to increase expenditures regardless of revenues. There is no responsibility link between the budget head at the department level and the source of revenues, which is ultimately the legislature and the taxpayer.

For example, at a state university the approved budget of the Biology Department calls for $50,000 in laboratory equipment for a given fiscal year (FY-1). Fiscal year (FY-1) starts on September 1, 19X1 and ends on August 31, 19X2. The head of the Biology Department has ordered and received $30,000 worth of equipment by the end of the fiscal year, waiting for impending technological changes before ordering more equipment. In a normal year the Biology Department expects a 10 percent budget increase for equipment, which means that in the next fiscal year the expected budget would have been $55,000. However, if the $50,000 is not spent the budget for next year will be $30,000 + $3,000 or $33,000.

The underlying motivation is to spend all of the budget, regardless of whether it is needed. There is no system of performance evaluation based on efficiency and conservation of resources. The department head is rewarded for spending the $20,000 for unneeded equipment and punished if he/she is conscientious and a good steward of the public tax money.

There is a major difference in the budgeting responsibilities of the public sector and that of the private sector. In the private sector, managers are responsible for revenues as well as costs, whereas, in the public sector managers are usually separated from the responsibility of raising revenues. Only those government agencies that are motivated by a code of high moral responsibility, by a tradition of good stewardship, or by a profession which demands strict ethical conduct will produce an efficient use of resources in the pursuit of their goals and objectives.

Although these philosophical and ethical differences exist between public and private organizations, the mechanical or procedural aspects of budget preparation are not materially different. The subsequent discussions of budgeting will refer to profit seeking manufacturing or merchandising companies that are part of the private sector.

BUDGET COMMITTEE

The chief executive officer, the chief financial officer and the executive vice presidents representing marketing, production and other major functions of the organization usually serve as the *budget committee.* It is important that the number of members of the budget committee remains as small as possible, and that all budget centers are represented. The organization chart shows the lines of authority and serves as a guide to whom should serve on the committee. The budget committee will normally follow a procedure such as that described below:

1. Establish guidelines for preparing the budget.
2. Set dates for submission of preliminary and final budget requests.
3. Review budget requests, reject and return unacceptable requests.
4. Interview budget heads where necessary.
5. Review and give approval to the final revised budget.

In a large corporation the individual members of the budget committee do not necessarily know the details about everything they have approved. For example, the advertising director plans to spend $2 million on national network television ads. This budget item is included in the total advertising budget of $50 million, that is a part of the total marketing budget of $300 million. The budget committee approves the total amount for marketing. Only the director of marketing will have reviewed the detail that is included in the marketing budget request.

The budget committee serves as a formal source of authority for budget review and approval. Keep in mind, however, that the chief executive officer cannot delegate the ultimate responsibility for the success of the budget process in meeting the company objectives. The chief executive officer alone answers to the board of directors for success or failure.

SALES BUDGET

As the key budget factor the *sales budget* is the beginning step in the preparation of the Master Budget. The annual sales budget is most helpful if divided into months or quarters. For demonstration purposes a quarterly budget is shown in Exhibit 4-1 where sales units are multiplied by a budgeted selling price for each period.

Exhibit 4-1
Porter Company
Quarterly Sales Budget for Year Ended December 31, 19X1

Estimated	1st Qtr.	2nd Qtr.	3rd Qtr.	4th Qtr.	Total Year
Units sold	400	800	1,200	600	3,000
Selling price	$ 30	$ 30	$ 30	$ 30	$ 30
Total sales revenue	$12,000	$24,000	$36,000	$18,000	$90,000

Exhibit 4-1 is the basis for further production schedules that use the units sold to predict units to be produced each quarter, or whatever period has been customary. Assume that the Porter Company is following a just-in-time (JIT) inventory policy and its suppliers have guaranteed them rapid delivery of production materials and supplies. This enables Porter Company to keep its finished goods inventory on hand at lower levels, because they have geared their production to meet current demand. However, it is necessary to maintain a minimum inventory level such as 10 percent to allow for contingencies.

PRODUCTION BUDGET

The *production budget* is based on sales units and projected finished goods inventory levels:

Units Produced (P) + Beginning Finished Goods Inventory (BI)	=	Units Sold (S) + Ending Finished Goods Inventory (EI)

The production equation is: P = S + EI - BI

This equation format is the conceptual basis for the production budget. Exhibit 4-2 shows the units to be produced for each of the four quarters and for the total year.

Exhibit 4-2
Porter Company
Production Budget for Year Ended December 31, 19X1

	1st Qtr.	2nd Qtr.	3rd Qtr.	4th Qtr.	Total Year
Budgeted sales units (Sch. A)	400	800	1,200	600	3,000
Add: Ending FG inventory	80	120	60	50*	50
Total units	480	920	1,260	650	3,050
Less: Beginning FG inventory	40#	80	120	60	40
Units produced	440	840	1,140	590	3,010

*Based on the first quarter of 19X2, estimated to be 500 units.

#Note that where the ending inventory is a given percentage of the following period (period 2), the beginning inventory is always the given percentage of the same period (period 1). For example, in the first quarter, the ending inventory is 80 or 10 percent of 800 units; and the beginning inventory is 40 or 10 percent of 400 units.

CASH COLLECTIONS BUDGET

After projecting the total sales dollars in the sales budget it is possible to estimate the cash collections for each quarter. In order to realistically forecast cash collections it is necessary to make two assumptions based on the company's historical data:

1. the proportion of sales on account
2. the collection history

Assume that a company's sales are 100 percent on account and that credit sales are collected as follows:

1st month (month of sale)	30%
2nd month	60%
3rd month	8%
Uncollectible	2%

Collections of credit sales would follow the pattern below. Note that the 2 percent uncollectibles is not included in the collections schedule.

Credit Sales In	Collections In				
	Month 1	Month 2	Month 3	Month 4	Month 5
Month 1	30%	60%	8%		
Month 2		30%	60%	8%	
Month 3			30%	60%	8%
Month 4				30%	60%
Month 5					30%

In a quarterly budget the cash collections would be spread over only the present quarter and the following quarter. For Porter Company it is assumed that 80 percent of sales are on account, 40 percent are collected in the same quarter, and 58 percent in the following quarter. Collections from the fourth quarter of last year due in the first quarter of 19X1 estimated at $5,000.

Exhibit 4-3
Porter Company
Cash Receipts Budget
Year Ended December 31, 19X1

	1st Qtr.	2nd Qtr.	3rd Qtr.	4th Qtr.	Total Year
Total sales revenue	$12,000	$24,000	$36,000	$18,000	$90,000
Proportion of credit sales	0.80	0.80	0.80	0.80	0.80
Sales on account	$9,600	$19,200	$28,800	$14,400	$72,000

Cash Collections From	1st Qtr.	2nd Qtr.	3rd Qtr.	4th Qtr.	Total Year
Last qtr. sales	$5,000				$5,000
First qtr. sales	3,840	$5,568			9,408
Second qtr. sales		7,680	$11,136		18,816
Third qtr. sales			11,520	$16,704	28,224
Fourth qtr. sales				5,760	5,760
Collections on credit sales	$8,840	$13,248	$22,656	$22,464	$67,208
Add: cash sales 20%	2,400	4,800	7,200	3,600	18,000
Total cash receipts	$11,240	$18,048	$29,856	$26,064	$85,208

CONTROL: PERFORMANCE MEASUREMENT

Control refers to the responsibility of top management to ensure that the objectives of the financial plan, the budget, are achieved, and that these objectives were met in compliance with company policies. The primary instrument of performance measurement is the periodic budget report. This report, usually issued on a monthly basis, or shorter periods when desired, compares actual expenditures with the pro-rated budgeted data. It is necessary to include year-to-date totals in addition to monthly or periodic data. As the year progresses, the cumulative year-to-date comparison reveals a pattern of performance, which allows for action before it is too late.

Operating Budget System

1. Sales Forecast -- The first step in preparing the master budget is the sales forecast. The budget committee must be careful to avoid extremes in either optimistic or pessimistic predictions. Optimism is favored over pessimism, but realism is preferred over both.

2. Finished Goods Inventory -- The appropriate level of finished goods inventory must be determined in order to prepare the production budget. The level of inventory depends on many factors and requires the expertise of production, marketing and financial managers.

3. Production Budget -- The current production must supply the requirements of sales and increases in inventory levels. In many industries the ending inventory is held constant, while in others it fluctuates with demand. Both increases and decreases will affect the quantities required by current production. The three input budgets are based on the production budget.

Direct Materials Budget
Direct Labor Budget
Factory Overhead Budget

4. Cost of Goods Sold Budget -- The cost of goods sold budget can be prepared from the information provided in the sales, inventory and production budgets.

5. Marketing and Administrative Expenses Budget -- All of the nonmanufacturing functions are classified as marketing or administrative. They represent period costs or expenses.

6. Budgeted Income Statement -- This income statement is based on estimated or budgeted data, but will provide the management with the projected effect on the net income if the goals of the budget are attained.

Financial Budget System

1. Cash Budget -- Much of the information provided by the operational budget system is needed to prepare the cash budget, as indicated below:

Schedule Of	Based On
Cash receipts	Sales budget
Cash disbursements	Materials purchases, labor, and overhead budgets
Expenses	Marketing and administrative expenses budgets

2. Capital Budget -- The subject of capital budgeting is reserved for a later chapter. Any cash outlays for purchases of equipment, machinery and other capital assets must be included in the cash budget.

3. Balance Sheet -- A budgeted (or pro forma) balance sheet may be prepared from all of the information provided in the master budget system. It presents the projected financial position assuming that the budget goals have been attained.

ILLUSTRATION OF OPERATING BUDGET SYSTEM

A comprehensive illustration of the *operational* budget system is presented to demonstrate the steps in preparing a master budget. A *financial* budget system will also be illustrated in this chapter.

Fleming Company uses a normal absorption-costing system. The company is preparing its master budget for the year 19X4. The management projects the following budget figures for 19X4.

Direct materials	
Material 1	$6.50 per pound
Material 2	$4.60 per pound
Direct labor	
Product A	$6.00 per hour
Product B	$12.00 per hour

Inputs Per Unit of Finished Product	Product A	Product B
Direct material 1	0.5 lbs	1.3 lbs
Direct material 2	0.8 lbs	0.4 lbs
Direct labor	2 hrs	0.5 hrs

Information regarding the year 19X4:

Finished Goods

	Product A	Product B
Expected sales in units	20,000	10,000
Selling price per unit	$40.00	$50.00
Projected ending inventory in units	2,500	5,000
Beginning inventory in units	3,500	4,000

Direct Materials

	No. 1	No. 2
Beginning inventory in lbs	4,000	7,000
Projected ending inventory in lbs	3,000	3,000

(Work in process inventory is to be ignored.)

At the budgeted level of volume, the following *factory overhead* costs will be incurred. Factory overhead is applied on the basis of *direct labor hours.*

Indirect materials	$41,000	Maintenance	20,000
Indirect labor	50,000	Depreciation	60,000
Supervision	65,000	Property taxes	40,000
Supplies	10,000	Insurance	25,000
Power and light	80,500	Total factory overhead	$391,500

Administrative and Marketing Expenses

Variable:	Amount	Fixed:	Amount
Uncollectible accounts	$65,000	Executive salaries	$60,000
Travel	26,000	Sales salaries	40,000
Supplies	13,000	Clerical wages	30,000
		Advertising	12,000
		Miscellaneous	4,000
Total Expenses			$250,000

Required: Prepare the following schedules for the year 19X4:

1. Sales budget
2. Production budget, in units
3. Direct-material-purchases budget
4. Direct-labor budget
5. Factory-overhead budget
6. Ending-inventory budget
7. Cost-of-goods-sold budget
8. Expense budget
9. Income statement (federal income tax rate is 30 percent)

Solution to Comprehensive Illustration

FLEMING COMPANY
Master Operating Budget -- 19X4

Schedule 1-- Sales Budget			
	Units	Selling Price	Total Sales
Product A	20,000	$40.00	$800,000
Product B	10,000	$50.00	500,000
Total Sales Revenue			$1,300,000

Schedule 2 -- Production Budget (units of finished goods)

Units required for:	Product A	Product B
Sales	20,000	10,000
Ending inventory	2,500	5,000
Total required	22,500	15,000
Less: Beginning inventory	3,500	4,000
Units to be produced	19,000	11,000

Schedule 3 -- Direct Materials Purchases Budget

Material 1		Material 2	
Ending inventory (lbs.)	3,000	Ending inventory (lbs.)	3,000
Production (see Sch. 1)		Production (see Sch. 1)	
Prod A (19,000 × 0.5)	9,500	Prod A (19,000 × 0.8)	15,200
Prod B (11,000 × 1.3)	14,300	Prod B (11,000 × 0.4)	4,400
Total lbs required	26,800	Total lbs required	22,600
Less begin. invent.	4,000	Less begin. invent.	7,000
Lbs to be purchased	22,800	Lbs to be purchased	15,600
Price per pound	$6.50	Price per pound	$4.60
Cost of Mat. 1 purch.	$148,200	Cost of Mat. 2 purch.	$71,760
Total cost of materials purchased			$219,960

Schedule 3A -- Direct Materials Usage Budget

Material	Quantity	Cost per lb	Amount
1	23,800	$6.50	$154,700
2	19,600	$4.60	90,160
Total cost of materials used in production			$244,860

Schedule 4 -- Direct Labor Budget

Product	Units Produced	DLH Per Unit	Total DLH	Rate	Amount
A	19,000	2.0	38,000	$6.00	$228,000
B	11,000	0.5	5,500	12.00	66,000
Total labor hours used			43,500		
		Total direct labor budget			$294,000

Schedule 5 -- Factory Overhead Budget

Indirect Materials	$41,000	Maintenance	$20,000
Indirect labor	50,000	Depreciation	60,000
Supervision	65,000	Property taxes	40,000
Supplies	10,000	Insurance	25,000
Power and light	80,500		
Total actual factory overhead			$391,500

Predetermined Overhead Rate (Based on total Direct Labor Hours)

$$\frac{\$391{,}500}{43{,}500 \text{ hrs}} = \$9.00 \text{ per DLH}$$

Schedule 6 -- Ending Inventory Budget

Direct Materials	Pounds	Price/Lb.	Amount
Material 1	3,000	$6.50	$19,500
Material 2	3,000	$4.60	$13,800
Direct materials ending inventory			$33,300

Finished Goods	Units	Cost Per Unit (See Sch A)	Amount
Product A	2,500	$36.93	$92,325
Product B	5,000	$20.79	$103,950
Finished Goods Ending Inventory			$196,275

Schedule 6A -- Computation of Unit Costs of Finished Goods

	Product A			Product B		
Input	Input Cost	Qty	Amount	Input Cost	Qty	Amount
Material 1	$6.50	0.5	$3.25	$6.50	1.3	$8.45
Material 2	4.60	0.8	3.68	4.60	0.4	1.84
Direct Labor	6.00	2.0	12.00	12.00	0.5	6.00
Overhead	9.00	2.0	18.00	9.00	0.5	4.50
Cost per Unit			$36.93			$20.79

Schedule 7 -- Cost of Goods Sold Budget

See Schedule	Manufacturing Costs	
3A	Direct material used	$244,860
4	Direct labor	294,000
5	Factory overhead	391,500
	Total manufacturing costs	$930,360
* ↓	Add: Beginning inventory-finished goods	212,415
6A	Subtract: Ending inventory-finished goods	(196,275)
	Cost of goods sold	$946,500

* ↑ Beginning inventory - finished goods

Product A	(3,500 × $36.93 #)	$129,255
Product B	(4,000 × $20.79)	83,160
Total		$212,415

(See Schedule 6A for unit costs)

Schedule 8 -- Expense Budget

Administrative Expenses:		Marketing Expenses:	
Executive salaries	$60,000	Sales commissions	$65,000
Clerical wages	30,000	Sales salaries	40,000
Supplies	13,000	Travel & entertainmnt	26,000
Miscellaneous	4,000	Advertising	12,000
Total administrative	107,000	Total marketing	143,000
Total expenses			$250,000

Schedule 9 -- Budgeted Income Statement

See Schedule		
1	Sales revenue	$1,300,000
7	Cost of goods sold	946,500
	Gross profit	$ 353,500
8	Expenses	250,000
	Operating income	$103,500
	Income Taxes @ 30%	31,050
	Net income	$72,450

ILLUSTRATION OF FINANCIAL BUDGET SYSTEM

The financial budget system consists mainly of the *cash budget*, which is dependent upon the estimation of cash receipts and cash disbursements. The *capital budget* in this system consists only of the current demands on cash. *Capital budgeting* is a specialized field overlapping both accounting and finance, and is treated in a separate chapter.

Small- and medium-sized companies may rely more on the analysis of cash flow than on the income statement as a measure of success. The owners depend on a steady flow of cash from which they withdraw their income. They invest heavily in depreciable assets to reduce their net income on the books and consequently pay less in income taxes. Larger corporations depend on the analysis of cash flow to guarantee that the current obligations will be met promptly, and to gain the financial advantages of wise cash management.

The master budget illustration of the Fleming Company is presented to show how an operational budget is prepared. The master budget is an annual budget, which may be *calendarized,* or divided into smaller calendar units, quarters, months, or weeks. Cash budgets are more helpful if prepared on a monthly, or even a weekly basis.

Based on the budget data from the Fleming Company a cash budget is illustrated on a quarterly basis. Although a shorter period is preferable in practice, it is less cumbersome to use an illustration with less detail. Also, many assumptions must be specified regarding the collection and payment practices of the company. These assumptions, along with additional information, are presented below

Cash Budget Information

The Fleming Company began the year, January 1, 19X4 with a cash balance of $27,000. It had budgeted total sales revenue at $1,300,000 with a quarterly breakdown of:

Last quarter 19X3	$300,000
First quarter 19X4	100,000
Second quarter 19X4	400,000
Third quarter 19X4	500,000
Fourth quarter 19X4	300,000
Total year 19X4	$1,300,000

In order to prepare the quarterly cash budget the company has made these assumptions based on past observations and other relevant observations.

1. Eighty percent of total sales are on account (credit sales) and the remainder are cash sales.

2. Of the sales on account, 75 percent are collected in the same quarter as the sale, and 20 percent are collected in the following quarter. The collections expected from the last quarter of 19X3 are $48,000.

3. Cash payments on purchases of direct materials are made, 70 percent in the quarter of purchase, and 30 percent in the following quarter. The terms of the industry are net 60 days, no cash discounts. Payments on last quarter, 19X3 purchases are budgeted at $15,000. Purchases of direct materials are budgeted at $219,960 for the year. The budget office has calendarized this amount quarterly.

First quarter	$20,000
Second quarter	70,000
Third quarter	80,000
Fourth quarter	49,960
Total year	$219,960

4. Direct labor and factory overhead are paid in the same quarter incurred. They are calendarized quarterly as follows:

	Direct Labor	Factory Overhead*
First quarter	$40,000	$65,000
Second quarter	80,000	110,000
Third quarter	104,000	120,000
Fourth quarter	70,000	96,500
Total year	$294,000	$391,500

*Factory overhead includes depreciation of $15,000 per quarter.

5. Expenses:

Variable Expenses:	
Uncollectible accounts	4% of total sales
Travel	3% of total sales
Supplies	1% of total sales
Fixed Expenses:	
Executive salaries	$15,000 per quarter
Clerical salaries	$ 7,500 per quarter
Sales salaries	$10,000 per quarter
Advertising	$3,000 per quarter

Also miscellaneous expenses of $1,000 were paid in the first quarter and $3,000 in the third quarter, which included $2,820 in interest.

6. Capital Expenditures
   Furniture and equipment

Second quarter	$42,000
Third quarter	$35,000
Fourth quarter	$26,000

7. Dividends -- Cash dividends of $7,000 are declared and paid in each of the first three quarters, and $7,560 in the fourth quarter.

8. Financing -- A minimum balance of $10,000 is required at the end of the quarter. Borrowing, in multiples of $1,000 only, is allowed up to $50,000 per quarter. The bank charges 1 percent per month, 12 percent per annum. Assume that borrowing takes place at the beginning of the quarter, and repayments take place at the end of the quarter.

The following schedules are based on information from the master operating budget, and on other assumptions.

Schedule C 1	Cash Receipts Schedule
Schedule C 2	Cash Disbursements Schedule
Schedule C 3	Expenses Schedule
Schedule C 4	Cash Budget

Schedule C 1

Fleming Company
Cash Receipts Schedule
For Year Ended December 31, 19X4

	1st Qtr.	2nd Qtr.	3rd Qtr.	4th Qtr.	Total 19X4
Sales revenue	$100,000	$400,000	$500,000	$300,000	$1,300,000
Proportion on acctount	0.80	0.80	0.80	0.80	
Sales on account	$80,000	$320,000	$400,000	$240,000	$1,040,000
Collections:					
Last qtr. 19X3	$48,000				$48,000
1st. qtr. 19X4	60,000	$16,000			76,000
2nd. qtr. 19X4		240,000	$64,000		304,000
3rd. qtr. 19X4			300,000	$80,000	380,000
4th. qtr. 19X4				180,000	180,000
Collections on credit sales	$108,000	$256,000	$364,000	$260,000	$988,000
Add: Cash sales	20,000	80,000	100,000	60,000	260,000
Total cash receipts	$128,000	$336,000	$464,000	$320,000	$1,248,000

Schedule C 2

Fleming Company
Cash Disbursements Schedule
For Year Ended December 31, 19X4

	1st Qtr.	2nd Qtr.	3rd Qtr.	4th Qtr.	Total Year
Direct material purch.	$20,000	$70,000	$80,000	$49,960	$219,960
Cash payments:					
Last qtr. 19X3	$15,000				$15,000
1st qtr. 19X4	14,000	$6,000			20,000
2nd qtr. 19X4		49,000	$21,000		70,000
3rd qtr. 19X4			56,000	$24,000	80,000
4th qtr. 19X4				34,972	34,972
Payment for direct material	$29,000	$55,000	$77,000	$58,972	$219,972
Direct labor	$40,000	$80,000	$104,000	$70,000	$294,000
Factory overhead (excluding deprec.)	50,000	95,000	105,000	81,500	331,500
Total cash disbursments	$119,000	$230,000	$286,000	$210,472	$845,472

Schedule C3

Fleming Company
Expenses Schedule
For Year Ended December 31, 19X4

	1st Qtr.	2nd Qtr.	3rd Qtr.	4th Qtr.	Total Year
Sales revenue	$100,000	$400,000	$500,000	$300,000	$1,300,000
Variable Exp:					
Uncollectible accounts 4 %	4,000	16,000	20,000	12,000	52,000
Travel 3%	3,000	12,000	15,000	9,000	39,000
Supplies 1%	1,000	4,000	5,000	3,000	13,000
Total variable expenses	$8,000	$32,000	$40,000	$24,000	$104,000
Fixed expense:					
Admin. exp:					
Executive salaries	15,000	15,000	15,000	15,000	60,000
Clerical wages	7,500	7,500	7,500	7,500	30,000
Miscellaneous	1,000		3,000*		4,000
Marketing exp.					
Sales salaries	10,000	10,000	10,000	10,000	40,000
Advertising	3,000	3,000	3,000	3,000	12,000
Total fixed expenses	$36,500	$35,500	$38,500	$35,500	$146,000
Total expenses	$44,500	$67,500	$78,500	$59,500	$250,000
Less unc.accts.	4,000	16,000	20,000	12,000	52,000
Total cash expenses	$40,500	$51,500	$58,500*	$47,500	$198,000

*Includes interest of $2,820.

Schedule C 4

Fleming Company
Cash Budget
For Year Ended December 31, 19X4

	See Sch	1st Qtr.	2nd Qtr.	3rd Qtr.	4th Qtr.	Total Year
Begin. cash bal.		$27,000	$10,500	$10,000	$47,500	$27,000
Add: cash receipts	C1	128,000	336,000	464,000	320,000	1,248,000
Cash avail.		155,000	346,500	474,000	367,500	1,275,000
Deduct:						
Cash disb.	C2	119,000	230,000	286,000	210,472	845,472
Expenses	C3	40,500	51,500	55,680	47,500	195,180
Income tax.	9	8,000	8,000	8,000	7,050	31,050
Capital exp.			42,000	35,000	26,000	103,000
Cash div.		7,000	7,000	7,000	7,560	28,560
Total cash payments		174,500	338,500	391,680	298,582	1,203,262
Receipts over (under) payments		(19,500)	8,000	82,320	68,918	71,738
Financing:						
Add: Loans		30,000	2,000			32,000
Repayment of loans				(32,000)		(32,000)
Repayment of interest *				(2,820)		(2,820)
Ending cash balance		$10,500	$10,000	$47,500	$68,918	$68,918

*Interest computations:

$30,000 for 9 months @ 1% per month	=	$2,700
$ 2,000 for 6 months @ 1% per month	=	120
Total interest		$2,820

Fleming Company
Budgeted Balance Sheet 19X3 and 19X4

ASSETS

See Sch	Assets	19X3		19X4	
C4	Cash	$27,000		$68,918	
C1	Accounts rec (net)	48,000		48,000	
6	Direct materials inventory (a)	58,200		33,300	
6	Finished goods inventory	212,415		196,275	
	Total current assets		$345,615		$346,493
	Property, plant, & equipment (b)	400,000		503,000	
	Less: accumulated depreciation (c)	(60,000)		(120,000)	
	Net P, P & E		340,000		383,000
	Land		120,000		120,000
	Total assets		$805,615		$849,493

LIABILITIES & OWNER'S EQUITY

See Sch	Liabilities and Owners Equity	19X3		19X4	
C2	Current liabilities (d)	$15,000		$14,988	
	Long-term liabilities	300,000		300,000	
	Total liabilities		$315,000		$314,988

	Capital stock		200,000		200,000
	Retained earnings, December 31		290,615		
9	Add: Net income 19X4			72,450	
C4	Deduct dividends			(28,560)	
	Retained earnings, December 31				334,505
	Total liabilities and owner's equity		$805,615		$849,493

Note (a)

Material 1	4,000 units @ 6.50	$26,000
Material 2	7,000 units @ 4.60	$32,200
Beginning inventory		$58,200

Note (b) Property, plant and equipment

Balance Jan. 1, 19X4	$400,000
Acquisitions	103,000
Balance Dec. 31, 19X4	$503,000

Note (c) Depreciation on factory property, plant, and equipment

Balance Jan 1, 19X4	$60,000
19X4 depreciation	60,000
Balance Dec 31, 19X4	$120,000

Note (d) $49,960 × 30% = $14,988

5

Allocation of Indirect Costs

One of the most important functions of managerial accountants is the capability of tracing costs and expenses to product lines, production departments, job orders, and to other cost objectives of the company. *Statement of Management Accounting (SMA) 1B*, which describes the objectives of management activity, includes traceability as part of the measurement process. In order to analyze and interpret accounting data, an effective effort must be made to trace costs and expenses to the appropriate cost objective whenever possible. Some costs, such as direct materials, are easily traced to product lines. The clerical expense of tracing this type of production cost is relatively low.

If time and expense were unlimited it would be possible to identify most costs and expenses with a cost objective, such as a product line, a department, or a function. In theory, almost all costs and expenses are traceable once the cost objective is defined. But, in practice, it may be too costly to establish elaborate systems of tracing production costs to product lines. A typical manufacturing firm may have several hundred different products. They may range in sales value from $1 to more than $1,000. The clerical expense of tracing all of the production costs and all of the administrative and marketing expenses to the low-priced products may actually exceed their total sales value. The result is that the preponderance of costs and expenses may be allocated rather than directly traced to the cost objective in actual practice.

A serious consequence of improperly allocating costs that cannot be economically traced directly to the product lines, is that unprofitable product lines could be carried, while profitable product lines could be discontinued. Marketing executives who are not sufficiently informed are forced to make product decisions based on intuition rather than profitability. It is imperative that the most precise methods of allocation within the practical limits of cost-effectiveness are used. The drastic effects of worldwide competition on some U.S. industries have caused a long overdue inquiry into the allocation methods used in the traditional cost accounting systems.

ASSUMPTIONS AND OBJECTIVES of COST ALLOCATION

A cost accounting system collects direct and indirect costs and assigns these costs to cost objects. The system should provide cost information for financial accounting requirements as well as for management decision-making purposes. The cost system should identify costs first by responsibility centers and ultimately with final cost objects. (In accordance with *Statement of Management Accounting 4G,* issued June 1, 1987.)

1. A single cost objective must be clearly identified, such as one product line, one activity, one patient bed-day in a hospital, or one production department in a factory.
2. It is assumed that allocation that takes place is both technically feasible and cost-effective.
3. All indirect costs and expenses must be allocated ultimately to the revenue producing divisions of the company in order to ensure accountability of total costs.

ALLOCATION CRITERIA

The four criteria commonly used in selecting an allocation base (*Statement of Management Accounting 4 B*) are

1. Benefit received from the cost
2. Cause of the incurrence of cost
3. Fairness to the cost objective
4. Ability to bear the cost

The first two, benefit and cause, are most commonly used in practice. They frequently coincide in those situations where the user cost objective may both benefit from and cause the incurrence of the cost in the service department. Fairness is difficult to administer because of its subjective nature. Using the ability to bear the cost as an allocation base criterion does not serve the purpose of measuring management performance. It should be used with discretion.

Activity-based costing emphasizes the *cause* of the incurrence of the cost. Cost drivers are the causes behind resource costs and are instrumental in measuring the performance of activities. Benefit received, fairness to the cost objective, and ability to bear the cost are theoretically ignored by the ABC/ABM advocates. This could be a major weakness in their system, unless the decision-making management recognizes the absence of these factors. All of the allocation methods described in this chapter may be applied to both traditional and activity-based systems. The activity-based philosophy is different, but any allocation method can be modified or applied directly to satisfy ABC/ABM criteria. Exhibit 5-1 illustrates the difference between the traditional and the activity-based costing philosophies of allocating indirect costs.

Exhibit 5-1
Traditional versus ABC Methods

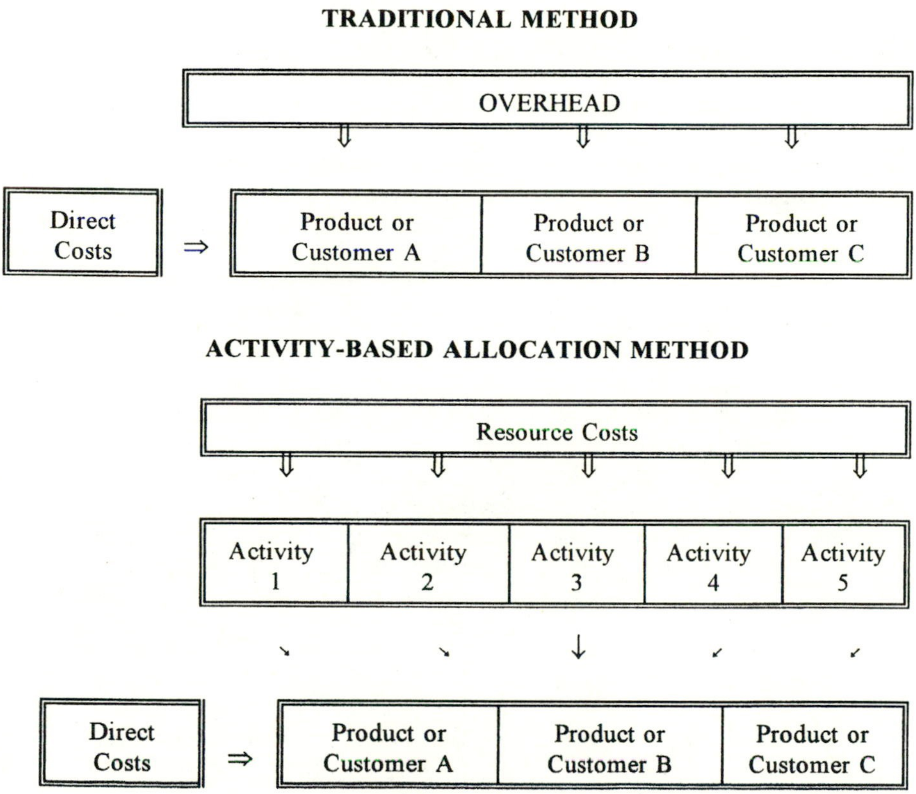

Costs and Expenses that are Traceable

Costs and expenses that can be directly traced to a revenue-producing division, a single product line, or to any defined cost objective need not be allocated. Traditionally, only direct materials and direct labor were assumed to be traceable to separate product lines. That assumption will no longer be followed. Instead, it will be assumed that elements of manufacturing overhead, administrative expenses, and marketing expenses may be economically traced to product lines, or revenue-producing divisions. Activity-based costing systems attempt to improve the allocation of indirect costs by identifying the activities that are responsible for the costs.

Below is a summary of the costs and expenses in a manufacturing firm that are traceable to a given cost objective or that can be traced to the cost objective, depending on the individual situation.

Manufacturing or Product costs	**Traceable to**
Direct materials and Direct labor	Individual jobs and/or product lines
Factory overhead identified with one cost objective	Activities, processes, departments or cells
Expenses or Period costs	**May be traceable to**
Administrative, Marketing, Engineering, Research and Development	Activities, cells, departments, individual jobs, processes, product lines

Costs and Expenses that are to be Allocated

Costs and expenses that cannot be economically traced to a cost objective are to be allocated on a rational basis. The specific types of indirect costs that are described in this chapter are listed here. Due to the importance of allocation methods in a changing economic environment both traditional costs and those that arise in response to the new technological changes in production methods are included. For accounting purposes, expenses are not normally allocated, but are charged to the accounting period in total. Nevertheless, there may be an attempt to trace expenses to cost objectives when it serves the purposes of management.

Nontraceable Cost Description	**Allocated to Cost Objectives**
Indirect manufacturing costs Joint manufacturing costs Service department costs	Activities, cells, production departments, service departments, individual jobs, processes, product lines
Administrative expenses: Controller Engineering	 Accounting services Product lines, processes
Marketing expenses: Selling Physical distribution	 Product lines, territories Activities, product lines, territories

Illustration of Traceability in a Flexible Manufacturing System

The painting work cell in an automobile assembly plant includes a flexible manufacturing system consisting of both robots and automatic machines that perform most of the operations to paint automobile bodies on a production line. The painting work cell requires no human labor. All costs are traceable to any specific model passing through the work cell.

Assume that there are two robots and four automatic machines in the system, and that 5,000 automobiles are produced annually. The costs of the machinery and the annual operating costs are:

Robots	$500,000 each
Automatic machines	$200,000 each
Annual operating costs	
Lubrication	$ 50,000
Power	$120,000

In traditional cost accounting systems, an estimated amount of depreciation of capital equipment is charged against operations, usually on a time period basis. Critics claim that these methods are inaccurate and that the new world-class systems can alleviate the inherent problems of the traditional systems. They point out that flexible manufacturing systems and other automated systems improve the tracing of costs to a cost objective. The costs of the robots and the automated machinery can be traced directly to each product or batch of products by merely following the flow of materials through the work cells. This is essentially an extension of the production method of depreciation, which estimates the number of operations or units of output the machine can produce during its lifetime.

What is overlooked by the critics is that it is impossible to eliminate the problem of estimation. For example, assume that each robot and each of the four automated machines has an estimated life expectancy of 10,000 paint operations. Thus, each machine is assumed to paint 5,000 autos per year for a two-year period. Depreciation is charged directly to each unit produced.

Cost Summary	Total Cost	Total Units	Per Unit
Robots (1)	$ 500,000	10,000	$ 50
Machines (1)	$ 200,000	10,000	$ 20
Lubrication	$ 50,000	5,000	$ 10
Power	$ 120,000	5,000	$ 24

Assume that the actual economic life of one of the robots and all four machines is the same as estimated and that the actual operating costs are equal to the estimated costs. The economic life of the other robot, named *Picasso* by the employees, will vary as described in the following three situations.

Situation A

Assume that the robot, Picasso, cost $500,000 and paints 10,000 automobiles before it becomes inoperable, obsolete, and is scrapped with no salvage value. Each automobile painted by Picasso will have received $50 in depreciation. A summary of the costs charged to each automobile passing through the paint work cell during both years is as follows:

Robots (2)	@ $ 50	$100
Machines (4)	@ $ 20	$ 80
Lubrication		$ 10
Power		$ 24
Total cost per auto		$214

Situation B

Assume that Picasso becomes inoperable with no salvage value after just 5,000 operations. Each automobile will have received the same $50 in depreciation, leaving an undepreciated balance of $250,000 in the robot's asset account. This balance must be disposed of in the accounting records. The products have already been sold assuming a cost of $50 for Picasso's operation, yet the true cost per automobile was $100. The error may be both significant and material. The cost of the paint work cell charged to one automobile during the first year should have been

Robot (1)	@ $ 50	$ 50
Picasso	@ $100	$100
Machines (4)	@ $ 20	$ 80
Lubrication		$ 10
Power		$ 24
Total cost per auto		$264

Situation C

Assume that Picasso continues to operate without loss of efficiency for 20,000 operations, after which it becomes inoperable with no salvage value. Each of the first 10,000 automobiles has been charged $50 in depreciation for Picasso. Because the actual life of Picasso was not anticipated, there is no balance left in the asset account to charge to the latter 10,000 automobiles. Each of the 20,000 automobiles should have been charged $25, therefore they have all been mischarged. The first 10,000 autos have been charged too much and the last 10,000 received no charge at all. At the end of the second year, although accountants may find ways to adjust some of the official records, there is no way to correct management decisions that may have depended on this cost data. The costs that should have been charged to each automobile during the first year are

Robot (1)	@ $ 50	$ 50
Picasso	@ $ 25	$ 25
Machines (4)	@ $ 20	$ 80
Lubrication		$ 10
Power		$ 24
Total cost per auto		$189

The following summary shows that during the first year, the charges to each unit will be the same regardless of the actual economic life of the robot, Picasso. Based on the actual life of Picasso, the cost of one automobile passing through the paint work cell during the first year should have been $50, or 23 percent more in Situation B and $25, or 12 percent less in Situation C.

Cost per unit	Accounting charge	Correct charge
Situation A	$214	$214
Situation B	$214	$264
Situation C	$214	$189

Observations

The situations presented are not exaggerated to stress a point. It is difficult to estimate the number of operations a specific machine will perform in its lifetime. Traditional cost treatment, which bases depreciation on time, not units of production, is equally unreliable for the same reason. The actual usable lifespan of almost any depreciable asset is difficult to estimate. The three situations illustrate that more sophisticated methods to trace the operations of Picasso, the robot, to each product line will not guarantee that the cost allocations will be accurate. It is the skill of estimating the usable life of the asset that is most important in the process.

TWO-STAGE ACTIVITY-BASED ALLOCATIONS

Indirect production costs may be allocated to final cost objects by following a two-stage allocation system that assumes that all service cost centers and production cost centers are identified separately. In stage one, indirect production costs are assigned either to a production cost center or to a service cost center. Total service center costs are reassigned to the production cost centers. In stage two, the total indirect costs of the production cost centers are allocated to products that are produced in the production cost centers. The following description may be applied to both traditional and activity-based applications.

The two-stage method was advocated in the late 1980's by Harvard professors Robin Cooper and Robert Kaplan for activity-based costing systems. Stage one allocations are based on resource cost drivers; the allocations are made from the resources to the activities. Stage two allocations are based on activity cost drivers; the allocations are made form the activities to the final cost objects.

Stage One Allocation

A *stage one allocation* is an assignment of costs or expenses to a cost objective that will be reallocated to a revenue-producing division, product line, job order, or another secondary cost objective. For example, the computer center provides services to other service departments as well as to production departments. The operating costs of the computer center represent stage one. They are not charged directly to products or jobs, but are allocated to other departments that may reallocate them to the final cost objective.

Stage Two Allocation

A *stage two allocation* is one that assigns production costs or expenses to revenue producing divisions, or to product lines. Product lines must be specified as to the individual, exact model in order to identify the appropriate basis for allocating costs and expenses. A company may have a large number of product lines that vary substantially in size, sales value, units produced and units sold. A stage two allocation is one that has reached its final destination within the overall organization or within a revenue-producing division of the organization.

Exhibit 5-2
Two-Stage Allocations

Stage One Allocations

(Based on resource cost drivers, or traditional methods)

Stage Two Allocations

(Overhead rate based on activity cost driver)

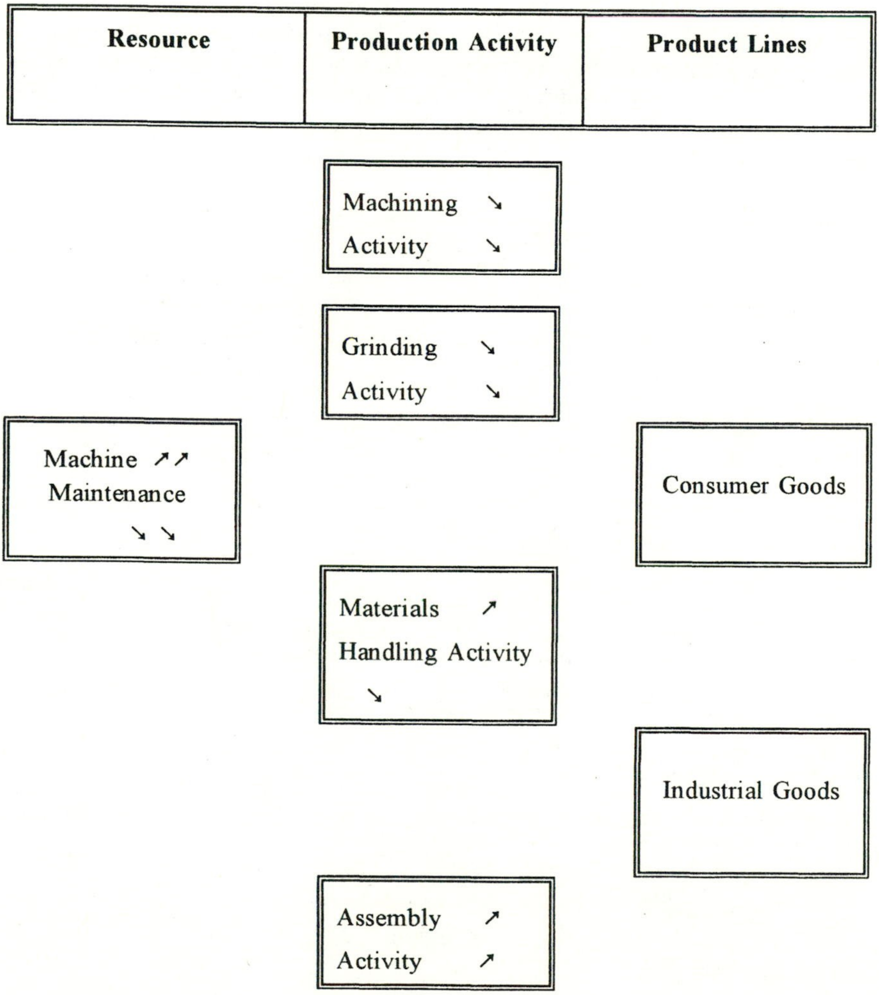

ALLOCATION RATE METHODS

The budgeted or actual indirect costs incurred by a service department or by a common cost production department may be allocated by use of a *single rate* or by a *dual rate*.

Actual Rates versus Budgeted Rates

The use of actual cost rates allows for a less uniform pattern of charges to the cost objectives. Actual rates are subject to fluctuations and variations that may distort the overall cost of the final product. Budgeted rates are averages that smooth out the unpredictable variations in the charges to the cost objectives and eventually to the final product. It is preferable to use budgeted rates whenever there is evidence that the use of actual rates would materially distort the cost allocation process.

Single-Rate versus Dual-Rate Methods

A single allocation rate may be used to allocate the indirect costs of a cost center to the cost objectives. For example, the duplication center serves only production department A, B, and C. The total monthly costs of the duplication center are $100,000 and are allocated on the basis of copies made by the user departments. Usage for last month was

	Copies
Department A	1,000
Department B	6,000
Department C	3,000
Total copies	10,000

The use of a single rate assumes that the cost driver is the number of copies made, or current use of the services. A single rate of $10 per copy was calculated and the allocated costs of the Duplicating Center to the Production Department was

Department A	$10,000
Department B	$60,000
Department C	$30,000

Dual-Rate Method

The use of dual allocation rates recognizes that there are two separate cost drivers based on the variability of the costs incurred by the provider department. Variable costs are driven by the current use of the user departments, but fixed costs are driven by a long-term commitment to provide services to the user departments. For example, the annual budget indicates that the expected use by the production departments will be

Department A	$30,000
Department B	$20,000
Department C	$50,000

Of the $100,000 monthly costs of the Duplication Center $40,000 are variable and $60,000 are fixed. Applying the dual-rate method would result in the following allocation of the $100,000 to the production departments.

Production Department

	A	B	C
Variable costs			
$40,000 × 1/10 =	$ 4,000		
$40,000 × 6/10 =		$24,000	
$40,000 × 3/10 =			$12,000
Fixed costs			
$60,000 × 3/10 =	18,000		
$60,000 × 2/10 =		12,000	
$60,000 × 5/10 =			30,000
Total costs	$22,000	$36,000	$42,000

There is a significant change in the amount allocated to all three departments with the use of the dual-rate method as compared with the single-rate method. Because the dual-rate method takes into consideration the long-term commitment that the Duplication Center made to service the three production departments, it is superior to the single-rate method.

ALLOCATION OF SERVICE DEPARTMENT COSTS TO PRODUCTION DEPARTMENTS

In a manufacturing facility, cost centers are established to provide support services to the production departments. In a hospital, functions such as nursing care that provide services to revenue producing functions, such as the operating room, have been designated as service cost centers. The costs of the service cost centers may be allocated to the revenue producing (profit) centers in one of three different methods, (1) direct allocation method, (2) step-down allocation method, and (3) reciprocal allocation method.

Huron Manufacturing Company has three service departments in its factory, which manufactures one product line. The Personnel Department handles all factory personnel matters, the Machine Maintenance Department services all machines in the factory as well as the office machines in the Personnel Department, and the Plant Engineering Department services the buildings and grounds, which are part of the factory. The factory has two production departments: Processing and Final Assembly. The allocation bases for the three service departments are as follows:

Department	Basis of Allocation
Personnel	Number of employees
Machine Maintenance	Number of machines
Plant Engineering	Floor space

The following information and data have been extracted from company records for the year 19X4.

Huron Manufacturing Company--19X4

	Service Departments			Production Departments	
	Personnel	Machine Maint.	Plant Engrg.	Processing	Assembly
Direct costs	$24,000	$12,000	$18,000	$150,000	$96,000
Number of employees	10	12	8	50	30
Number of machines	4	8	6	15	35
Floor space in sq. ft.	10,000	15,000	12,000	45,000	30,000

Direct Allocation Method

The first step in the direct allocation method is to determine the percentages of allocation of the service department costs based on production department data only.

Allocation basis	Processing	Assembly
Number of employees	50/80 = 0.625	30/80 = 0.375
Number of machines	15/50 = 0.30	35/50 = 0.70
Floor space (000s)	45/75 = 0.60	30/75 = 0.40

The second step is to allocate the incurred costs of the service departments directly to each production department in accordance with the percentages of allocation derived in step 1.

Allocation of Service Department Costs--Direct Method

	Service Departments			Production Departments		Total
	Person nel	Mach. Maint.	Plant Engrg.	Proces sing	Assem bly	
Dir costs	$24,000	$12,000	$18,000	$150,000	$ 96,000	$246,000
	(24,000)			15,000	9,000	24,000
		(12,000)		3,600	8,400	12,000
			(18,000)	10,800	7,200	18,000
Costs allocated to production departments				$ 29,400	$ 24,600	$ 54,000
Total costs after allocation				$179,400	$120,600	$300,000

Reconciliation Schedule

	Before Allocation	After Allocation
Personnel	$ 24,000	$ 0
Machine Maintenance	12,000	0
Plant Engineering	18,000	0
Processing	150,000	179,400
Assembly	96,000	120,600
Total	$300,000	$ 300,000

Step-Down Allocation Method

The step-down method of allocation is mentioned specifically in SMA 4G as a preferable method of allocating service department costs. It is one of the methods required by federal agencies in allocating hospital service departments costs to revenue-producing departments in order to receive Medicare benefits.

Determination of Step-Down Order

The order of the service departmental costs to be stepped-down is essential. A change in the order of step-down will change the amounts allocated. Other than for reimbursement from federal or state agencies, such as the Medicare and Medicaid payments to hospitals, the order is determined independently by each firm. Two recommended methods are described below

Method 1

Arrange the service departments in order of the largest dollar amount of directly incurred costs. Referring back to the Huron Manufacturing Company data, the order would be (1) Personnel $24,000, (2) Plant Engineering $18,000, and (3) Machine Maintenance $12,000.

Method 2

Arrange the service departments in order of the highest percentage of service given to other service departments. Referring back to the Huron Manufacturing Company's original data, the following analysis is made:

Department	Personnel	Machine Maintenance	Plant Engineering	Total Factory
Number of employees	- #	12	8	100
Percentage	0%	12%	8%	100%
Number of machines	4	- #	6	60
Percentage	7%	0%	10%	100%
Floor space	10,000	15,000	- #	100,000
Percentage	10%	15%	0%	100%

The allocating service department omits its own data.

Ranking Procedure

Department	Percentage of service to other service departments
Plant Engineering	25%
Personnel	20%
Machine Maintenance	17%

The ranking is based on the sum of 10 percent of Plant Engineering services to the Personnel Department and 15 percent to Machine Maintenance. This sum, 25 percent, of services to other service departments is the highest of the three service departments included in the data. While this ranking procedure (Method 2) may be conceptually superior to the highest dollar method (Method 1), it is more difficult to administer. For the sake of simplicity, Method 1 is used to demonstrate the step-down method of allocation in the following table.

Step-Down Allocation Order
Computation of Allocation Percentages

Departments	Person-nel	Plant Engrg	Mach. Maint.	Process-ing	Assem-bly	Total
Personnel: No. of employees	-	8	12	50	30	100
Percentage		8%	12%	50%	30%	100%
Plant Engrg. Floor space (sq ft)	-	-	15,000	45,000	30,000	90,000
Percentage			16.7%	50%	33.3%	100%
Mach. Maint. No. of mach.	-	-	-	15	35	50
Percentage				30%	70%	100%

The Personnel Department is the first department to step down costs. Its directly incurred costs are to be allocated to all other service departments and to all production departments. Based on the number of employees, Plant Engineering will receive 8 percent, Machine Maintenance 12 percent, Processing 50 percent, Assembly 30 percent of the total $24,000 to be allocated from the Personnel Department. At the end of the allocation procedure, the Personnel Department and all other service departments will have zero costs. The second department, Plant Engineering, will allocate costs to all other service departments, except Personnel, and to all production departments. The last service department, Machine Maintenance, will allocate costs only to the two production departments. The following table demonstrates the dollar amounts to be allocated to each production department using the step-down method of allocation.

Allocation of Service Department Costs--Step-Down Method

	Service Departments			Production Departments		Total
	Personnel	Plant Engrg.	Machine maint.	Processing	Assembly	
Direct costs	$24,000	$18.000	$12.000	$150,000	$ 96,000	$246.000
Alloc. of Personnel costs	(24.000)	1.920	2.880	12,000	7.200	19.200
Sub-total		19.920				
Plant Engrg. costs		(19.920)	3.320	9.960	6.640	16.600
Sub-total			18.200			
Machine Maint. costs			(18.200)	5.460	12.740	18.200
Total costs allocated to production departments				$ 27.420	$ 26.580	$ 54.000
Total costs after allocation				$177,420	$122.580	$ 300.000

Personnel costs of $24.000 were allocated to the two other service departments and to the two production departments. The allocated costs of $1,920 from Personnel added to the direct costs of $18,000 from Plant Engineering, totalling $19,920, were allocated to the remaining service department and to the two production departments. Machine Maintenance picked up $2,880 from Personnel and $3,320 from Plant Engineering, which added to its direct costs of $12,000, was distributed to the two production departments, Processing and Assembly. After completing the step-down method of allocation, the total of $54,000 direct costs of the three service departments has been distributed to the two production departments, leaving a zero balance in all three service departments.

Reciprocal Method of Allocation

The step-method of allocation requires that the service departments be ranked to determine the step-down order. The ranking process has an effect on the final allocation outcome as does the allocation method used. A change in the order of step-down will result in a change in the amounts allocated. Judgment is required in the selection of the ranking order in the attempt to allocate the costs equitably.

The *reciprocal* method of allocating service department costs is a mathematical application using simultaneous equations. There is no need to establish a ranking order of allocation, which eliminates one element of potential misallocation. The reciprocal method allows the costs of the service departments to be allocated and reallocated by the precise percentages of service provided to other service departments and ultimately to the producing departments.

other service departments and ultimately to the producing departments.

For demonstration purposes, a new set of data will be provided by the Midland Printing Company. The following table shows the distribution of services from the service departments to all other departments in the company.

Midland Printing Company

	Service Departments		Production Departments	
	Materials Handling	Payroll	Printing	Binding
Direct costs incurred	$ 12,000	$ 10,000	$ 60,000	$ 80,000
Services from: Materials Handling	-	20%	30%	50%
Services from: Payroll	10%	-	60%	30%

The Midland Printing Company has two service departments and two producing departments. The schedule shows the percentages of service provided by the service departments to all other departments, and the direct costs incurred by each department.

The first step in the reciprocal method is to formulate the two simultaneous equations, one for each service department. A simple way is to start at the top of the first service department column and read down. Let MH equal Materials Handling and P equal Payroll.

Material Handling:	MH	=	\$12,000 + .10 P
Payroll:	P	=	\$10,000 + 0.2 MH
	MH	=	\$12,000 + [.10 (10,000 + 0.2 MH)]
	MH	=	\$12,000 + 1,000 + 0.02 MH
	0.98 MH	=	\$13,000
	MH	=	\$13,265
	P	=	\$10,000 + 0.2 (\$13,265)
	P	=	\$10,000 + \$2,653
	P	=	\$12,653

Allocation of Service Department Costs--Reciprocal Method

	Service Departments		Production Departments		Total
	Materials Handling	Payroll	Printing	Binding	
Direct costs	$ 12,000	$ 10,000	$ 60,000	$ 80,000	$140,000
Allocations: Materials Handling	(13,265)	2,653	3,980	6,632	10,612
Payroll	1,265	(12,653)	7,592	3,796	11,388
Total	0	0	$ 71,572	$ 90,428	$162,000

The reciprocal (simultaneous equation) method redistributes the service departments' direct costs to each other in proportion to the services performed before distributing them to the production departments. This method is theoretically superior to both the direct method and the step-down method. It is, however, mathematically complicated in realistic situations. The typical large manufacturer may have as many as fifty service departments.

The above manual solution method would be most difficult with a large number of service departments. The use of computers and electronic spreadsheet software packages makes it relatively easy to apply the reciprocal method to real-world situations. The computer performs the intricate and tedious mathematical computations. Regardless of the number of service departments or production departments, the conceptual formulation of the method remains the same.

Allocation of Joint Costs

Joint costs are common to more than one process, department, or product line. Those industries that use the process costing method are particularly likely to incur joint, or common, costs. Chemical companies such as DuPont and Dow Chemical, use raw materials that are common to a large number of final products. For example, one chemical mixture, which is used in making insecticides, becomes a volatile explosive with only a minor change in its mixture.

Because joint costs are not traceable to a single cost objective, a method of allocation must be used in order to account for the full costs of production. The method used should be in harmony with the production process. However, there are so many variations in production processes that it is not possible to explore all of them. An example of a few typical production processes involving joint costs demonstrates the basic principles.

Example

St. Clair Chemical Company mines and processes industrial products. One of its product, Buron, is a basic material that is mined, processed, and delivered to the processing plant for $40 per barrel. In March 19X1, 10,000 barrels were received from the company mines. The 10,000 barrels of Buron cost $400,000. Additional costs of $20,000 are incurred at the plant site. Buron may be used without additional processing in three separate chemical products with the following market values:

Product	Barrels	Market Value at Split-off
A	2,000	$200,000
B	3,000	180,000
C	5,000	300,000

All three products may be processed further in order to increase their market value. The market values after further processing and the additional costs of processing are shown in the table.

Product	Incremental Processing Costs	Market Value After Further Processing
A	$ 40,000	$ 280,000
B	20,000	200,000
C	60,000	480,000

There are three methods of allocating the joint costs to products A, B, and C in order to account for the full cost of production. The three methods are (1) the physical units method, (2) the sales value at split-off method, and (3) the net realizable value method.

Physical Units Method

The physical units method bases the allocation of joint costs on the barrels (physical units) of each product line.

Product	Units (barrels)	Allocation Ratio	Joint Costs	Allocated Joint Costs
A	2,000	0.20	$ 420,000	$ 84,000
B	3,000	0.30	420,000	126,000
C	5,000	0.50	420,000	210,000
Total	10,000			$ 420,000

The physical units method meets the allocation base selection criteria of benefit and cause in the example, because there appears to be no difference in the incurred joint costs due to the physical differences in a barrel of A, B, or C. This method does not satisfy the criteria of fairness or ability to bear the cost where there is a significant difference in the unit value of each product. In this example, product A would benefit more than either product B or C as demonstrated in the table

Product	Unit Sales Value at Split-Off	Allocated Joint Costs	Sales Value Less Allocated Costs
A	$ 110	$ 42	$ 68
B	60	42	18
C	60	42	18

Sales Value at Split-off Method

The sales value at split-off method stresses the market value of the products in allocating the joint costs. Value as an allocation base recognizes the selection criteria of fairness and ability to bear the cost. This emphasis is reasonable as long as the criteria of benefit and cause are not clearly present.

Product	Market Value at Split-Off	Allocation Ratio	Joint Costs	Allocated Joint Costs
A	$ 220,000	22 ÷ 70 ×	$ 420,000 =	$ 132,000
B	180,000	18 ÷ 70 ×	420,000 =	108,000
C	300,000	30 ÷ 70 ×	420,000 =	180,000
Total	$ 700,000			$ 420,000

An alternative mathematical solution is to divide $420,000 by $700,000, which equals 60 percent, and multiply the market value at split-off of each product by 60 percent. By using the market value at split-off method, product A bears a significantly greater share of the joint costs than in the physical units method. Products B and C both share a smaller portion of allocated joint costs when value is the allocation base used.

Net Realizable Value Method

Products that have joint costs can be processed further in order to increase their market value (MV). Production costs, including a combination of direct materials, direct labor, and variable overhead are incurred in processing the product further. The *net realizable value* of a product is the market value after further processing less the incremental processing costs. The three products that separate from Buron have net realizable values as shown in the table.

Product	Market Value After Further Processing	Incremental Processing Costs	Net Realizable Value
A	$ 280,000	$ 40,000	$ 240,000
B	200,000	20,000	180,000
C	480,000	60,000	420,000
Total	$ 960,000	$ 120,000	$ 840,000

The allocation of the joint costs of $420,000 using the net realizable value method assumes that all three products are processed further. As in the market value at split-off method, the results emphasize fairness and ability to bear the cost as selection criteria.

Product	Net Realizable Value	Allocation Ratio	Joint Costs	Allocated Joint Costs
A	$ 240,000	24 ÷ 84 ×	$ 420,000 =	$ 120,000
B	180,000	18 ÷ 84 ×	420,000 =	90,000
C	420,000	42 ÷ 84 ×	420,000 =	210,000
Total	$ 840,000			$ 420,000

The decision to process further or not is based on the incremental revenues and incremental costs incurred subsequent to the split-off point. This decision is *not* affected by the joint costs or by the method selected for allocation. The decision to process further or not is illustrated in the table.

Product	MV after Further Processing	Market Value at Split-off	Incremental Revenue	Incremental Cost	Revenue Over (Under) Cost	Process Further ?
A	$280,000	$220,000	$ 60,000	$ 40,000	$ 20,000	Yes
B	200,000	180,000	20,000	20,000	0	No
C	480,000	300,000	180,000	60,000	120,000	Yes

Where the incremental revenue exceeds the incremental cost, the product should be processed further. In the above example, product A and product C should be processed further. Any product whose incremental cost exceeds its incremental revenue should not be further processed, and product B, whose incremental revenue and cost are equal, should not be processed further, because it has not increased the income of the firm.

SUMMARY

The allocation methods presented in this chapter represent those acceptable for generally accepted accounting principles. They can be equally applicable to traditional and to activity-based costing systems. The popularity of activity-based costing and management concepts has caused the accounting personnel as well as the operating managers to innovate in the area of cost allocation. The techniques and methods of cost allocation preferred by the ABC/ABM advocates are included in the activity-based costing chapters.

II

Activity-Based Costing Systems

6

The Environment for Activity-Based Systems

THE GLOBAL ENVIRONMENT

The principles and concepts of managerial accounting have not drastically changed since the 1920s, but the production environment has. When Henry Ford introduced the assembly line for the Model T, there was a need for cost control. Henry Ford was reported to have detested cost accounting, but became a multimillionaire in spite of his continued antipathy toward cost control methods.

The world has changed drastically since the Model T. Worldwide competition has forced U.S. manufacturing companies to examine their production systems. Some major U.S. industries will not survive unless they make pervasive changes in the utilization of both physical and human resources. This is the stage that challenges management accountants today. There is pressure to modify the methods, techniques, and procedures that have been used for several decades. Many business practitioners and some of their former professors have already joined forces to modify and adapt the managerial accounting practices to the needs of production system changes in response to worldwide competition.

World Class Competition

The United States dominated the industrial world for three decades after World War II. It also aided the war-devastated countries, particularly its enemies, to rebuild their industries for a world of peaceful trading partners. Not until the late 1970s did the United States recognize that West Germany and Japan were producing high-quality products more efficiently. They were slow to recognize the drastic change in the quality of products coming from Japan.

World-class competition, although nurtured by the United States, is now challenging our major industries. American industries that were slow to change are now forced to improve their production methods and revise their cost control systems in order to survive. The prevailing attitude of the free-world governments is free-trade, even though protectionism is still a major obstacle. The United

States thrives in a free trade environment, growing stronger when challenged and rallying when threatened. American industries are now going through a stage of overhauling their production systems to meet the challenge of world-class competition.

Traditional Systems

The traditional cost accounting systems used in the United States are being challenged by corporate financial and production executives and by professors of both accounting and production management. A major controversy over the relevance of the traditional cost accounting systems has emerged. There are two opposing viewpoints, one that points directly to the cost accounting system is not a direct cause of production problems. Those who support the first position propose a major overhaul of traditional accounting systems in order to solve production problems resulting from world-class competition. Those who take the opposing viewpoint are convinced that the production systems need the overhaul and that the traditional accounting systems cannot directly cause production problems. They point out that management accounting cost systems are already flexible and custom designed so that only minor tune-ups are necessary to accommodate the changes brought about by world-class competition.

THE FACTORY OF THE FUTURE

The factory of the future will have a computer-integrated manufacturing system (CIMS). The CIMS will coordinate and control the various flows of materials, labor, and overhead through the automated machinery and processes in the factory. Included in the CIMS are:

Computer-Aided Design (CAD)--which consists of the use of computers in drafting and design, engineering, and process planning.

Computer Automated Manufacturing (CAM)--which includes numerically controlled machines and machine tools, process control, and automatic inspection devices and mechanisms.

Flexible Manufacturing System (FMS)--which is a series of computer-controlled interlocking machines that perform one production process from start to finish. The FMS replaces production lines that would require human labor involved in materials handling, setups, and other nonvalue activities.

Production and Inventory Management (PIM)--which includes inventory control methods, such as materials requirement planning (MRP), just in time (JIT), which is an inventory reduction system, manufacturing resource planning (MRP II), which is a fully MRPsystem used as the basis of business planning.

Computer-Integrated Manufacturing Systems

The following list describes the most important objectives of computer-integrated manufacturing systems.

1. Increase product quality.
2. Shorten the time required for non-value added activities, such as machine set up time.
3. Reduce inventory levels and push-through versus pull-through methods.
4. Develop flexible manufacturing systems where feasible.
5. Work toward a fully integrated and coordinated production system operated by a centralized computer.

Improve Product Quality

Although Japanese automobiles and electronic equipment are noted for their high quality, it was not long ago that "made in Japan" was a synonym for cheap and breakable. After World War II, the Japanese borrowed many industrial techniques from the United States, and while the U.S. manufacturers were enjoying a seller's market and built obsolescence into their products, the Japanese and European countries began to improve quality.

Some U.S. manufacturers have fallen behind their foreign competitors and must improve quality. Major efforts to improve quality have been made in the automobile industry and other highly competitive industries. A major objective of the new manufacturing environment is to improve quality. The computer-integrated manufacturing system and its related technological changes provide the means for improved product quality.

Shorten Time for Nonvalue Added Activities

The just-in-time concept represents a continuing effort to reduce waste and the time taken by nonvalue added activities in the production process. The objective of JIT is to reduce overall product cost by conserving all resources used in the process.

Non-value added activities are those factory operations that add costs, but not value. Inspection time, job setup time, storage time, and physical movement are such factory activities that may be reduced or even eliminated. The rearrangement of the work stations and the installation of flexible manufacturing systems eliminate much physical movement time and reduce the time taken for the other non-value added activities.

Reduce Inventory Levels

The JIT philosophy centers around inventories. The reduction of inventories saves the associated costs of the physical handling and storage and also saves the financial costs. Historically the emphasis of U.S. manufacturers has been on satisfying the customer by always having the merchandise available. The larger the inventory levels, the less chance of not filling the order.

The JIT philosophy emphasizes lower inventories accompanied by perfect timing of materials, parts, and supplies with the production process. The demands of production are now just in time, not weeks or even days before. This emphasis places pressure on suppliers throughout the entire system. They are all pressured to shorten the timing in order to meet the demands of the primary producer.

Push-Through versus Pull-Through Philosophy

It has been common practice for U.S. manufacturers to mass produce goods in order to lower unit costs. A push-through philosophy has dominated the system. The products are pushed through the production system by the manufacturer's estimates of demand. Automobile dealers have for decades been forced to sell automobiles that no one has ordered.

The pull-through method, which has been promoted under the JIT philosophy, emphasizes the customer's order. The customer's order triggers the system into action. The ordering of parts and materials in smaller quantities is possible, and because of automated machine systems, frequent changes in setups are possible. It must be understood, however, that this approach will not work in all types of manufacturing systems, and the savings accompanying the pull-through method may be lost entirely by the sacrifice of quantity discounts on large purchases of materials, parts and supplies.

Flexible Manufacturing Systems

The flexible manufacturing system is a series of computer-controlled interlocking machines that perform one production process from start to finish. The materials are fed through the FMS without being touched by human hands. The system may consist of both robots and automated machines. The system represents a series of operations that complete one phase in the production process. The FMS eliminates non-value added activities such as materials handling and setup time.

Many U.S. industries are adopting flexible manufacturing systems into the production process. They are complex and require expensive technological research and engineering expertise. They will not be adopted unless they prove to be economically beneficial. Some robotic operations have already been abandoned by manufacturers who found them unsatisfactory under actual conditions.

COST ACCOUNTING SYSTEM OF THE FUTURE

The cost accounting system of the future that will be necessary to accompany the factory of the future will have the following features.

1. The future cost system will emphasize the flow of materials and parts. As materials flow through the production process the system tracks costs at the operational level. Costs are accumulated in cells, processes, or departments.

2. Recognition that automated factories require a redefinition of production costs. The traditional definition of direct and indirect costs no longer serves the needs of modern industry. Emphasis should be on material and conversion costs

classified into (a) direct material costs, (b) resource and activity-based costs of labor, (c) resource and activity-based costs of machines and automation, and (d) resource and activity-based costs of factory support.

3. Allocation methods must be revised or modified to match the changes of the new technology. For example, the production machinery used in a flexible manufacturing system should be depreciated using the production method based on estimated total machine hours and traced to each product or other cost object passing through the system. The traditional method is to charge the straight-line depreciation to factory overhead and allocate the overhead to product lines on an activity base, such as direct labor.

4. The cost accounting system must be refocused to identify the cost drivers (or causal factors) behind nonvalue-added processes and functions, as well as those that directly add value to the product. Storage time, setups, physical movement, and inspection time are costs that do not directly add value to the product. The cost system of the future must attempt to identify the cost drivers behind these nonvalue-added functions.

5. The system of the future will place greater emphasis on estimates and allocations of cost. The decision-making process will depend more on quick responses, which cannot wait for the collection of actual cost data.

The Direct Labor Controversy

One of the main arguments of the critics of traditional cost accounting systems is that the use of direct labor in the allocation of factory overhead is becoming inappropriate as it decreases as a proportion of the total manufacturing costs. Direct labor, which in most cases varies directly, but not always proportionately with output, has traditionally been the reason for a greater proportion of overhead than any other activity factor. People use the cafeteria; the rest rooms; the payroll office; the personnel office; the health services; the utilities that provide heat, lighting, and air conditioning; and numerous other overhead requirements in the factory. A large proportion of these services that are caused by people, no matter how few there are in the factory, are fixed costs and will not disappear as the machine-to-direct-labor ratio increases.

The major objective of allocation is not to justify a specific factor, but to justify that activity base that causes, or is most directly related to the overhead item. Scholars have not limited this causal factor to direct labor, instead they have warned against recommending the use of only one activity base, without examining the true causal factors. Routinely, statistical methods are recommended that assist decision makers in determining the correlation between activity bases and overhead occurrence. Multiple regression techniques are recommended for nonlinear causal factors.

Direct Costs: Time for a Redefinition

The major characteristic of a direct cost is traceability to the cost object, such as the product. In the traditional financial accounting system, only direct materials and direct labor are assumed to be traceable to the product. A computer-integrated manufacturing system incorporates production changes that make it possible to trace some overhead directly to the product.

There is one significant change in cost accounting terminology that may be necessary because of the pressure to change the production process; the change is in the definition of overhead. At present, all factory overhead is assumed to be indirect, not traceable to the product. This definition is strongly challenged by the proponents of activity-based costing.

If some of the overhead costs under CIMS production processes can be directly traced to each product line, then overhead should no longer be assumed to be inherently indirect, and should be divided into direct overhead and indirect overhead. Direct overhead is that which can be traced to the product just as direct material and direct labor. Indirect overhead will have to be allocated to product lines as before. This concept is not new, but it has not been emphasized or foreseen as a panacea for the problems created by the pressures to change the production process.

Total Cost Management

The system of the future must a total cost management (TCM) system, such as activity-based management (ABM). In a total cost management system, as illustrated in Exhibit 6-1, the top level managers must oversee the processes of the entire company. It is their responsibility to see that the research and development (R & D), product engineering, process engineering, manufacturing, service performance, and marketing activities all operate efficiently to serve the customer. Serving value to the customer efficiently is an assurance of profits.

The Effect of Changing Technology on Cost Analysis

The three situations that follow Exhibit 6-1 illustrate the effects of changing production technology on the cost analysis and control system. The first situation represents the traditional production and cost system, which is labor intensive. The second situation represents the introduction of automation, but no change in the cost analyses and control system. The third situation represents the most advanced technological changes in production accompanied by changes in the cost analysis and control system.

The purpose of the illustration is to reveal the positive and negative effects of production changes on the costing system, and to demonstrate the specific changes in the costing system that are necessary to support effective management decision. It has become popular to blame the costing system for the lack of relevant cost information. Cost analysis and control systems are instituted by top management in contrast to financial accounting reporting systems, which must adhere to GAAP rules and regulations. If management wants more specific cost data they must be willing to pay for it. The illustrations reveal the necessity for more detailed and accurate cost tracking under more automated production systems.

Exhibit 6-1
Total Cost Management

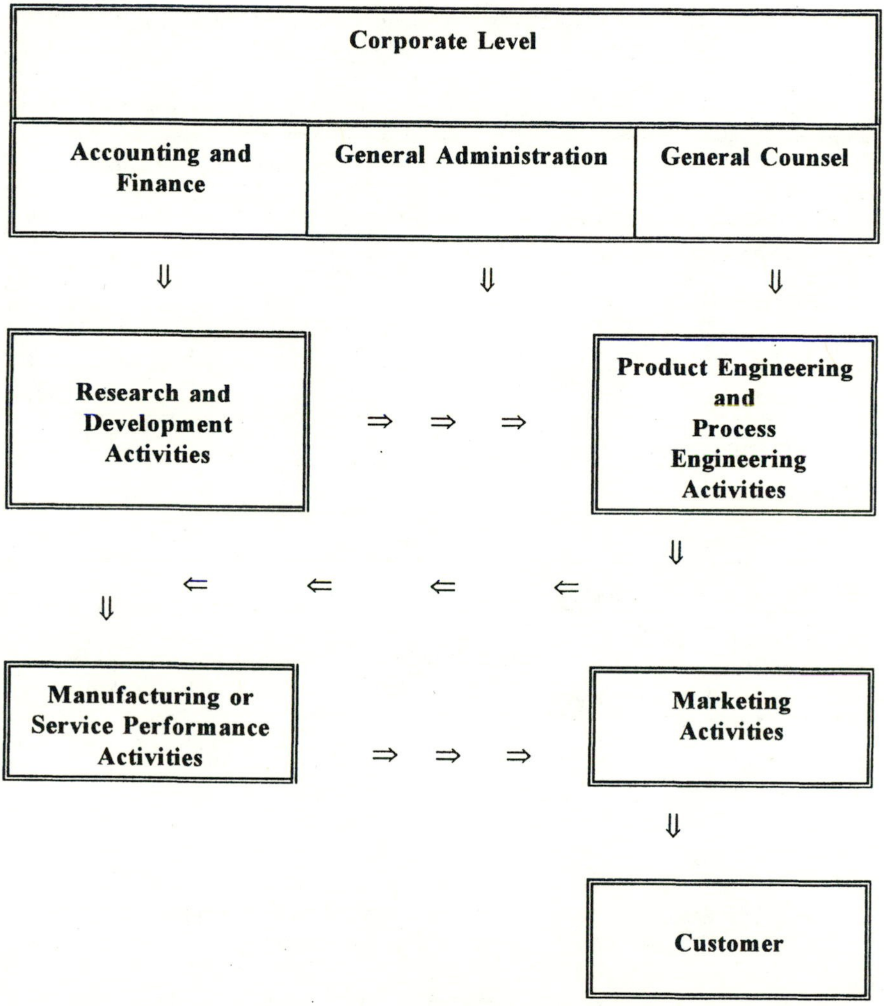

Situation A: Traditional Labor Intensive Manufacturing

Assumptions:

1. Riker Company manufactures industrial containers that are separated into ten product lines.
2. The company is labor intensive.
3. Only direct material and direct labor are traceable to product lines.
4. Direct labor cost is used to apply manufacturing overhead to product lines.
5. No attempt is made to trace expenses to product lines.

	Total	Traceable to Product Lines	Costs to be Allocated
Production costs:			
Direct material	$ 20,000	$ 20,000	
Direct labor	30,000	30,000	
Manufacturing overhead	20,000		$ 20,000
Full absorption cost	$ 70,000	$ 50,000	$ 20,000
Expenses:			
Administrative	10,000		10,000
Marketing	10,000		10,000
Engineering, R & D	10,000		10,000
Total costs and expenses	$100,000	$ 50,000	$ 50,000

Situation B: Machine Intensive Manufacturing

Assumptions:

1. Robots and automated machinery are purchased to replace direct labor. The machines are depreciated on a straight-line basis.

2. Machine depreciation is included in manufacturing overhead, which is allocated on the basis of total machine hours.

3. No attempt is made to trace manufacturing overhead or expenses to product lines.

	Total	Traceable to Product Lines	Costs to be Allocated
Production costs:			
Direct material	$ 20,000	$ 20,000	
Direct labor	10,000	10,000	
Manufacturing overhead	40,000		$ 40,000
Full absorption cost	$ 70,000	$ 30,000	$ 40,000
Expenses:			
Administrative	10,000		10,000
Marketing	10,000		10,000
Engineering, R & D	10,000		10,000
Total costs and expenses	$100,000	$ 30,000	$ 70,000

Observations:

1. The traceable manufacturing costs have decreased with greater automation.

2. There is more reliance on estimated costs and arbitrary allocation of costs than with the labor intensive--situation A.

3. The traditional cost accounting system has become less reliable because of changes in technology, not because of inherent deficiencies in the system. If management desires more traceability in the cost system, they will require it. The cost of acquiring more detail must not exceed the benefits to be derived.

Situation C: Computer-Integrated Manufacturing System

Assumptions:

1. Flexible manufacturing systems are introduced in production and materials handling. The factory layout is rearranged to facilitate the flow of materials through the production processes.

2. Machine time and materials handling time is traced to product lines. The production system along with ordering, billing and payment systems are computerized and coordinated.

	Total	Traceable to Product Lines	Costs to be Allocated
Production costs:			
Direct materials	$ 20,000	$ 20,000	
Direct labor	5,000	5,000	
Manufacturing overhead	45,000	25,000	$ 20,000
Full absorption costs	$ 70,000	$ 50,000	$ 20,000
Expenses:			
Administrative	10,000	2,000	8,000
Marketing	10,000	8,000	2,000
Engineering, R & D	10,000	6,000	4,000
Total costs and expenses	$100,000	$ 66,000	$ 34,000

Observations:

1. The traceable production costs in the labor intensive--Situation A, using traditional costing methods, are at high level because direct labor is assumed to be traceable.

2. Under Situation B--machine intensive, the traceability is diminished. Overhead is assumed to be indirect and no attempt is made to trace the machine time directly to product lines. Even if it were, straight-line depreciation is an estimate and cannot accurately be traced to each unit of output.

3. Under Situation C, with a computer-integrated manufacturing system and the introduction of flexible manufacturing systems, there is greater traceability of machine time and other nonproduction activities. The overall traceability of production costs returns to the level of Situation A, which had more traceable direct labor. However, there is an attempt to trace nonmanufacturing costs, such as engineering, materials handling, ordering, and billing, directly to product lines. This is where Situation C, with CIMS, challenges the traditional cost accounting system. The traditional system does not provide for the attachment of administrative, marketing and engineering expenses to the units of product. The computer integrated manufacturing system provides a computerized cost accounting system that accumulates, classifies, and traces those items of overhead and expenses, which attach specifically to separate product lines.

CONCLUSIONS

It is the change in technology, the production process, that has made it more difficult to trace production costs to product lines. The reduction of the proportion of traceable direct labor and the increase in manufacturing overhead and expenses such as engineering, research and development, and marketing expenses, have made it more difficult to reliably estimate the cost of producing a single product line.

Traditional cost accounting system is not the direct cause of the problems associated with the changes in technology. However, the reduction in traceable production costs calls for a significant and substantial revision in traditional cost accounting concepts.

The emergence of activity-based costing and activity-based management concepts and techniques has challenged both the financial accounting and the management accounting professionals to modify their existing systems to meet the needs of the manufacturing, marketing, and service functions of the organization. Even more important are the demands of the customers.

The factory of the future will require the following modifications in the traditional cost accounting system: (1) Manufacturing overhead must no longer be assumed to be indirect. Those items of overhead that can economically be traced to product lines should be classified as direct manufacturing costs along with direct materials and direct labor (2) Allocation methods that assign estimated costs to product lines must be reexamined in order to more accurately identify the cause-effect relationship (3) Expenses, particularly engineering and marketing expenses, that can be economically traced to product lines should be considered in estimating total product costs. They should be considered as part of total product costs rather than charged to the period. This is a major break with accounting tradition, but as with other management accounting techniques, such as the contribution margin approach, this modification need not be incorporated into the financial accounting system.

7

Activity-Based Systems

ACTIVITY-BASED COSTING CONCEPTS

Activity-based costing is a part of total cost management. It is a relativity new term in accounting. It refers to the basis for cost accumulation, either direct or indirect, to products or services. The activity-based costing system will differ from the traditional system in two ways: (1) cost pools are defined as *activities* rather than production cost centers and (2) the *cost drivers* used to assign activity costs are ***structurally different*** from those used in traditional cost systems.

Direct materials and direct labor are traceable to the product regardless of the costing system. The cost of direct materials is relatively stable and normally a substantial portion of the total product costs, but direct labor costs have been declining as a proportion of total costs in many industries. Indirect overhead costs, marketing, engineering, and administrative costs have become proportionately greater due to the decrease in direct labor. These are the costs that are not traced to the product under the traditional costing models.

Total cost management and ABC recognize that many of these costs, which have been assumed to be nontraceable, are now traceable because of changes in the production process, to plant reorganization, or to technological changes. The rapid growth of computer technology has made it possible to accumulate and classify the enormous amount of data needed for a variety of management information systems.

The activity-based costing system models the usage of the organization resources on the activities performed by these resources, and then links the cost of these activities to outputs, such as products, customers, and services. This linking of resource costs to activities to outputs, a concept essential to management decision making, is the major difference between ABC and traditional costing systems. This characteristic of the ABC concept is referred to as *activity-based management* by scholars and practitioners. Because of these characteristics, activity-based cost systems would be more appropriately referred to as management planning, budgeting, and control systems, than as cost systems.

The traditional approach to assigning costs to products is to attach those costs that are directly traceable to the product and allocate the indirect costs by a measure of volume, such as direct labor hours, direct labor dollars, or machine hours. In the traditional system of cost accounting, the pricing of products is based on a cost plus percentage, modified by market limitations. There is no attempt to itemize nonmanufacturing expenses in the costing process. The primary costs of labor, materials, and manufacturing services are charged directly to the cost objective, such as the product, or allocated on some logical basis to a cost center or cost pool, which in turn is reallocated to the product.

The activity-based costing approach begins with the same general ledger accounts that are incurred for indirect labor, indirect material, indirect factory services, direct and indirect marketing services, and direct and indirect administrative services. These are the basic resources, which the firm uses to perform all of its administrative, manufacturing, and marketing functions in order to achieve its goals. The ABC costing system then identifies the activities performed, and traces the resource costs to the activities. The activities are then linked with the final cost objects, such as products, territories, or customers.

The concept of basing cost assignment by activities was developed for physical distribution costs in the 1960s, but was never accepted formally by the accounting profession. Activity-based costing requires cost pools for each defined activity. Costs are attached to only those products that pass through the activity. Indirect costs that cannot be traced to each unit of product are allocated on the basis of cost drivers, which are responsible for the variability of the activity.

Activity-based costing has been developed to satisfy some of the weaknesses of the traditional systems of accounting for and controlling costs. It is important to recognize the place of ABC systems in the overall picture of cost management. In traditional cost systems, direct materials and labor are the only costs traced directly to the product. Manufacturing overhead costs, by definition, are not traced, but allocated to the product. They may be traced to an activity or a service department or some other cost objective, but not to the product itself. Administrative, engineering and marketing expenses are not included in production costs even when they can be traced directly to the product.

ABC along with other new concepts such as computer-integrated manufacturing (CIM) and total cost management (TCM) advocate changes in the traditional system to coincide with technological changes in the production process. Once the factory has been reorganized to provide maximum efficiency and minimum wasted resources, the cost system can be streamlined to serve the needs of managers, not just to satisfy the presentation of data in the financial statements.

The proponents of ABC/ABM view the requirements of the costing system from the customer's viewpoint. The demands of the customers cause the activities to happen. Exhibit 7-1 illustrates the viewpoint of the advocates of activity-based costing and activity-based management.

Exhibit 7-1
Customer and Product Costs as
Viewed by Activity-Based Costing/Activity-Based Management

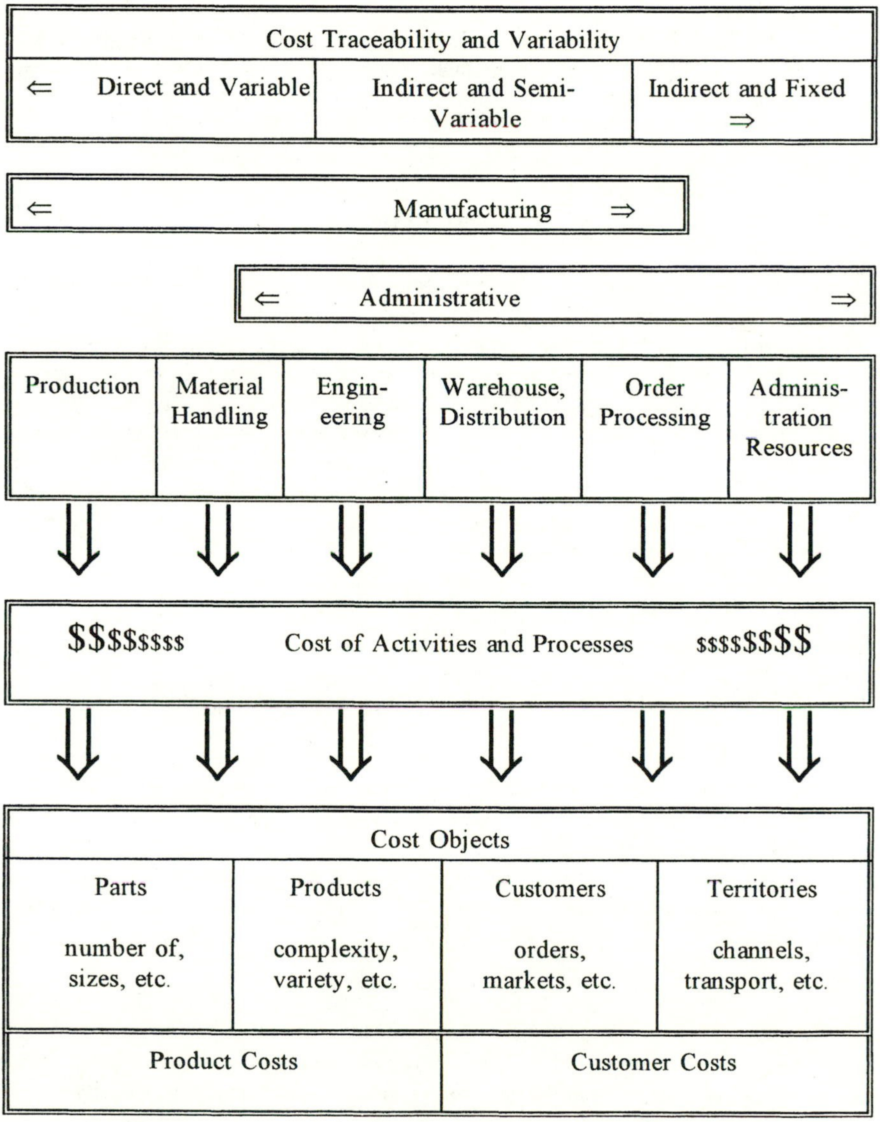

The Consortium for Advanced Manufacturing-International (CAM-I) gives the following definition for activity-based costing:

Definition of Activity-Based Costing

- A method that measures the cost and performance of process-related activities and cost objects
- Assigns cost activities based on their use of resources, and assigns costs to cost objects, such as products or customers, based on their use of activities
- Recognizes the causal relationship of cost drivers to activities

ACTIVITY-BASED MANAGEMENT (ABM)

The concept of *activity-based management* was a natural outgrowth of the activity-based costing (ABC) concept. Although ABC may be a valuable accounting tool, providing more accurate product and process costs, it must also be applied to management decision-making in order to make a significant impact on the firm. Activity-based costing emphasizes the assignment of resource costs to activities, and activity costs to cost objectives, such as products, territories, and customers. Activity-based management focuses on managing the functions or processes, and their activities. ABM evaluates activity performance for the purpose of improving product quality, logistics and time, costs of performing the activity, and other activity characteristics.

The Consortium for Advanced Manufacturing-International gives the following definition for activity-based management.

Definition of Activity-Based Management

- A discipline focusing on the management of activities as the route to continuously improve both the value received by customers and the profit earned by providing this value
- Includes cost driver analysis, activity analysis, and performance analysis
- Draws on activity-based costing as a major source for data and information

Activity-based costing traces the costs of resources to the activities necessary to perform the functions of the firm. By focusing on activities rather than departments, or other traditional cost centers, ABC enables activity-based management to become a dynamic catalyst for product quality improvement, and business process reengineering.

In the following diagram the ABC side emphasizes the tracing of resource costs directly to the activities, and the assignment of activity costs to the cost objectives. The ABM side emphasizes the management of resources by identifying the cost drivers that cause the activities to consume resources, identifying and defining the activities, and establishing criteria to evaluate the effectiveness of the work performed.

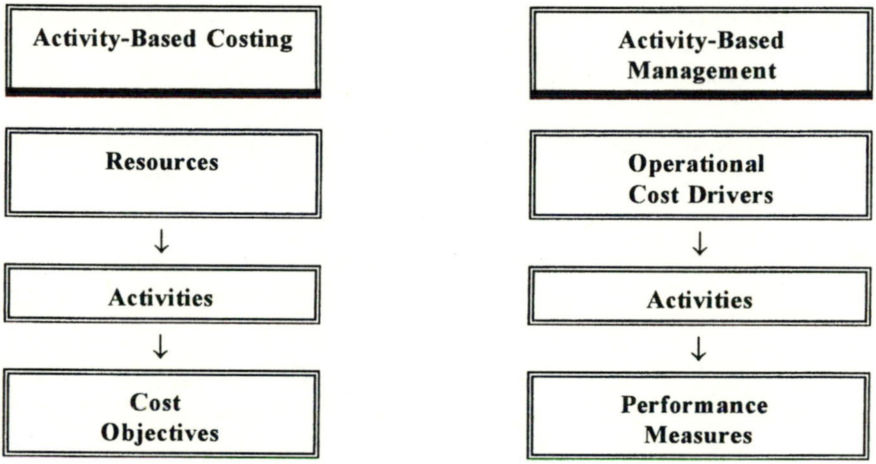

Improving Activity Performance

An article entitled "Activity-Based Management" by Peter Turney lists the goals of ABM as (1) to improve value received by customers and (2) to improve profits. The article presents a cogent description of:

A. *Analyze* activities to find areas for improvement.

1. Identify nonessential activities. Activities *with value* fall into two categories:
   a. Those that are essential to the customer.
   b. Those that are essential to the functioning of the organization. All other activities are non-value added and are judged to be nonessential.
2. Analyze *significant* activities only. Some activities that have a nominal cost should be given low priority.
3. Compare activities with those known to be best. Compare the activity with a similar activity of another division, or with that in another firm that is known to be a standard of good practice.
4. Examine the links between activities; one activity leads to the next, so moving a product from one work station to the next is a nonvalue-added activity. When a move is eliminated in the process, such as in FMS installations, the process is almost always improved.

B. Look for *factors causing waste* (cost drivers).

C. Measure what the activity should be doing to contribute to customer satisfaction.

Limitations of Activity-Based Costing Systems

Thomas H. Johnson sounded the alarm in his article entitled, "It's Time to Stop Overselling Activity-Based Concepts" in the September 1992 issue of *Management Accounting*. Quoted below are several of his strong statements warning practitioners about activity-based costing.

Activity-based panaceas, along with activity-based information and thinking, are recommended to any company striving to achieve world-class status as a profitable competitor.

As someone who helped put the ABC concept in motion, I feel compelled to warn people that *I believe it has gone too far*. It should be redirected and slowed down, if not stopped altogether.

Many erroneous *histories* of ABC concepts have appeared in the cost management literature, often written by people who are selling some kind of product--- such as consulting services, seminars, or software.

One frequently hears the claim that activity-based cost management tools help companies achieve long-term profitability and competitiveness in the global economy. I believe that anyone who understands the original purpose and nature of activity-based tools *realizes the absurdity of that claim.*

The article by Professor Johnson concludes that:

1. ABC does not help companies achieve continuous improvement of globally competitive operations.

2. ABC does nothing to change old management behavior.

3. Does not drive companies to change their fundamental views about how to organize work and to satisfy customers efficiently.

As one of the pioneers of the "relevance lost" movement, Professor Johnson appears to be dissatisfied with both traditional and activity-based methods of costing. The ABC/ABM momentum was brought on by the critics of traditional costing. ABC systems have been successfully applied to many segments or divisions of large companies that have had the appropriate product and organizational characteristics. ABC/ABM has been applied successfully to both marketing functions and service industries. It has made both accountants and operating managers more aware of the the substance (the how and why) of cost incurrence and the costing process, rather than just the framework (the what and where) of the cost system. Activity-based costing systems are not expected to apply to all situations and to solve all problems, but, in many installations they have changed management attitudes and achieved positive results.

SUMMARY

Activity-based costing is not a solution for all product costing problems. In many production processes, the preponderance of costs are directly related to labor dollars, machine hours, or some other direct measurement of volume. Modern concepts and techniques, such as automation, computers, innovative production and inventory systems, and global competition, have all contributed to the decrease in direct labor as a percentage of total production costs. The evidence inexorably calls for less dependence on direct labor dollars as the major basis for allocating indirect costs to product lines. Activity-based costing and activity-based management have been implemented by many companies to replace their traditional costing systems because they do provide timely, decision-making cost information.

The activity-based costing method, based on the assumed data in the preceding illustrations, provides a more detailed tracing of indirect costs to cost objectives. The functions of production were separated into activities that became resource consumers. The cost drivers most likely to cause cost variation in the activities were identified and used as the basis for cost attachment in the activity. Finally, the cost objectives (products) were traced through the activities to determine the amount of activity cost to be attached to each product line.

Although activity-based costing has contributed positively to the practices of accounting for costs in many companies, there are limitations that must be recognized before considering ABC as a panacea for all American industries. Evidence indicates that Japanese manufacturers use primitive allocation methods; they do not seem to care what the total product line costs are. They follow a strategy of underpricing the competition until they control the market. After controlling the market they merely raise the price to make a profit. Why should they waste money on a more expensive allocation system that contributes nothing to their long-range strategy.

All allocation methods, no matter how sophisticated, yield estimates. A cost-benefit analysis must be made to decide whether an activity-based costing system will be beneficial. The laws and ethical trade practices in the United States require that accurate cost information be maintained by domestic manufacturers. American companies must follow the generally accepted accounting rules that affect allocation, and managers need accurate cost data to make correct decisions. Those who advocate activity-based management techniques have demonstrated that in many cases an ABC system does improve the accuracy and relevance of the costing of products, services, activities, and functions performed by the firm.

8

Designing Activity-Based Systems

PRELIMINARY IMPLEMENTATION PROCEDURE

The road to implementing an activity-based costing and activity-based management system will vary from firm to firm. Activity-based costing systems are custom designed to the individual needs of the firm. For each model installation, a special team of involved *operations* personnel within the company must direct the changes necessary to implement the new ABC system. If only accounting people advocate and spearhead the new ABC changes, it will be perceived as just another modification in the book entries and the financial statements. The changes must be designed to meet the needs of the operational personnel.

Exhibit 8-1 illustrates the procedural steps to be followed in order to prepare the operational personnel and top management for the changes that are necessary to implement the new system. Before committing any resources to an ABC/ABM installation, the management should examine these procedural steps. Not all of the steps must be taken for a successful installation, but all of these steps should be considered. Some consulting firms recommend additional steps, involving their services, that are costly and not necessarily beneficial. It is recommended that all of the steps in Exhibit 8-1 be followed.

Exhibit 8-1
Implementation Procedure for Activity-Based Costing

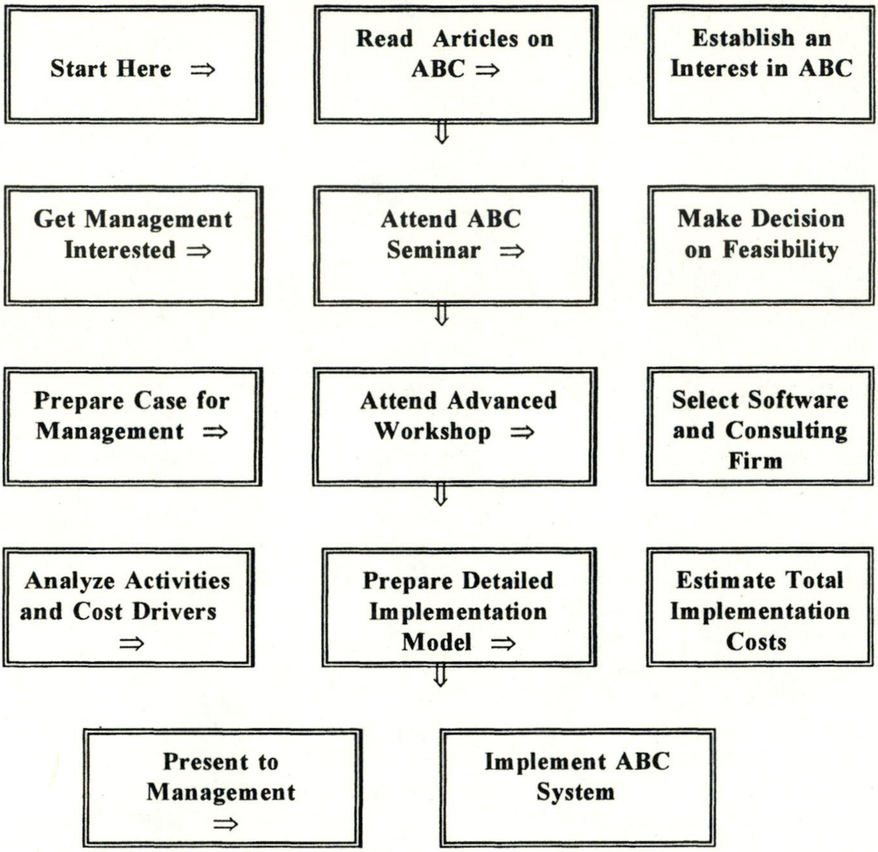

DESIGNING ACTIVITY-BASED COSTING SYSTEMS

Implementing Activity-Based Cost Management, a joint study by the Institute of Management Accounting, KPMG Peat Marwick, Robert S. Kaplan and Robin Cooper, and the Maisel Consulting Group, and published by the IMA in 1992, includes case studies of eight separate companies. The study, which includes models for manufacturing, marketing, and service functions, has identified *four primary steps* that the ABC system designers take for either a service organization or a manufacturing company.

Step 1. Identify and analyze the activities performed to produce outputs.
Step 2. Trace the usage of organizational resources to these activities.
Step 3. Define the outputs produced.

Step 4. Link the activity costs to the outputs, using activity cost drivers.

Once these steps are completed by the ABC team, the data are entered into the activity-based costing system that calculates the cost of activities, activity drivers, and output. After validating the data, the model development and analysis stage has been completed.

Identify and Analyze Activities

Activity-based costing systems, by focusing on the custom designed activities, provides periodic reports that are more informative than those produced from the natural accounts in the general ledger. Note in Exhibit 8-2 that the activities are defined in terms of an action. In the traditional view, salaries *are incurred*. In the ABC view there are obviously salaries involved in the activities, such as administering the department, or processing special orders. The emphasis, however, is on the dynamic nature of the action, not on the passive incurrence of the journal entry, salaries. The ABC method helps to explain *how and why* the cost is incurred, rather than just *how much* is incurred.

Exhibit 8-2
Traditional versus Activity-Based Costing View

Engineering Department Traditional View Using Chart of Accts./Gen. Ledger		Engineering Department Activity-Based View Using ABC Database	
Salaries	$400,000	Create Bills of Materials (BOM)	$25,600
		Maintain BOMs	82,500
Travel expense	80,000	Create routings	24,900
		Maintain routings	84,500
Occupancy costs	70,000	Process special orders	107,800
		Improve processes	42,400
Equipment costs	150,000	Study capacities	76,000
		Design tooling	125,700
Supplies used	50,000	Train employees	35,600
		Administer department	145,000
Total	$750,000	Total	$750,000

Common sense must be used in identifying activities. An activity can be described in one action, such as: prepare purchase orders; or it can be described in several more detailed actions, such as: open the drawer, take out a form, pick up a pencil, fill out lines 1 through 14, place the form in the bin marked purchase orders. Unnecessary activities will merely increase the cost of implementing the system. A typical ABC system will have from 25 to 100 identifiable activities. The IMA sponsored joint study has provided a list of typical activities in manufacturing settings in Exhibit 8-3.

Exhibit 8-3
Typical Activities in Manufacturing Settings

Procurement

Purchase Order Processing	Determine order quantities, timing issues, complete the P.O.
Contract Negotiations	Negotiate, develop, and sign vendor contracts
Inventory Material-Receiving	Record the receipt of material, verify incoming quantities
Incoming Material Inspection	Assess the quality of incoming material
Processing Accounts Payable	Accumulate documents and provide authorization to pay

Production

Equipment, Maintenance, and Repair	Maintain and repair existing production equipment
Shop Floor Control	Supervise production and production personnel
Facility Maintenance	Plant construction and facility maintenance

Production Management

Sales Forecast	Obtain a regular short-term sales forecast
Schedule Production-Normal	Schedule orders per customer request
Monitor Production	Collect production data at the shop floor level
Expedite	Speed up the process of production and material procurement
Inventory Material	Track material available within the factory premises
In-Process Material	Manage in-process inventories

Quality Control

Customer Complaints	Customer contact regarding complaints about quality, shipping, etc.
Product Service Testing	Testing results from customer complaints
Shop Floor Process Control	Monitor shop floor processes to ensure quality output
Quality Complaint Analysis	Determine the cause of quality problems
Testing for Quality Evaluation	Perform tests required to analyze a quality problem
Final Inspection	Final inspection of finished product

Trace the Usage of Resource Costs to Activities

After identifying the activities, the costs of the resources must be traced to them. The general ledger contains all of the recorded costs, but not traced to the activities. Exhibit 8-4 illustrates the activity-based costing philosophy of assigning resource costs to activities.

Exhibit 8-4
Activity-Based Costing Philosophy

Indirect material **Indirect labor** **Indirect factory services** **Direct marketing services** **Direct administrative services** **Indirect marketing services** **Indirect administrative services**	**Are the *Resources* ⇒ for**	**Activities**

⇩

Resources ⇒	**Are Consumed By ⇒**	**Activities**

⇩

Activities ⇒	**Are Performed For ⇒**	**Products, Customers, or Service Units**

Define the Outputs

The outputs in the activity-based costing system are the cost objectives, such as products, customers, territories, services, or special projects. In designing the new ABC system, the team must be careful to specify outputs with distinct, identifiable activities. If the activities are ambiguous, the assignment of resource costs to activities will be inaccurate. All outputs must be identified so that total activity costs will be accounted for and not arbitrarily charged to the wrong output.

Link Activity Costs to Outputs

There are three ways to link activity costs to the outputs, direct charge, estimation, and arbitrary allocation. The IMA-sponsored study stated that because of the large number of differing outputs in many organizations, direct charging of activities to outputs is not feasible. In manufacturing processes, only direct material and direct labor are charged directly to the product. For almost all indirect manufacturing and nonmanufacturing costs the link of activities is estimated. Arbitrary allocation is a last resort.

In activity-based costing, as illustrated in Exhibit 8-5, the first preference is to trace the resource costs directly to the cost objects through the activities. The second preference is to charge the resource costs to the cost objects by estimating.

The estimating is based on the cost drivers associated with each activity. The last resort is to allocate the resource costs on an arbitrary basis, which has no management decision-making benefits.

Exhibit 8-5
Tracing Resources

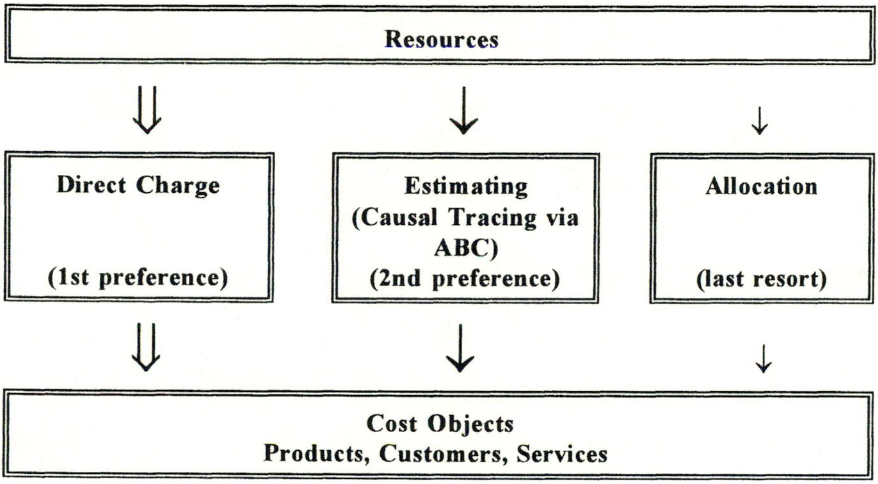

Activity Coding

A variety of coding schemes are used in designing the activity-based costing system in order to summarize the classes of activities. Some are *reason codes*, based on why specific activities are performed; others are *purpose codes*, which provide insights into whether the purpose of the activity is central or secondary to the goals of the firm; and some are *process codes*, which identify the type of production process involved. A common coding scheme is to classify the activities into:

1. Activity centers
2. Activity hierarchies
3. Value added \ non-value added rankings

Activity Centers

Activity centers are groups of activities that are related to one specific business process. Activity centers can be designed around existing departments, functions, or business processes, or they can be completely new. Exhibit 8-6 shows some of the activity centers in a manufacturing setting.

Exhibit 8-6
Typical Activity Centers--Manufacturing

Principal Activity Centers

Production	All activities except direct labor that can be directly attributed to the production process
Customer Admin.	All activities related to dealings with customers
Procurement	All activities required to provide the business with all the materials needed for operation
Production Management	All plantwide activities of scheduling, monitoring, and quality control of all production areas
Quality Control	All quality-related activities dealing with production processes, incoming material, and product service
Production Tooling	All activities relating to maintenance, repair, or replacement of existing tooling
Maintenance	All activities performed to maintain, repair, or replace existing equipment and facilities
Warehouse and Shipping	All activities involved in the handling and distribution of finished goods transferred from the production area

Change-Related Activity Centers

Internally Generated Modifications	All activities for dealing with internal requests for product or process changes
Customer Driven Changes	All activities for dealing with product or process changes due to customer request or requirement
New Products and Processes	All activities to develop new products or processes

Support-Related Activity Centers

Business Information Systems	All activities related to development of new information systems and computer systems
General Administration and Finance	All activities related to external financial reporting, general accounting, special studies, and reserves
Human Resources	All activities related to administration of employee and community services and programs, and workforce maintenance
Environment and Safety	All activities performed to ensure a safe, secure work environment

Activity Hierarchies

The second coding scheme, described in the IMA-sponsored study for classifying the characteristics of activities, is:

Unit-Level Activities	Performed each time a unit is produced
Batch-Level Activities	Performed each time a batch of goods is produced
Product-Sustaining Activities	Performed to support the diversity of products in a plant
Facility-Sustaining Activities	Performed to support a facility's general manufacturing process

Unit-level activities are unit volume related activities, such as attaching material to one unit of product, or a final inspection. Setting up a machine, moving a batch of products, and placing an order for a purchased part are examples of batch-level activities. Product-sustaining activities include product engineering, warehousing, and other marketing functions. A facility-sustaining activity would include plant engineering, providing light, heat, and air conditioning, and providing landscaping and janitorial services.

Value Rankings

The definition of what constitutes value added is a custom decision made by each firm. Classifying an activity as value added may not be clear cut. The criteria for deciding what creates value may vary from firm to firm. Managers who operate in manufacturing, marketing, and service areas may all have different criteria for defining value added. One company, cited in the IMA-sponsored study, has devised a four-category value-added coding scheme, which will serve as an example:

1. An activity required to produce the product or improve the process; the activity *cannot*, on a cost justification basis, be improved, simplified, or reduced in scope at this time.

2. An activity required to produce the product or improve the process; the activity *can be* cost justifiably improved, simplified, or reduced in scope.

3. An activity *not* required to produce the product or improve the process; the activity can be eliminated *eventually* by changing a process or a company procedure.

4. An activity *not* required to produce the product or improve the process; the activity can be eliminated *in the short run* by changing a process or a company procedure.

The value-ranking coding scheme allows managers to focus on the non-value added activities, or on those that are performed inefficiently. These are the activities that can be instrumental in reducing costs of operation. Some teams assign grades on a scale to the value added and non-value added content, but establishing the guidelines for assigning the grades can be challenging.

Cost Driver Analysis

A *cost driver* is any factor that causes the incurrence of costs in the designated activity. Activity-based costing systems may use different types of cost drivers. *Transaction drivers* represent the number of times an activity is performed. *Duration drivers* represent the time it takes to perform an activity. It is important to caution that the determination of causation is a judgment matter, not an unequivocal fact. Some costs drivers are easy to trace, such as machine hours, which can be used to trace direct material from the machining activity to the product. Activity-based costing does not conceptually improve the tracing of direct materials and direct labor to the product. It improves the accuracy of allocating the indirect costs, those that are not directly traceable to the product, but that are traceable to the activity. These are the costs that require more accurate methods of allocation. Cost drivers provide the causal relationship between the activity's total costs and the product that passes through the activity.

Activity Drivers and Operational Cost Drivers

An *activity driver* reflects the consumption of an activity by its cost objects. The activity driver must distribute activity dollars into each cost object in proportion to some characteristic or diversity that is unique to that cost object. It is the link between the activity and the cost object, but it does not explain the true cause of the cost incurrence. The number of parts on the product's bill of materials is selected by the ABC/ABM team to represent the activity driver for the issuing of purchase orders.

An *operational cost driver* reflects and measures how efficiently an activity is performed. It is the true driver that explains what causes the costs to occur. It represents the cost of the *process*, not the product. The operational cost driver identified by the ABC/ABM team is the number of purchase orders issued.

Product	Number of Purchase Orders	Total Amount of Orders	Number of Parts per BOM
A	400	$4,000	120
B	600	25,000	540
C	1,200	2,000	60
D	1,000	35,000	1,200
E	500	12,000	500
F	300	22,000	80
Total	4,000	$100,000	2,500

Operational Cost Driver Rate

The operational cost driver is the output of issuing purchase orders. The operational cost driver rate is the total cost of purchases, $100,000, divided by the total number of purchase orders, 4,000, or $25 per purchase order. The operational cost driver rate ***measures the performance, or efficiency***, of issuing the purchase orders.

Activity Driver Rate

The activity driver for issuing purchase orders is identified as the number of parts on the product bill of materials (BOM). In the above example, the activity driver rate is the total cost of purchases, $100,000, divided by the total number of parts, 2,500, or $40 per part. The activity driver rate ***measures the consumption of the activity by the product***, which is the cost object.

Selection of Cost Drivers

Many of the sites in the IMA-sponsored study reported that measuring the cost drivers was the most difficult task. Some activity centers do not have clear-cut cost drivers. Materials handling and maintenance are examples of activities that may not have a quantifiable cost driver. Their costs are then charged on the basis of arbitrary or proxy drivers that do not provide the accuracy needed to satisfy the objectives of the ABC system. Regardless of the problems involved in selecting the appropriate cost drivers, they represent a more accurate method of tracing costs and expenses to cost objectives than the more arbitrary traditional methods. Exhibit 8-7 illustrates typical cost drivers for manufacturing, marketing, and service organizations.

Exhibit 8-7
Typical Cost Drivers

Manufacturers	
Number of engineering change notices	Number of labor hours
Number of customer complaints	Number of times hauled
Number of shipments processed	Distance moved
Number of orders processed	Number of machine hours
Number of inspections performed	Number of setups performed
Marketing/Retailers	
Items purchased	Stock outs
Employees-direct and indirect	Inventory items
Customer complaints	Returned items
Product lines carried	Locations
Employee turnover	Shrinkage
Service Organizations	
Employees-direct and indirect	Orders
Employee turnover	Service calls
Customer complaints	Returned items
Clients/customers	Services offered
Total vendors added	Locations

FORMAT OF AN ABC MODEL

One of the eight companies in the IMA sponsored joint study developed a separate model for each of its production processes. Two of these models are demonstrated to *illustrate the actual formats* used by a company. The company selected for the demonstration of an ABC Model is a large manufacturer of integrated curcuit devices. The firm designs, manufactures, and markets integrated circuits, such as microprocessors, memory devices, and programmable logic devices. They are used in a wide range of applications, such as telecommunications, office automation, and networking. Their sales run over $1 billion and they employ more than 12,000 people. The manufacturing process consists of three production steps, each usually performed in a separate, specialized plant.

The actual pilot site selected for the ABC Model, situated in Asia, performs *test and assembly* operations. The plant employs 4,000 people in assembling and testing the company's latest and most complex microprocessors. The key steps followed to complete the ABC implementation were:

1. Define scope	6. Hold activity driver interviews
2. Carry out activity interviews	7. Develop activity driver quantities
3. Collect labor activity data	8. Load and run the model
4. Analyze nonlabor activity	9. Verify and analyze data
5. Analyze activity	10. Expect continuous evolution

Resource Costs

The project team identified all indirect factory costs to be included in the overhead (resources) categories. Direct labor and direct materials, not included in the resource groups, were traced directly to the product. The manufacturing equipment was classified into groups of machines with similar processing characteristics. Indirect materials were grouped by similar usage characteristics. The total resource costs (shown in the two models) of the machine categories assigned to these machine groups included:

1. Repair and maintenance	4. Depreciation
2. Spare parts costs	5. Preventive maintenance
3. Utilities costs	6. Statistical process control

Activity-Based Costing System
Assembly Model

Overhead (Resources)

Indirect Labor	Indirect Material	Variable Expenses	Maintenance & Repair	Deprec-iation	Fixed Expenses

↙ ↘ ↙ ↘ ↙ ↘ ↙ ↘

Activity Pools -- 26

Unit		**Batch**		**Product-Sustaining**	**Facility-Sustaining**
Die Attach	Centrifuge	Produc-tion	Expedite	Carrier	
Frame Attach	Trim & Form	Schedul-ing	Tubes /Roll	Product Transfer	Facility-Sustaining
B Side Mark	Temp Cycle	Setup	Pack	Quality Analysis	
Mold	Hormel	QA Sustain	Ship		
Seal	Lead Fin	QC Sustain			
Bond	Oven	Die Prep			

Activity Cost Drivers

Machine Hours	Machine Hours No. of Tubes No. of Boxes No. of Line Items No. of Lot Sampled	No.of Quality Problems No. of Failures, etc.	No. of Units

↘ ↓ ↓ ↓

Direct Labor	→	**Product**
Direct Material	→	

Activity-Based Costing System
Test Model

Overhead (Resources)

Indirect Labor	Indirect Material	Variable Expenses	Maintenance & Repair	Deprec-iation	Fixed Expenses

↙ ↘ ↙ ↘ ↙ ↘ ↙ ↘

Activity Pools -- 19

Unit	**Batch**		**Product-Sustaining**		**Facility-Sustaining**
Program	Production	Expedite	Process Sustain	Product Transfer	
Erase	Scheduling	Tubes/Roll	Quality Analysis	Yield & Quality	Facility-Sustaining
Oven	Setup	Pack	Carrier		
Handler	QC Sustain				
Tester	QA Sustain				

Activity Cost Drivers

Labor Hrs	Machine Hrs No. of Tubes No. of Boxes No. of Line Items No. of Lot Sampled, etc.	No.of Quality Problems No. of Failures, etc.	No. of Units

↘ ↓ ↓ ↓

Direct Labor	→	**Product**

ACTIVITY-BASED MANAGEMENT BENCHMARKING

Benchmarking is comparing the ABC-derived activity costs of one segment of a company with those of other segments. Benchmarking requires consistency in the definition of activities and the measurement of their costs. It also requires cooperation and full disclosure among company segments. Benchmarking allows the less efficient segments of the company to replicate the processes of the most efficient segments. It can be applied to individual activities or to activity centers (business processes).

Assume that a company has four plants with some of the same activities. The company has implemented an ABC/ABM system with one team determining the definitions and measurements of activity costs. An analysis of the ABC/ABM determined costs of order processing, materials handling, and maintenance, using the benchmarking technique, follows.

Activity	Order Processing	
Plant	Rank	Cost Driver Rate
Detroit	#2	$ 0.459
Atlanta	#4	0.675
Topeka	#1	0.328
Ontario	#3	0.566
Average		$0.507

Activity	Materials Handling	
Plant	Rank	Cost Driver Rate
Detroit	#4	$45.13
Atlanta	#1	38.56
Topeka	#2	42.65
Ontario	#3	43.98
Average		$42.58

Activity	Maintenance	
Plant	Rank	Cost Driver Rate
Detroit	#3	$12.47
Atlanta	#4	13.75
Topeka	#1	9.34
Ontario	#2	10.88
Average		$11.66

The benchmarking analysis allows us to observe the costs of these three activities performed at the four plants. The ABC/ABM team for the overall company has defined these activities the same, and has assigned the same cost drivers. Each plant can compare their individual activity cost with the average and with the most efficient. The Topeka plant is ranked number one for both order processing and maintenance, and is ranked number two for materials handing. It ranks as the most efficient plant in regard to these three activities. Atlanta is ranked number one for materials handling, but is ranked fourth for the other two activities. The Detroit and the Ontario plants can both benefit from studying these activities at the most efficient plants. Benchmarking provides the data necessary to improve the efficiency of the overall company and its processes.

9

Activity-Based Costing for Manufacturing

ACTIVITY-BASED MODEL FOR MANUFACTURING

The ABC model described is based on an actual case reported in the Institute of Management Accountants (IMA) sponsored joint study of eight companies that incorporated activity-based systems into manufacturing, service, or marketing functions of their companies. The study includes two processing facilities of a large manufacturing company, Plant A, a small focused facility, with approximately 200 employees, and Plant B, a large complex facility, with approximately 1,000 employees. Both plants have the same general product lines so that they can be compared. The implementation procedure outlined and described is designed to fit *manufacturing processes* only.

Objectives of the Project

The ABC project team defined the specific objectives of the study:

1. Identify key cost drivers.
2. Compare traditional product cost to ABC product cost.
3. Compare product costs between plants.
4. Compare process implementation between the two different size plants.
5. Evaluate any model differences between the two different size plants.

Activity-Based Costing System Design

The ABC model for manufacturing functions in this research study follows, in principle, the *four primary steps* listed below that the system designers (Cooper, Kaplan, KPMG Peat Marwick, Maisel, and the IMA) recommend for implementing an ABC system.

Step 1. Identify and analyze the activities performed to produce outputs.
Step 2. Trace the usage of organizational resources to these activities.

Step 3. Define the outputs produced.
Step 4. Link the activity costs to the outputs, using activity cost drivers.

Each situation is as different as the companies and their outputs. The ABC project team for this manufacturing implementation used its own procedure and methodology as follows:

1. Define activities.
2. Analyze nonlabor expenses.
3. Analyze each activity.
4. Group functions and subfunctions (activity centers).
5. Define resource cost drivers.
6. Define activity cost drivers.
7. Calculate product costs.
8. Analyze and present results.

Cost Objects

In a manufacturing operation the cost objects are the products. Plant A in the study manufactures approximately 35 different products, while Plant B manufactures approximately 250 different products, but in the same product line as Plant A. At the end of the study a total of only 200 different products were analyzed.

Exhibit 9-1 diagrams on the left, the general concept of an ABC system, and on the right, shows the activities, resource groups, and cost objects selected by the ABC project team. The cost of the resources are traced to the activities and to the business processes directly or by use of resource cost drivers, and the cost of the activities are linked to the cost objects by use of activity cost drivers.

Exhibit 9-1
Project Team Selections

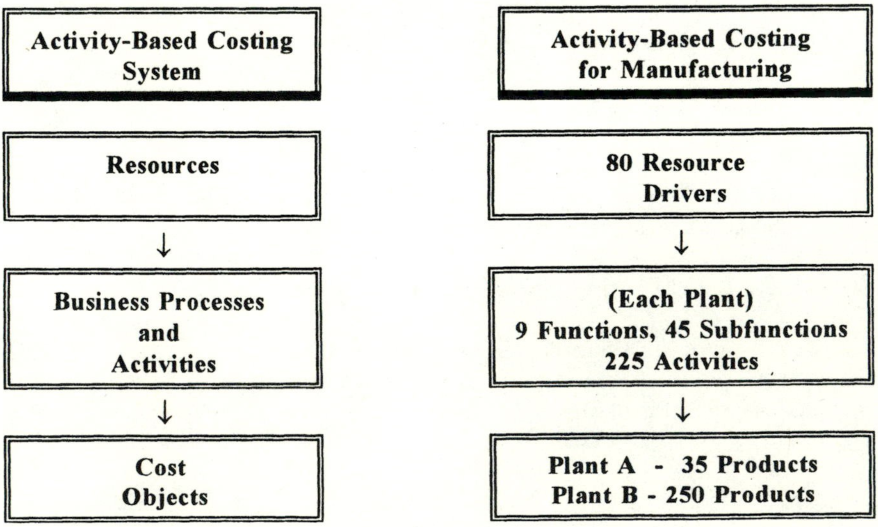

Activity-Based Resources

The resources of the two plants are the costs of indirect labor, materials and supplies, utilities, equipment, buildings, and capital, which appear in the general ledger accounts and are traced to the traditional departments and responsibility centers. Before using resource drivers to trace the resource costs to the activities, each department's costs were categorized as:

1. Management payroll
2. Hourly or staff payroll
3. Nonpayroll expenses (i.e. supplies)

The nonlabor and machine-related expenses were assigned to approximately 25 separate machine groups that included:

1. Depreciation
2. Energy expenses
3. Maintenance costs
4. Replacement and spare parts

Resource Cost Drivers

The ABC/ABM project team identified approximately 80 resource cost drivers. Resource drivers are Stage One drivers that link the cost of the resources to the individual activities, and eventually to functions and subfunctions (activity centers).

Partial List of Resource Drivers

Supervision time	Cleanup time
Breakdown hours	Capital project dollars
Maintenance part usage	No. of changeovers
No. of maintenance work orders	Line hours
Sanitation supervision time	No. of SKUs
Case volume Training time	Maintenance supervision time
Amount of salvage	Line mechanic hours

Activity Cost Drivers

The ABC project team identified the most conceptually accurate activity cost drivers to assign activity costs to products. Activity cost drivers are Stage Two drivers that link the cost of activities to the cost objects. Most of the activity cost drivers were volume (unit-level) based. A partial list of the activity cost drivers and their respective activities is shown below:

Activities	Cost Driver
Maintenance; Depreciation; Sanitation Quality Control Supervision	Line hours
Expediting; Purchasing; Salvage	Pounds of product
Production Supervision; Training	Labor hours
Material Handling	Number of cases

Activity Coding

The ABC project team eatablished three classifications of activities:

1. By activity hierarchy
2. By value analysis
3. By activity center analysis

Hierarchy Analysis

The team classified each activity as unit, batch, product-sustaining, and facility-sustaining. The classification of batch-related did not work well. In a practical sense, it was difficult to identify uniform batches.

Unit-Level Activities	Performed each time a unit is produced
Batch-Level Activities	Performed each time a batch of goods is produced
Product-Sustaining Activities	Performed to support the diversity of products in a plant
Facility-Sustaining Activities	Performed to support a facility's general manufacturing process

Value Analysis

The ABC project team attempted to rank activities by their value added contribution to the company. They found that it was difficult to classify activities as having little or no value and decided that a value ranking was not important to their project.

Activity Centers (Functions and Subfunctions)

Plant managers wanted a two-tiered grouping of activity centers, one at a higher level. To satisfy the plant managers, the ABC project team, using their own methods and terminology, organized the approximately 225 separate *activities* that they had identified into 9 major groups and 45 subgroups that they called *functions and subfunctions*. All activity centers are called subfunctions. For example, each production line was classified as a subfunction. Similar subfunctions are then grouped into broader groups, called functions, listed below:

Function	No. of Activities	Function	No. of Activities
1. Logistics	25	6. Bus unit managers	
2. Quality control	39	per product line	256
3. Human resources	9	7. Sanitation	7
4. Accounting	11	8. Maintenance	13
5. Asset management	15	9. Engineering	

Results of the Activity-Based Analysis Implementation

The two pilot studies proved to management that the ABC concepts were feasible, and gave them insight as to how activities affected their product costs. Although the overall costs were not substantially different as compared with traditional methods, individual products varied significantly. As expected, the low-volume items were the most affected, showing increases in costs when measured by the ABC system.

The ABC model provided direct visibility to activities performed by production line. One of the project leaders summarized that the system identifies where you add value, in procurement, in conversion, and in distribution, to the production process. Traditional systems do not provide this insight.

ILLUSTRATION OF ABC SYSTEM FOR MANUFACTURING

Activity-based costing focuses on activities, rather than departments, as the basic units of cost attachment. Costs pools are established to match the activities. The costs attached to the activities are direct in regard to the activity but indirect in regard to the product. They must be ultimately allocated to the final cost object, the product. Allocations to the activity from other cost centers are Stage One allocations. Allocations from the activities to the product lines are Stage Two allocations.

Following is an example of an activity-based costing system for manufacturing costs. Aspro Company produces three grades of aspirin in one plant. The monthly quantity of output of the three product lines is approximately equal. The process is highly automated. Direct labor is less than 5 percent of total manufacturing costs and is included in the work cells. All other labor, such as that used in handling materials and quality control inspections, is indirect.

All three products use the services of the electric power, materials handling, and quality control inspection activities. In addition to the three service activities, there are four cost centers called work cells. Product E, enteric coated aspirin, which requires the largest number of process operations, goes through all four work cells; product B, buffered aspirin, goes through three work cells; and product P, plain aspirin, which requires the least number of process operations, goes through only two work cells.

Aspro Company--Estimated Annual Budget 19X3

Activity	Total Cost	Estimated Activity Driver
Electric power	$ 500,000	1,000,000 kWh
Materials handling	1,000,000	25,000 moves
Quality control	1,200,000	40,000 inspections
Work cell 1	1,000,000	50,000 MH
Work cell 2	500,000	10,000 DLH
Work cell 3	800,000	80,000 runs
Work cell 4	200,000	2,000 MH
Total work cell costs	$2,500,000	

Calculation of Activity Rates	
Electric power	$500,000 ÷ 1,000,000 kWh = $ 0.50 per kWh
Materials handling	$1,000,000 ÷ 25,000 moves = $ 40 per move
Quality control	$1,200,000 ÷ 40,000 inspections = $30 per insp.
Work cell 1	$1,000,000 ÷ 50,000 = $ 20 per MH
Work cell 2	$ 500,000 ÷ 10,000 = $ 50 per DLH
Work cell 3	$ 800,000 ÷ 80,000 = $ 10 per run
Work cell 4	$ 200,000 ÷ 2,000 = $100 per MH

Summary for the Month of October 19X3

Activities	Cost Driver	Product Line E	Product Line B	Product Line P	Total
Electric power	kWh	30,000	28,000	24,000	82,000
Materials hdlg.	Moves	800	700	600	2,100
Quality control	Inspections	1,000	1,000	1,000	3,000
Work cell 1	MH	1,200	1,600	1,800	4,600
Work cell 2	DLH	300	300	300	900
Work cell 3	Runs	3,000	4,000		7,000
Work cell 4	MH	200			200

Cost Allocation to Product Lines

Activity	Product Line E	Product Line B	Product Line P	Total
Electric power	$ 15,000	$ 14,000	$ 12,000	$ 41,000
Material handling	32,000	28,000	24,000	84,000
Quality control	30,000	30,000	30,000	90,000
Work cell 1	24,000	32,000	36,000	92,000
Work cell 2	15,000	15,000	15,000	45,000
Work cell 3	30,000	40,000		70,000
Work cell 4	20,000			20,000
Total costs	$166,000	$159,000	$117,000	$442,000

This analysis follows the activity-based costing concept. Each product line was allocated costs on the basis of the activities consumed. Product B was not allocated any costs from work cell 4, and product P was not allocated costs from work cells 3 and 4. The cost driver that was determined to most directly cause variations in cost within the activity was used as the basis for allocating costs to the product lines. Product line E, which required the greatest number of processing operations was allocated the largest amount of costs, $166,000, whereas, product line P, which passed through the fewest number of activities, received the lowest cost allocation, $117,000.

Traditional versus Activity-Based Costing Methods

The following analysis illustrates the differences between activity-based costing and the more traditional cost allocation methods. In the traditional procedure the indirect costs will be allocated on the basis of machine hours. The costs to be allocated to the three product lines using the traditional procedure are:

Electric power	$ 500,000
Materials handling	1,000,000
Quality control	1,200,000
Work cell 1	1,000,000
Work cell 2	500,000
Work cell 3	800,000
Work cell 4	200,000
Total costs	$5,200,000

The 19X3 annual budget for Aspro Company indicates that there are 50,000 machine hours in work cell 1 and 2,000 machine hours in work cell 4, for a total of 52,000 machine hours (MH).

$$\text{Allocation Rate} = \frac{\$5{,}200{,}000}{52{,}000 \text{ MH}} = \$100 \text{ per MH}$$

Referring back to the Summary for the Month of October 19X3, the actual machine hours for product E were 1,200 from work cell 1, and 200 from work cell 4, for a total of 1,400 MH. Product B had 1,600 actual machine hours from work cell 1, and product P had 1,800 actual machine hours from work cell 1. Actual machine hours times the rate of $100 yields the allocation shown in the table.

Allocation of Indirect Costs Based on Machine Hours

Product Line	Actual Machine Hours	Rate	Allocated Costs
Product E	1,400	$ 100	$ 140,000
Product B	1,600	100	160,000
Product P	1,800	100	180,000
Total			$ 480,000

The use of the traditional method of allocating costs places the emphasis on only those activities that generate machine hours. The summary of the differences in the two methods shown below indicates that product E is charged with $26,000 more under the ABC method, product B has only a small difference, but product P is charged considerably less under the ABC method as compared with the traditional method using machine hours. Product E is more complex and utilizes more activities than product P, logically it should be allocated a greater proportion of the total indirect costs.

Product Line	Activity-Based Costing Method	Traditional Method Based on Machine Hours	Difference ABC over (under) MH
Product E	$ 166,000	$ 140,000	$ 26,000
Product B	159,000	160,000	(1,000)
Product P	117,000	180,000	(63,000)
Total	$ 442,000	$ 480,000	$ (38,000)

10

Activity-Based Analysis for Services

ACTIVITY-BASED ANALYSIS MODEL FOR SERVICES

The Services Model described in this chapter is based on an actual service function installation reported in the IMA-sponsored study of eight companies that incorporated ABC/ABM systems into their companies or segments of their companies. The implementation procedure outlined and described is designed to fit the financial services performed by the Controller's Group in an organization. The model in the study is designated as an *Activity-Based Analysis (ABA)* model and can be applied to the financial functions performed in a manufacturing company, a marketing organization, or in another service organization.

The ABA model for service functions in the IMA-sponsored research study followed the *four primary steps* listed below that the ABC system designers recommend for implementing an ABC/ABM system.

Step 1. Identify and analyze the activities performed to produce outputs.
Step 2. Trace the usage of organizational resources to these activities.
Step 3. Define the outputs produced.
Step 4. Link the activity costs to the outputs, using activity cost drivers.

Objectives and Scope of the Project

The Controller's Group in the study is organized into five key functional areas with a professional staff of 175 people. The five key functional areas reporting to the Controller are:

1. Financial Reporting & Analysis
2. Policy & Internal Control
3. General Accounting
4. Business Manager--Profit Center A
5. Business Manager--Profit Center B

In the implementation process these five high-level functional groups were expanded to 25 resource groups based on the activities performed. The major activities performed are:

1. Consolidate and analyze all forecasts and budgets.
2. Coordinate internal controls and policies.
3. Manage accounts payable and materials.
4. Audit all co-ownership agreements.
5. Handle all revenue, production, and tax accounting.
6. Write reports for shareholders.
7. Provide financial support for field operations.

The four main objectives of the ABA Model, set by the Controller, are:

1. Develop an activity-based analysis (ABA) of the staff functions of the Controller's Group.

2. Study and document the cost behavior of the functions performed by Controller's Group staff members.

3. Evaluate the activity-based analysis for the Controller's Group and its application to other staff and operating units.

4. Present the findings and recommendations to the Controller and other management.

Business Processes (Activity Centers)

The ABA team organized the more than 200 separate *activities* that they had identified into the ten major *business processes* listed.

1. Accounts Payable	6. External Reporting
2. Administrative Management	7. Fixed Assets Management
3. Allocations	8. Operational Reporting
4. Budget	9. Systems Development and Support
5. Audits	10. Revenue Accounting

Cost Objects

In a manufacturing operation the cost objects are the products. The cost objects in a service function are not easy to identify. In the Controller's Group the *outputs* are the budgets, audits, and the various types of financial reports that are generated for the divisions, other profit centers, and the cost centers. Activities are performed to produce these outputs. The *cost objects* are the divisions, profit centers, and cost centers that require, by contract or government regulation, or have requested the reports from the Controller's Group. The ABA team identified a total of 14 cost objects in the study. The cost objects represented separate sites of operation, either profit centers or cost centers, that required the budget, audit, and reporting functions of the Controller's Group.

Exhibit 10-1 diagrams, on the left, the concept of an activity-based costing system, and, on the right, shows the activities, resource groups, and cost objects selected by the ABA team for the Controller's Group. The cost of the resources are traced to the activities and to the business processes directly or by use of resource cost drivers, and the cost of the activities are linked to the cost objects by use of activity cost drivers.

Exhibit 10-1
Activity-Based Analysis

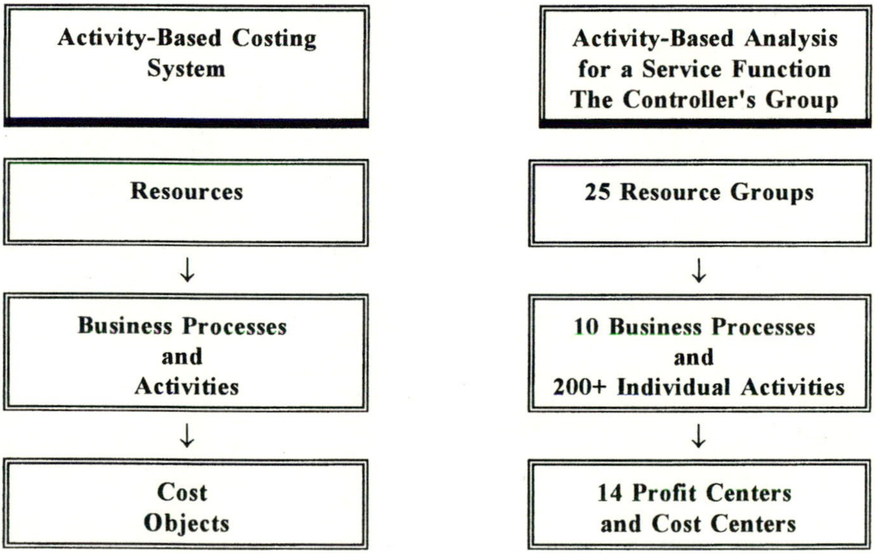

Cost Drivers

The ABA team identified the cost drivers used to assign activity costs to the cost objects, based on the cost object's request for and use of the activity. The team found that quantifiable cost drivers did not exist for many of the activities performed by the staff members. When objective drivers were not identified, manager's estimates were used to measure the usage of the activities by the cost object. Examples of cost drivers used for selected activities are shown in the table.

Activity	Cost Driver
Accounts payable management	Number of invoices
Material control	Number of transactions
Administrative management	Headcount
Technical labor reporting	Number of time sheets
Fixed asset control	Net assets
Audit reporting	Number of contractor audits

Value and Reason Code Analysis

The ABA team questioned the preponderance of high value estimates, (71 percent) of all activities. The value code analysis indicated that the managers believed that only 4 percent of their activities were low value and did not support the mission of their specific group. The unusually small percentage of low value activities was due to the procedure followed. The evaluators had written their own mission statement, and had ranked the activities in regard to their own group's mission. So their opinion of the necessity or value of the activities that they performed were biased on the high side. The ABA team noted this practice and recommended that the value placed on the activity should be based on the activity's effect on the mission of the overall controller's function and the company.

Value Estimate

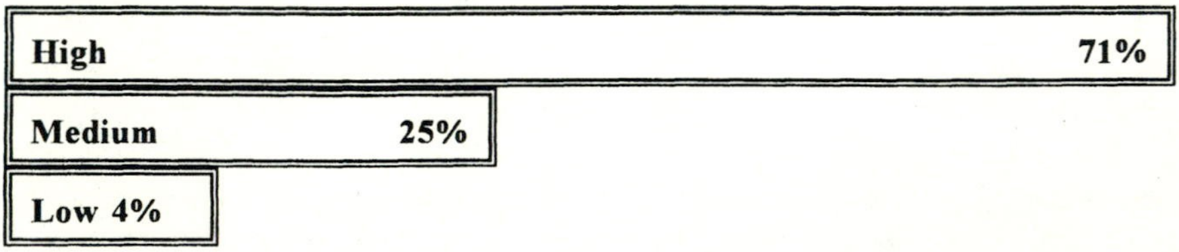

Reason Code

The reason codes indicate that the greatest number of requests, 36 percent, came from managers. Contractual requirements of 27 percent, and regulatory requirements, 18 percent, comprised a total of 45 percent.

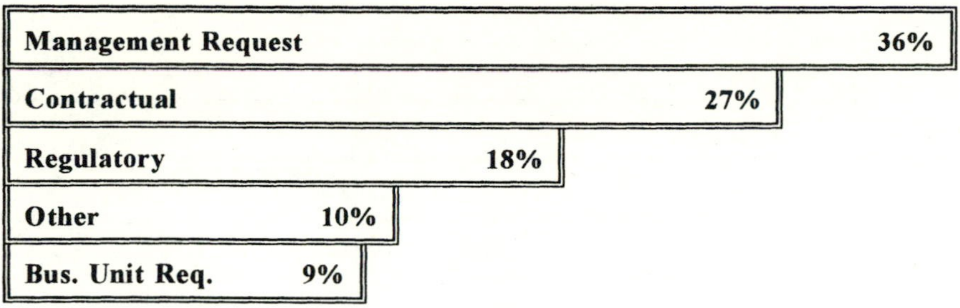

Business Process Resource Consumption

The business process analysis showed that, as expected by the team, accounts payable consumed the greatest percentage of resources. The team members had not expected that administrative management, which consisted of hiring and firing, staff meetings, and performance evaluation efforts, would be the next highest consumer of resources.

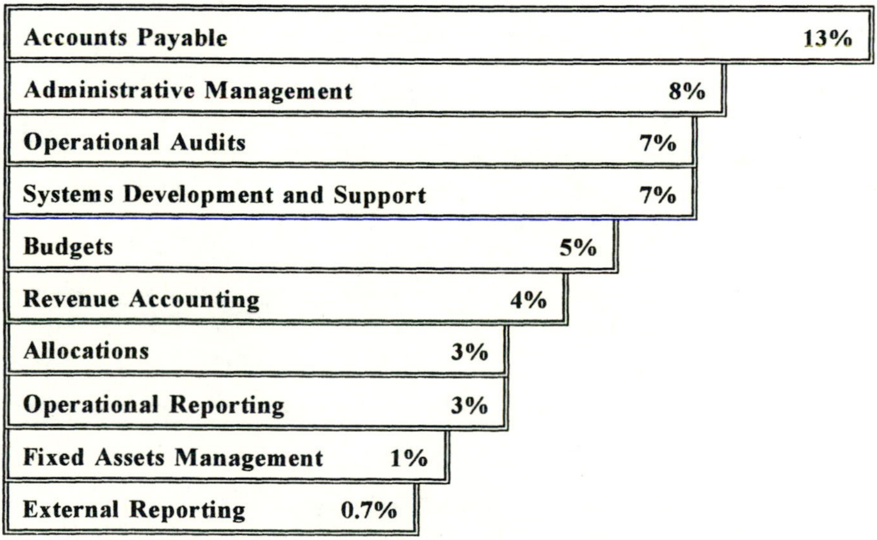

Accounts Payable Business Process Analysis

The consumption of resources showed that accounts payable, at 13%, was the highest individual consumer. The seven activities that are performed in the accounts payable process, as identified by the ABA team, are as follows:

Accounts Payable Activities

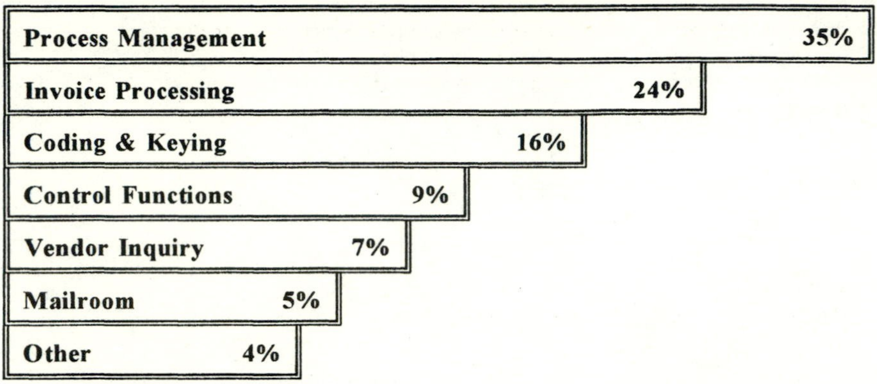

Value by Reason Code

The first cross-functional analysis made in the study revealed that the greatest percentage of low-value activities were performed at management request, not because they were required by regulation or contract. The highest percentage of activities performed for both regulatory (23 percent), and contractual (30 percent) reasons were classified as high value. The highest percent of management requested activities (57 percent), were classified as low value. After reviewing these results, the ABA team set the theoretical goal, optimistic considering the actual data, that low-value activities be performed only when legally or contractually required.

High Value

Mgmt Request 29%	Contractual 30%	Regulatory 23%	Other 11%	Bus. Req. 7%

Medium Value

Management Request 54%	Contract 19%	Reg 8%	Other 8%	B R 11%

Low Value

Management Request 57%	Con-tract 11%	Regula-tory 14%	Other 15%	Bus. Req. 3%

Cost Object Analysis

The cost object analysis revealed, as expected, that Profit Center B, the largest operational unit in the company, consumed the greatest share of activities. The corporate headquarters consumed more activities than expected, to the delight of the controller's staff.

Consumption of Activities by Cost Object

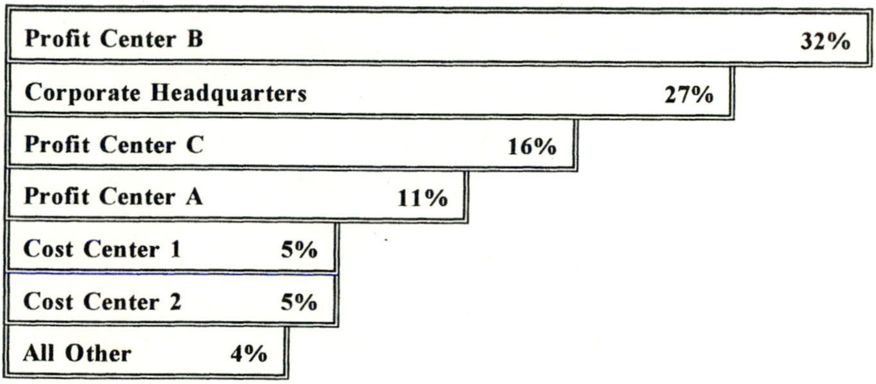

Results of the Activity-Based Analysis Implementation

The ABA team calculated the equivalent person-years required for each business process, using the data from the study. The equivalent-person calculation indicated how many people should be able to perform the process, rather than how many actually did perform the process. By using the equivalent-persons measurement the ABA team also calculated the headcount required in each cost object. This measurement indicated the total amount of resources required by the cost object. All cost objects not only received services from other resource groups, but also provided services to other cost objects, such as operating divisions and support groups.

Profit Center B had an actual headcount of 25. The study indicated that a total of 37 equivalent-persons were required to perform the functions of the operating unit. The analysis showed that Profit Center B provided the equivalent of 3 person-years to other operating divisions. It received the services of 10 additional equivalent-persons from the Controller's Group, and Corporate Headquarters provided the remainder.

This is an example of the information that is revealed from implementing an activity-based analysis system for a service function, such as the controller's office. The ABA model described can be applied equally as well to any service function. Since every company has its own unique characteristics, no model can be a perfect fit. The framework, however, is conceptually similar, and may help in implementing an activity-based system.

11

Activity-Based Costing for Marketing

MARKETING RESOURCES AND ACTIVITIES

Marketing embraces two basic functions: identifying or creating demand for the product or services of a company and satisfying that demand. Costs of identifying or creating demand include market research, advertising, and sales force remuneration. Costs of satisfying demand include warehousing, transportation, order processing, inventory holding costs, and customer service costs. Exhibit 11-1 illustrates the activities that are included in the marketing function.

Exhibit 11-1
Marketing Activities

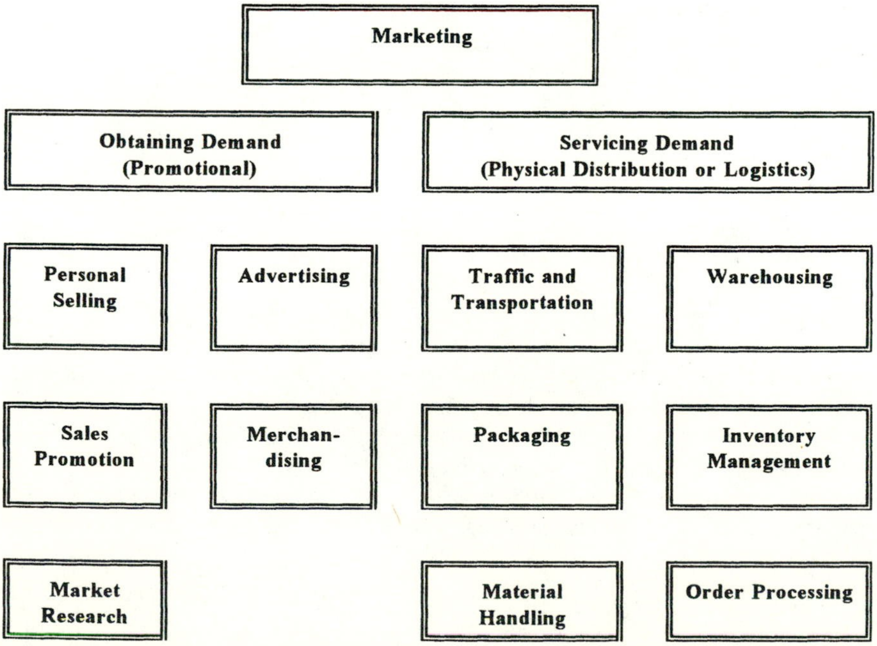

MARKETING COST ANALYSIS

The principles and techniques of marketing cost analysis are similar to those of production cost accounting. There are unique characteristics, however, in the nature of marketing costs. These characteristics are:

1. Marketing cost data are not usually represented by financial accounts. They tend to be used more for informal and statistical purposes than for the preparation of financial statements.
2. Marketing costs are often incurred outside the place of production. They may occur at geographically scattered centers.
3. Marketing costs are examined and classified functionally in order to assist management in appraising the contribution of products, sales territories, customers order sizes, and other marketing activities.
4. Marketing costs are generally treated as period costs rather than product costs, and are seldom if ever capitalized in inventory.
5. There is usually more flexibility in the choice of alternative methods of distribution than of production. This explains managerial interest in marketing cost analysis.

Marketing cost analysis provides information for decisions concerning

1. Commodities to be sold
2. Prices to be charged
3. Extent of territory to be served
4. Classes of trade to be cultivated
5. Distribution channels and agencies to be used
6. Profitable size of order to handle
7. Profitable size of unit of sale
8. Credit terms to be granted
9. Favorable time to expand
10. Size of inventories to be carried
11. Control of individual distribution operations and cost
12. Results to be obtained from marketing expenditures

Classifying Marketing Costs

There are two methods of classifying marketing resource costs. First is the *primary account* method, which identifies the natural origin or subject of expenditure, such as salaries, rent, insurance, and utilities. This is the *traditional* method of classification used in financial accounting.

Second is the *activity-based costing* method, which identifies the activities performed in the pursuit of cost objectives. The marketing objectives of obtaining demand (promotional) and servicing demand (physical distribution) include activities such as materials handling, advertising, market research, and order processing.

Under the primary account method, costs, which are collected in the natural expense accounts, are divided into direct and indirect to be charged or allocated to each product, territory or customer. This method follows traditional accounting procedures.

Under the activity-based costing method, all costs are directly traced or allocated to the specific *activity*, or to a *business process*. A business process consists of two or more activities that have the same or similar cost drivers. A unit rate for each activity is developed in terms of the activity's cost driver, the principal cause of the cost incurrence.

The objective of marketing cost analysis is to enable the accountant to produce data for management decisions, either by the analysis of the past or the projection of the future. In large organizations, the cost accounting activity may be performed within the marketing division by a marketing controller. Such an accountant may report to the manager of the marketing division and the controller of the corporation as a whole, having a staff relationship with the one and a line relationship with the other. In a small company, the accountant should be prepared for the analytical tasks that marketing cost accounting calls for, even though the greater part of the accounting duties lies elsewhere.

Marketing Resource Costs

Marketing resource costs are not determined by types of expenses; most of the categories of expense encountered in manufacturing are also encountered in distribution. However, certain types of costs typically relate only to marketing, namely,

- Salaries and wages of market researchers, product value analysts, artists and photographers, and others engaged in production of advertising and publicity
- Salaries and expenses of salesmen and commissions on sales
- Printing advertising materials
- Entertaining customers
- Rental of space at exhibitions
- Packing, shipping, and postage on advertising materials as well as products
- Gifts and other promotional items
- Transportation by land, water, or air
- Credit and collection salaries and expenses
- Rent of storage for finished products

MARKETING ACTIVITY-BASED COSTING PROCESS

The process of marketing activity-based cost analysis involves the following steps.

1. Define the marketing cost objectives, such as product lines, territories, and customers, and identify the activities and business processes that are involved in accomplishing the objectives. It is likely that costs will be accumulated in

traditional departments, rather than in activities or processes. The materials handling activity may be a marketing function even though it is physically located in the factory and charged to a manufacturing account.

2. Define the output of the marketing activity or the business process. ***A business process is defined as two or more related activities.*** This is not always measurable in terms of number of products. For example, the output of an advertising department may be information provided, inquiries received from new markets, or number of readers of material published as well as goods and services sold.

3. Determine the *cost drivers* that are most likely to cause variability in each *activity or business process.* In developing the cost drivers, relate the incurrence of the natural costs to the activities performed, which may be the outputs of the individual cost center. Shipping department costs may be expressed as per piece shipped or per ton/mile of product delivered. Billing costs may be expressed per line of invoice typed or per bill mailed.

4. Identify all relevant *direct* marketing and nonmarketing costs that are traceable to the marketing cost objective. Traceable manufacturing, engineering, and administrative costs may be considered relevant depending on the purpose of the analysis.

5. Based on the cost drivers selected, allocate the costs of the activities or business processes, to the major marketing cost objectives, such as product lines, territories, or customers.

This procedure serves as the framework for decision making. In studies of actual company practices, more product lines are added or dropped because of the personal attitudes or prejudices of a top executive than for any other reason. This activity-based analysis provides the objective evidence for adding or dropping product lines or territories. A comprehensive illustration of the procedure follows.

ACTIVITY-BASED COSTING MODEL FOR MARKETING

The ABC/ABM model described is based on actual cases reported in the IMA sponsored study of eight companies that incorporated ABC/ABM systems into their companies or segments of their companies. The implementation procedure outlined and described is a general model to fit the marketing functions of an organization. The model will apply to marketing organizations, or to the distribution functions in a manufacturing company.

Key Steps to Complete the ABC/ABM Implementation:

1. *Determine the scope, timing, and objectives of the project.* What product lines, facilities, employees, and other resources are to included in the study?

2. *Develop a project team, a work plan, and train the personnel involved in the project.* If only accounting and finance personnel are involved the results may be suspect. It is necessary to include all key operating personnel who

participate in the activities involved in the study.

3. *Make an activity analysis.*
Identify activity centers and business processes. Assemble the activities that make up business processes, such as, purchasing and procurement, customer administration, and materials handling. Determine the activities performed by all the employees included in the study.

4. *Make a cost driver analysis.*
Identify potential cost drivers for each activity and/or business process. Each individual activity needs a link to a product or service. This link is made through a second stage cost driver that is measurable in regard to the end product/service.

5. *Establish a value analysis and value-added coding scheme.* A value coding scheme was specifically designed for this model. Each situation requires its custom designed scheme.

6. *Develop a hierarchy analysis for activities.*
The activity hierarchy for the ABC/ABM Model is tailored to fit a distribution segment or an independent marketing organization. Both payroll-related and nonpayroll-related activities (expenses) need to be split into logical activity centers and coded to hierarchy categories (unit, batch, product-sustaining, and facility-sustaining).

Objectives and Scope of the Project

1. *Product class, location, and customer profitability analysis.*
Use the ABC/ABM model to quantify individual product and customer profitability. Which are the most profitable product lines? How can profitability of an order be determined? There are some 20,000 distinct stock-keeping units (SKUs) in the ABC/ABM model. Although the model marketing organization doesn't manufacture a product, it identified 23 separate classes of products that it stores, handles, and delivers. Both products and customers represent the cost objects of the ABC/ABM analysis.

2. *Cost reduction opportunities.*
Where and how can costs be reduced without affecting efficiency and quality of service?

3. *Customer satisfaction.*
How can the cost of on-time, accurate deliveries be measured? What is the cost of entering and processing orders, and of specialized packaging?

4. *The complexity of interbranch transactions.*
   What is the cost of delivery to a customer when transfers and transshipments are involved?

Business Processes (Activity Centers)

The ABC/ABM team organized the business processes and activity centers into groupings that followed functional rather than organizational patterns. The major groups of business processes are listed below. Within these categories there were 35 activity centers and 250 individual activities that were identified for the ABC/ABM model.

1. *Customer management.*
   Activities related to selling, marketing, and maintaining customers, including an imputed cost of carrying accounts receivable at each site.

2. *Product processing.*
   Activities related to processing material.

3. *Distribution management.*
   Activities related to loading, packing, and outbound material handling.

4. *Inventory management.*
   Activities related to unloading trucks, scheduling, procurement, transfers, and transshipments.

5. *Support.*
   Activities related to personnel management, finance, MIS, and general administration.

Cost Drivers

The ABC/ABM team established criteria for selecting cost drivers that fit the needs of the company. The final model for this project had 20 activity cost drivers. Some of the cost drivers were:

Delivery cost driver: the delivery costs varied by the number of stops made, the weight of the material, and the distance traveled.

Loading cost driver: the loading costs varied by the number of items in each order, the weight, and the handling difficulty.

Sales and Marketing cost driver: the sales and marketing costs varied by the number of inquiries, the number of orders, and the size of the orders.

Common Costs

The team established a total of five sites, which included the three stocking sites, a mill direct site, and a common site. Corporate costs for support activities are charged directly to the common site. The mill direct site is for the costs of servicing orders delivered directly to the customer from the mill. The support costs charged to the common site are distributed to the three stocking sites and the mill direct site. Their assignment is based on the activities performed at the common site and their appropriate cost drivers, such as the number of sales orders.

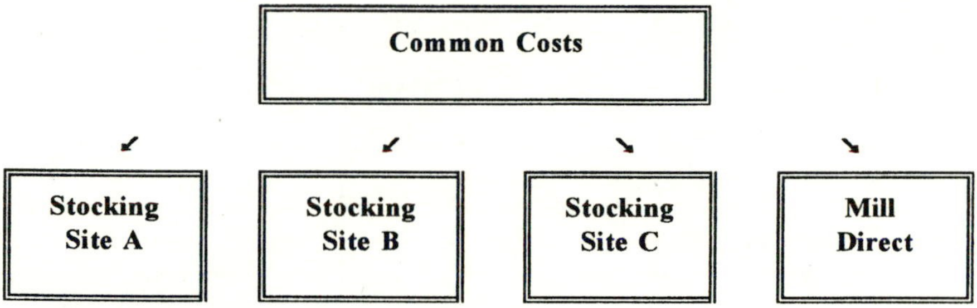

Cost Driver Information Collection

Resource cost drivers are an innovation aspect of ABC/ABM modeling, eliminating the traditional step-down or reciprocal methods, and replacing departments with activities. Data collection methods are especially important in the activity-based systems. An example of the data collection method for wage-related resource cost drivers is percentage estimates based on interviews with employees who perform the key functions. The most common sources of estimating resource cost drivers are interviews, survey forms, observation, and timekeeping systems.

Activity	Bill Bates	Jane White	Brad Smith		Total in ($000's)
Study capacities	15%	-	10%	→	$ 120
Design tooling	-	40%	-	→	80
Train employees	5%	-	-	→	45
Maintain routings	-	-	20%	→	106
↓	↓	↓	↓		↓
Total	100%	100%	100%	→	$1,500

The determination of time spent on activities by each employee is used along with the payroll information to assign total wage-related costs to each activity. This is an example of the Stage 1 allocation process. In Stage 2, the activity costs determined, by using the above procedure, are assigned to the cost object.

Profit Centers

The ABC/ABM team determined that the *profit center* would be the *stocking site*. The stocking site is the warehouse that stocked and processed inventory prior to sale, and where most of the costs are incurred. The revenues for orders, and the costs related to fulfilling the order are transferred to the stocking site. There are two kinds of cost transfers, transfers and transshipments.

Transfers of Cost

Transfers		Transshipments
Transfers are physical movements of materials without a customer order. Material is received by one warehouse, unloaded, processed, reloaded, and then moved to another warehouse for additional processing or to be stored in inventory. The final warehouse becomes the stocking site to the customer when a sale is made and the goods are pulled from that warehouse's inventory. The costs to unload, process, and load at each warehouse prior to the customer sale are transferred to the stocking site.		Transshipments are intermediate handling points, or staging points, prior to delivery to a customer. The costs of loading and unloading at each warehouse has to be transferred back to the stocking site where the sales revenue is credited.

Stocking Site	Transshipment Site	Customer
Profit center Sales revenue credited to and costs of transfers and transshipments charged to the stocking site	Costs transferred back to stocking site ⇐	Receives delivery from the stocking site or the transshipment point ⇐
Material delivery ⇒	Material delivery ⇒	

Activity Analysis

One of the activity centers/business processes identified was Customer Administration. The activity cost analysis for the Customer Administration business process revealed that some activities were more or less important than expected by management. The analysis gave managers a more objective basis to estimate activity costs.

Activity Center/Business Process: Customer Administration

Activities	Activity Costs as a Percent of Total Activity Center
Credit and collections	32%
Process order entry	27%
Customer service	21%
Support to sales force	16%
Testing	4%
Total	100%

Activity Center/Business Process: Distribution Management
Specific Activity Costs by Location

Activity	Site A	Site B	Site C	Total
Truck loading	$500	$200	$150	$850
Equipment maintenance	400	90	300	790
Packaging	350	150	100	600
Common carriers	150	180	160	490
Transfers	200	80	200	330
Fleet	1,200	500	400	2,100
Material handling	800	200	190	1,190
Total	$3,600	$1,400	$1,500	$6,500
Volume in lbs.	900	500	600	2,000
Cost per lb.	$4.00	$2.80	$2.50	$3.25

The analysis reveals that Site A, which handles more small orders than the other sites has a greater cost in terms of volume. The activity costs were based on the cost drivers selected by the company's ABC team.

Value Analysis

The coding scheme used by the ABC/ABM model was designed to assist in understanding the value of the specific activities and for cost reduction.

Value Rating	Description
9	High value: adding value to the product and/or customer
7	Medium to high value
5	Medium value, but necessary
3	Activity not necessary, or one that could be improved
1	Non-value added: should not occur

Activity Costs for All Sites by Value Code

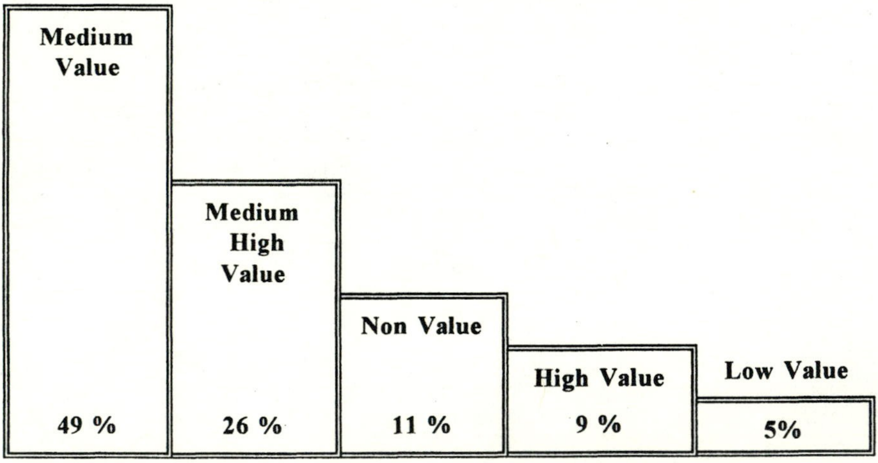

Hierarchy Analysis

The hierarchy analysis consisted of establishing categories that identified the volume or functional characteristics of the activities. The hierarchy analysis adopted for the ABC/ABM model and the results of the project are:

Unit level activities are defined as individual customer orders.
Batch level activities are defined as shipments or movements of products to fulfill customer orders.
Product-sustaining activities include such activities as machine maintenance and product management.
Facility-sustaining activities include non-product-related general plant and support service activities.

Activity Costs for All Sites by Hierarchy Classification

Unit Level	Facility-Sustaining	Batch Level	Product-Sustaining
41%	22%	21%	16%

Results of ABC Implementation

The activity-based analysis helped management to better evaluate both product and customer profitability. The review of activities within business processes provided insight into the potential to improve the organization. The hierarchy analysis revealed that facility costs, at 22 percent, represented the high cost of operating at three or more locations. The unit level (order activities) costs of 41 percent indicated that volume was a major factor in the distribution business. The value analysis revealed that 84 percent of the activities were considered necessary, medium to high value. However, that left 16 percent of the activities that could be improved or eliminated.

The ABC/ABM model described above is constructed from one of the eight actual case studies conducted by Professors Cooper and Kaplan, Lawrence Maisel, and KPMG Peat Marwick, and sponsored and published under the title, *Implementing Activity-Based Cost Management,* by the Institute of Management Accountants in 1992. It is not an academic model. It is the epitome of the practical application of ABC/ABM concepts to real-life situations. Although only a summary of the extensive effort and details that went into developing this model, it describes each step that was followed in the implementation process.

ILLUSTRATION OF ACTIVITY-BASED MARKETING ANALYSIS

This illustration shows the calculation of the profitability of product lines by territories using the activity-based costing approach. The previously described procedures are followed in principle. These procedures are as follows:

1. Identify the *activities,* such as, developing an advertising campaign, traveling to the sales territory, filling the orders, preparing orders for shipping, and storing orders in the warehouse.

2. Combine the activities into *business processes*, where possible, such as those shown in the table below.

3. Determine the *cost driver*, which is the basis of variability for each activity. These three steps are illustrated in the table.

Activities/Business Processes	Cost Driver
Selling	Gross sales, orders received, or salesmen's calls
Order filling	Number, weight, or size of units ordered
Shipping and warehousing	Units shipped
Credit and collection	Number of invoice lines

4. Calculate the unit cost of the activity or business process. The unit cost of each activity is determined by dividing the total activity cost by the basis of variability selected. Where conditions justify the practice, the unit cost can be used as the basis for budgeting and for the establishment of standards in a standard cost system.

5. Perform a marginal cost analysis. The accumulation of direct costs and the allocation of indirect costs to marketing cost centers enables management to assign total cost responsibility to each marketing activity. However, the identification of total costs does not always provide relevant information for specific decisions concerning such important functions as salesmen's performance and territorial profitability.

For example, salesmen are tempted to select products, customers, and territories that yield them the greatest personal commissions, not those that yield the highest profit margins to the company. Only by applying margin analysis will the company be able to determine profit contribution by product lines, territories, or other major marketing objectives.

Exhibits 11-2 through 11-8 were prepared by the controller of Auburn Company to provide information about marketing profitability. Exhibit 11-2 shows selling prices, unit manufacturing costs, units sold, and other bases of variability.

Exhibit 11-2
Auburn Company--Product Line Data, Year 19X3

Product Line Information	Product Line A	Product Line B	Product Line C
Selling price	$ 10.00	$ 8.00	$ 12.00
Unit manufacturing cost	$ 8.00	$ 5.00	$ 11.00
Quantity of units sold and shipped	50,000	30,000	20,000
Average weight of units sold	2.0 lb	3.0 lb.	4.0 lb.
Number of customer's orders	100	200	200
Variable portion of mfg. cost	60%	60%	60%

Exhibit 11-3 shows total variable and fixed costs for each business process and develops unit rates for variable and fixed costs of each major marketing activity, which are explained in the following paragraphs.

Selling: The selling activity is represented by the dollar value of sales. There may be justification for basing variability of selling cost on other factors, such as number of salesmen's calls, or orders obtained, and the controller must select the basis that has the main causal effect on cost variability. Auburn uses the dollar value of sales.

Advertising: Advertising is a promotional activity, similar to selling, which could logically be attributed to the same factors. Units of product sold was selected by Auburn. Note that advertising may or may not have variable cost characteristics. Some companies increase advertising when sales are down, so the cost may bear an inverse relationship with sales. Auburn found that a portion of advertising varies with sales and a larger portion is fixed.

Warehousing: This is the physical distribution activity of storage and terminaling. The factor of variability selected by Auburn is weight of products sold.

Packaging and Shipping: Another physical distribution activity, packaging and shipping normally has a greater proportion of variable expenses and is related to the quantity of units of product shipped. Auburn assumed units shipped are equal to units sold.

General Office: Auburn needs clerical, accounting, credit and collection, and other activities to service the overall marketing function. Each service has its own variability but Auburn assumed that number of orders affects all.

Exhibit 11-3
Auburn Company--Business Processes:
Calculation of Total Costs and Cost Rates per Unit

Business Process	Cost Driver	Total Volume	Total Cost	Unit Rate
Selling	Dollar value of sales	$ 980,000	$ 49,000	5.0%
Advertising	Quantity of units sold	100,000	$ 40,000	$ 0.40
Warehousing	Weight of units shipped	270,000 lb	$ 27,000	$ 0.10
Packaging and shipping	Quantity of units shipped	100,000	$ 20,000	$ 0.20
General office	Number of customer's orders	500	$ 10,000	$20.00

Calculation of Variable and Fixed Cost Rates				
Business Process	Variable Cost	Unit Rate	Fixed Cost	Unit Rate
Selling	$ 29,400	3.0%	$ 19,600	2.0%
Advertising	$ 10,000	$ 0.10	$ 30,000	$ 0.30
Warehousing	$ 13,500	$ 0.05	$ 13,500	$ 0.05
Packaging and shipping	$ 12,000	$ 0.12	$ 8,000	$ 0.08
General office	$ 2,000	$ 4.00	$ 8,000	$ 16.00

Exhibit 11-4 provides additional product and territory transactions data. For example, the quantity of product C sold in the West territory during the period is 14,000 units. Customers' orders for product A in the South territory total 50. These data form the basis for the determination of the cost calculations in subsequent exhibits.

Exhibit 11-4
Auburn Company--Sales and Orders by Territory in Units, Year 19X3

Transactions by Territory	Total	Product A	Product B	Product C
Products sold: West	60,000	26,000	20,000	14,000
South	40,000	24,000	10,000	6,000
Total	100,000	50,000	30,000	20,000
Customers orders: West	280	50	80	150
South	220	50	120	50
Total	500	100	200	200

Exhibit 11-5 shows an analysis of profitability by territory for all products for the year 19X3.

Exhibit 11-5
Auburn Company--
Profitability Statement by Territory, All Products, Year 19X3

	Allocation Basis	Total Company	West Territory	South Territory
Sales revenue		$ 980,000	$ 588,000	$ 392,000
Less cost of sales		770,000	462,000	308,000
Gross margin		$ 210,000	$ 126,000	$ 84,000
Selling expense	5% of sales	$ 49,000	$ 29,400	$ 19,600
Advertising exp.	$ 0.40/unit sold	40,000	24,000	16,000
Warehousing exp.	$ 0.10/lb. ship.	27,000	16,800	10,200
Packaging and shipping exp.	$ 0.20/unit sold	20,000	12,000	8,000
Gen. office exp.	$ 20/order	10,000	5,600	4,400
Total expenses		$ 146,000	$ 87,800	$ 58,200
Operating income (loss)		$ 64,000	$ 38,200	$ 25,800

The profitability analysis by territory reveals that both territories show a profit from operations. Exhibit 11-6 shows the total company profitability by product line.

Exhibit 11-6
Auburn Company--
Profitability Statement by Product Line--All Territories, Year 19X3

	Allocation basis	Total Company	Product Line A	Product Line B	Product Line C
Sales revenue		$980,000	$500,000	$240,000	$240,000
Cost of sales		770,000	400,000	150,000	220,000
Gross margin		$210,000	$100,000	$ 90,000	$ 20,000
Less expen.					
Selling	5% of sales	$ 49,000	$ 25,000	$ 12,000	$ 12,000
Advertising	$0.40/unit sold	40,000	20,000	12,000	8,000
Warehousing	$0.10/lb shipped	27,000	10,000	9,000	8,000
Packaging and shipping	$0.20/unit sold	20,000	10,000	6,000	4,000
General office	$20/order	10,000	2,000	4,000	4,000
Total expenses		$146,000	$ 67,000	$ 43,000	$ 36,000
Operating income (loss)		$ 64,000	$ 33,000	$ 47,000	$(16,000)

The profitability statement by product line provides additional information for marketing managers. Product lines A and B are both profitable, whereas product line C shows an operating loss of $16,000. This statement has revealed that although the overall company shows a profit and that both territories are profitable, there is one product line that requires further analysis. Exhibits 11-7 and 11-8 present data by product line for each territory separately to further isolate the operating loss of product C.

Exhibit 11-7
Auburn Company--
Profitability Statement for West Territory, All Products, Year 19X3

	Allocation Basis	All Products	Product A	Product B	Product C
Sales revenue		$588,000	$260,000	$160,000	$168,000
Cost of sales		462,000	208,000	100,000	154,000
Gross margin		$126,000	$ 52,000	$ 60,000	$ 14,000
Less expenses					
Selling	5% of sales	$ 29,400	$ 13,000	$ 8,000	$ 8,400
Advertising	$0.40 / units sold	24,000	10,400	8,000	5,600
Warehousing	$0.10 / lb shipped	16,800	5,200	6,000	5,600
Packaging and shipping	$0.20 / units sold	12,000	5,200	4,000	2,800
General office	$20 / order	5,600	1,000	1,600	3,000
Total expenses		$ 87,800	$ 34,800	$ 27,600	$ 25,400
Operating income (loss)		$ 38,200	$ 17,200	$ 32,400	$(11,400)

Exhibit 11-7 shows that in the West territory product C has an operating loss of $11,400 and that products A and B show a profit of $17,200 and $32,400 respectively. Exhibit 11-8 presents a similar profitability analysis for the South territory.

Exhibit 11-8
Auburn Company--
Profitability Statement for South Territory, All Products, Year 19X3

	Allocation Basis	All Products	Product A	Product B	Product C
Sales revenue		$392,000	$240,000	$ 80,000	$ 72,000
Cost of sales		308,000	192,000	50,000	66,000
Gross margin		$ 84,000	$ 48,000	$ 30,000	$ 6,000
Less expenses					
Selling	5% of sales	$ 19,600	$ 12,000	$ 4,000	$ 3,600
Advertising	$0.40/unit sold	16,000	9,600	4,000	2,400
Warehousing	$0.10/lb. shipped	10,200	4,800	3,000	2,400
Packaging and shipping	$0.20/unit sold	8,000	4,800	2,000	1,200
General office	$20/order	4,400	1,000	2,400	1,000
Total expenses		$ 58,200	$ 32,200	$ 15,400	$ 10,600
Operating income (loss)		$ 25,800	$ 15,800	$ 14,600	$ (4,600)

Exhibit 11-8 reveals that only product C shows an operating loss in the South Territory. Just as in the West territory, products A and B show an operating income. The sum of the losses of product C in the two territories is equal to the $16,000, which is shown in Exhibit 11-6.

CONTRIBUTION MARGIN APPROACH

Profitability statements have provided valuable information for the marketing managers in measuring the profitability of both territories and products. In the long run, a total cost approach must be made to determine which products and territories are profitable. It is cautioned, however, that a total cost approach to decisions regarding dropping a product line or territory may be detrimental to the overall company.

Instead of using the profitability statements in Exhibits 11-7 and 11-8, a contribution margin analysis is presented to determine whether product line C should be dropped. In order to present a contribution margin analysis, the relevance of cost categories must be determined. The following assumptions are provided for the Auburn Company: (1) the fixed production costs are unavoidable if product line C is dropped and (2) the fixed portion of the marketing and general office expenses are unavoidable if product line C is dropped.

Exhibit 11-9 presents the contribution margin approach for the West territory and Exhibit 11-10 for the South territory, both for product line C. Exhibit 11-11 presents a pro forma profitability statement for the Auburn Company assuming that product line C is dropped.

Exhibit 11-9
Auburn Company--Contribution Margin Approach for West Territory, Product C, Year 19X3

Sales revenue			$168,000
Less variable cost of sales	60% × $154,000		92,400
Gross contribution margin			$ 75,600
Less variable expenses: Selling	3% × $168,000	$5,040	
Advertising	$0.10 × 14,000 units	1,400	
Warehousing	$0.05 × 56,000 lb	2,800	
Packaging and shipping	$0.12 × 14,000 units	1,680	
General office	$4.00 × 150 orders	600	
Total variable expenses			11,520
Contribution margin			$ 64,080
Less fixed cost of sales	40% × $154,000	$61,600	
Less fixed: Selling	2% × $168,000	3,360	
Advertising	$0.30 × 14,000 units	4,200	
Warehousing	$0.05 × 56,000 lb	2,800	
Packaging and shipping	$0.08 × 14,000 units	1,120	
General office	$16 × 150 orders	2,400	
Total fixed expenses			75,480
Operating income (loss)			$ (11,400)

Exhibit 11-10
Auburn Company--Contribution Margin Approach for South Territory, Product C, Year 19X3

Sales revenue			$72,000
Less variable cost of sales	60% × $66,000		39,600
Gross contribution margin			$ 32,400
Less variable expenses: Selling	3% × $72,000	$2,160	
Advertising	$0.10 × 6,000 units	600	
Warehousing	$0.05 × 24,000 lb	1,200	
Packaging and shipping	$0.12 × 6,000 units	720	
General office	$4.00 × 50 orders	200	
Total variable expenses			4,880
Contribution margin			$ 27,520
Less fixed cost of sales	40% × $66,000	$26,400	
Less fixed expenses: Selling	2% × $72,000	1,440	
Advertising	$0.30 × 6,000 units	1,800	
Warehousing	$0.05 × 24,000 lb	1,200	
Packaging and shipping	$ 0.08 × 6,000 units	480	
General office	$16.00 × 50 orders	800	
Total fixed costs and expenses			$ 32,120
Operating income (loss)			$ (4,600)

Exhibit 11-11
Auburn Company--Pro Forma Profitability Statement
Elimination of Product C, Year 19X3

Sales revenue			$740,000
Less cost of sales	60% × $550,000 + $308,000		638,000
Gross margin			$102,000
Selling exp.	3% × $740,000 + $19,600	$41,800	
Advertising exp.	$0.10 × 80,000 units + $30,000	38,000	
Warehousing exp.	$0.05 × 190,000 lb + $13,500	23,000	
Packaging and shipping exp.	$0.12 × 80,000 units + $8,000	17,600	
General office exp.	$4.00 × 300 orders + $8,000	9,200	
Total expenses			129,600
Operating income (loss)			$(27,600)

The elimination of product line C will result in a reduction of operating income from $64,000 (see Exhibit 11-5) to a loss of $27,600, a total reduction in income of $91,600. The contribution margin of product C in the West territory is $64,080 (see Exhibit 11-9), and the contribution margin of product C in the South territory is $27,520 (see Exhibit 11-10). The sum of product C's contribution margin is $91,600, which explains the overall loss in income if product line C were to be dropped. The Auburn Company would be better off to keep Product C.

III

Managerial Accounting Analysis and Control

12

Cost Behavior

INTRODUCTION

In a manufacturing company, increases in volume are assumed to be accompanied by increases in total costs. Volume is measured by total units of output or by total sales dollars. Total costs include costs of production and expenses that are related to the volume of sales. Some of the costs incurred in manufacturing a physical product, by nature, increase in direct proportion to the volume. Assembly line products receive equal amounts of direct labor. The inputs of material and labor are *engineered* costs, meeting standardized quality control tests for uniformity. These costs are direct in regard to the product and vary directly in proportion to the number of units produced.

Some factory overhead costs do not directly attach to the product but are consumed in quantities proportionate to the number of units produced. Indirect materials and supplies, indirect labor, and electric power for operating production machinery, are observed to be consumed in proportion to the number of units produced. These costs are indirect in regard to the product, but vary in direct proportion to volume.

Other indirect factory overhead costs are contracted on the basis of time rather than volume. The general plant manager's salary, property taxes, depreciation and insurance are observed to be fixed during the current fiscal period, that is, they do not increase or decrease with changes in volume.

A third category of factory overhead costs increase, but less than in proportion with increased in volume. Under observation, the costs of production line supervision; office services, such as payroll, personnel, timekeeping, and clerical; machine repair, and maintenance; and building utility bills are indirect in regard to the product and are mixed or semivariable with respect to volume.

Cost behavior refers to the reaction of total cost to a change in one unit or a batch of units of input or output. For example, if one additional unit of the finished product is produced, what would the effect be on total costs of production? The change in total costs would be the *incremental* or *decremental* cost. The average cost at the new level of output would be the *unit* cost.

Output (volume) is the primary, but not the only basis for determining cost behavior. Inputs are also used to measure cost behavior. Machine hours may be used to measure the behavior of electricity or lubrication costs, whereas direct labor hours may be used in determining the behavior of other factory overhead costs.

DIFFERENCES IN TRADITIONAL AND ACTIVITY-BASED COST BEHAVIOR

Is there a difference in traditional costing and activity-based costing methods in regard to cost behavior? The answer is yes and no. There are no differences in the principles of cost behavior. The principles are:

1. Variable costs or expenses increase or decrease in exact proportion with increases or decreases in the activity base.
2. Fixed costs or expenses do not increase or decrease with changes in the activity base.
3. Mixed costs or expenses contain both variable and fixed behavior characteristics.

There are also no differences in the general assumptions. But there are differences in specific assumptions, and in the definitions of organizational structures. Activity-based costing assumes that activities, not organizational units or departments, are the basic cost centers. It emphasizes how and why the activities are performed, and the causes behind them. It redefines many terms.

In both traditional and activity-based costing, the allocation of indirect costs is based on the most direct causal factor, such as square feet for building costs, number of employees for personnel costs, or machine hours for repair and maintenance of production machinery costs. In activity-based systems these causal factors are called *cost drivers* and are related to the *activity* rather than the output volume. Activity-based costing concepts do not alter the definition of variability as it relates to output. Activity-based systems may, however, improve the accuracy in identifying the behavior of specific production costs. For example, activity work cells may include costs that were assumed to be fixed, but actually vary proportionally with each unit passing through the work cell.

GENERAL ASSUMPTIONS OF COST BEHAVIOR

The general assumptions on which the following discussion of cost behavior is based are:

1. Cost behavior is related to one specified activity base.

2. There is a defined time period, and a range of activity, within which cost behavior is examined.
3. The relationship between the cost and the activity is linear.

THE ACTIVITY BASE

The activity base is the principal volume-related factor that causes a specified cost to behave in a predictable manner. The single most common activity base for defining the variability of the production costs--direct materials, direct labor and factory overhead--is *units of output*. The most frequently used activity bases for nonmanufacturing service or merchandising firms are *service units*, *sales units*, or *sales dollars*. In activity-based costing the activity bases are expanded and reclassified. The activity base is conceptually similar to the cost driver.

In nonmanufacturing service firms there is no physical product. Revenue is in the form of fees for contractors and professional services, taxes for governmental services, or tuition for educational services. The variability of costs is directly related to dollars of revenue, which in most service industries, is based on a specific unit of service. For example, where college students pay tuition on the basis of credit hours, the credit hours are proportional to tuition revenue.

Because of inflation, sales dollars are not as reliable as nonmonetary activity bases are for comparative purposes. Therefore, the service unit, such as student credit hours, can be substituted for dollars of revenue as the activity base. This activity base is called the service unit. In hospitals, the service unit may be the number of patient bed days; in airlines it may be passenger seats occupied, or passenger miles.

The most appropriate base for defining the variability of production costs, direct material, direct labor, and factory overhead is units of output. Activity-based costing systems do not alter the definition of variability as it relates to output. Activity-based costing systems may, however, improve the accuracy in identifying the behavior of specific production costs.

Administrative and marketing costs are period expenses that are subtracted from revenues. They are directly related to units sold not units produced. It is thus more appropriate to measure variability of these expenses with sales units or sales revenues as an activity base.

The most appropriate activity base for merchandising firms, wholesalers, and retailers is sales revenue. Although quantities, rather than dollars, would normally be preferable (because of inflationary influences on the value of the dollar), there is no acceptable activity unit for most retailers and wholesalers. They purchase large quantities of heterogeneous products for resale at a wide range of prices. No single unit of quantity would be representative enough to serve as an activity base. Sales revenue is the only common denominator for merchandising firms.

The most appropriate activity base for service industries is that which represents a common denominator for measuring services rendered. This is the service unit such as student credit hours or passenger miles. Where no unit of service is appropriate, service revenue is used as the activity base.

Below is a summary of the major production costs and expenses showing examples of activity bases:

Source of Cost or Expense	Activity Base
I. Manufacturing industries	
A. Costs of production	
Direct material	Units of output
Direct labor	Units of output
Factory overhead	Various bases
B. Administrative expenses	
Executive offices	Square feet
Accounting and finance	Invoices
Personnel Office	Number of employees
Security and maintenance	Buildings, square feet
Engineering	Change orders, projects
Research and development	Various bases
C. Marketing expenses	
Selling and promotional	Sales dollars/units
Physical distribution	Various bases
II. Merchandising companies	Sales dollars/units
III. Service industries	Service unit/dollars

RELEVANT TIME PERIOD AND RELEVANT RANGE

Theoretically all costs are avoidable in the long run. That is, plant capacity can be expanded or contracted. Entire divisions of large corporations can be closed, which would eliminate all costs, variable or fixed. In order to analyze cost relationships for practical applications, an assumption concerning a ***relevant time period*** (RTM) must be made. The normal period of time during which costs are considered fixed is the budget year. Budgets are normally based on one fiscal year. Budgets approved by the corporate executives are authority to commit the company to annual salary contracts and other major contracts for the entire year or for a considerable portion of the year.

For practical purposes the relevant time period is one (fiscal) year. In the relevant time period, fixed costs are either *committed* or *discretionary*. Committed fixed costs cannot be changed during the RTP. Annual salaries, contractual legal agreements, and various building occupancy costs such as insurance and depreciation, are not avoidable within a defined time period. These are called *committed fixed costs*.

Those fixed costs that can be avoided within the relevant time period are called *discretionary fixed costs*. They include such items as advertising, company parties, charitable donations, and budgeted positions that have not yet been filled. In conjunction with the relevant time period assumption is the *relevant range of activity* assumption. This assumption confines the output in units or dollars to minimum and maximum limits. It also reconciles the economist's more realistic analysis of cost behavior with that of the accountant's more pragmatic interpretation.

LINEARITY

In management accounting, it is assumed that the behavior of production costs and of expenses has a linear relationship with the activity base. To explain and to predict cost variability the formula $Y = a + b(X)$ is used, which is a linear equation. Projections of costs using this linear regression formula appear as a straight line when plotted on a graph.

The assumption of linearity is consistent with the accountant's relevant range assumption. In the relevant range of activity, fixed costs remain at only one level and the variable rate per unit remains constant during the relevant time period, that is, one year for budgeting purposes. This assumption avoids the nonlinear portions of the economist's total cost curve that are caused by diseconomies of scale.

In order to obviate the use of ***multiple regression*** techniques, which are mathematically more complex, it is further assumed that there is only one independent variable, X (the activity base), which is related to the cost behavior of the dependent variable, Y. This assumption allows us to confine our mathematical solutions to linear equations.

VARIABLE, FIXED, AND MIXED COSTS

Variable Costs (Proportionally Variable)

Cost behavior refers to the degree to which costs vary with respect to the activity base. ***Variable*** costs increase or decrease directly and in proportion with changes in volume. Consequently, a 10 percent increase in units of output is accompanied by a 10 percent increase in variable costs of production. The categories of variable costs are:

1. Production costs (variable in relation to units of output)
   - Direct material
   - Direct labor
   - Variable overhead
2. Expenses (variable in relation to units sold or sales dollars)
   - Variable administrative
   - Variable marketing

Some typical examples of variable factory overhead are

1. Indirect materials, such as lubricants and abrasives
2. Indirect labor, such as fork lift truck operators
3. Factory supplies
4. Power for machinery
5. Machine maintenance
6. Factory payroll fringe benefits
7. Small tools

Few administrative expenses are variable in regard to sales. Several marketing expenses, however, are variable in response to increases or decreases in sales, such as

1. Sales commissions
2. Packing materials
3. Shipping room labor
4. Delivery expenses

Let us assume that all costs of producing product *X* are proportionally variable at $10 per unit. A cost schedule for product *X*, from 1 to 10 units is shown in the table.

Units of Output	Total Production Cost	Units of Output	Total Production Cost
X	*Y*	*X*	*Y*
1	$10	6	$ 60
2	20	7	70
3	30	8	80
4	40	9	90
5	50	10	100

From the above cost schedule we note that as units of X increase by one the total production costs increase by \$10. There is proportionality in each increment of output:

\$10 / 1, \$20 / 2, \$30 / 3 ... \$100 /10 = 10 to 1

The same data plotted on the graph below reveals that they fit a linear pattern. The algebraic equation for a straight-line (linear regression) is $Y = a + b(X)$.

Let
Y = total costs of production
X = units of product
a = total fixed costs (assumed to be zero for a proportionally variable cost)
b = variable costs per unit
also,
b = $\Delta Y / \Delta X$, the change in Y accompanied by a change in one unit of X

The *cost formula*, $Y = a + b(X)$, can be use to estimate total production costs at any level of output. For example, let

X = 8 units of output

$Y = a + b(X)$

a = fixed costs = \$0

b = variable costs per unit of output = \$10 / 1 = \$10

Y = \$0 + \$10(8)

Y = \$80

Fixed Costs

Fixed costs do not change in response to an increase or decrease in the activity base within the relevant range. As production increases, total fixed costs remain constant, whereas average fixed costs per unit of output decrease. A manufacturing company, has the following categories of fixed costs and expenses:

1. Production costs
   Fixed overhead
2. Expenses
   Fixed administrative
   Fixed marketing

The fixed factory overhead includes costs such as:

1. Plant manager's office
2. Supervision
3. Factory depreciation
4. Factory insurance
5. Property taxes
6. Utilities such as heat and light
7. Plant security and maintenance

Fixed expenses include:

1. General administrative offices, for example, president's office.
2. Research and development
3. Engineering staff
4. Promotion and advertising
5. Depreciation on office and sales property and equipment
6. Insurance & taxes on office & sales property & equipment

An example of the behavior of fixed costs is shown below:

Units of Output--X	Total Production Costs
1	20
2	20
3	20
4	20
...	...
10	20

As product X increases by one unit the total production costs remain the same. Algebraically the cost formula is: $Y = a + b(X)$

where a (total fixed costs) is assumed to be \$20, and
where b (variable costs per unit) is assumed to be zero

$Y = a + \$0(X)$
$Y = \$20$

Total production costs (Y) remain constant at \$20 at all levels of output (X). Graphically, the above relationship appears as follows:

Fixed Costs

Total Costs

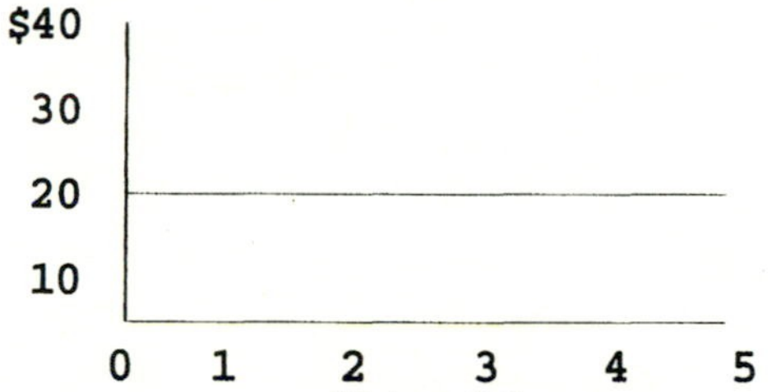

Units of Output

Step-Fixed Costs and the Relevant Range

There are costs that increase or decrease in steps rather than proportionally to activity changes. As production increases there is a point at which an increase in capacity is necessary. For example, one production machine has a capacity of 5,000 units per year. The depreciation on one machine is \$10,000 per year. At levels of production from 5,001 up to 10,000 units, two machines are required. These ***step-fixed costs*** would appear as shown in the graph.

Total Costs

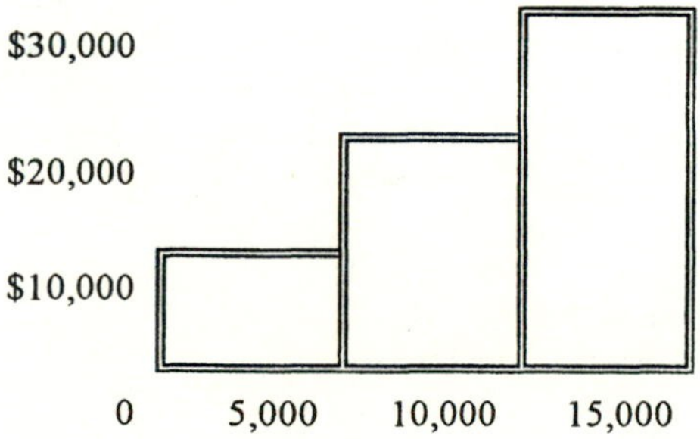

Units

Assuming that the normal production falls between 5,001 and 10,000 units, this activity level is defined as the ***relevant range***. By confining our activity level to this range, we are assured that fixed costs in total will not change. Fixed costs are budgeted at $20,000 per year. Should we venture outside of the relevant range the original budget equation will no longer be valid. For example, within the relevant range the budget equation presumes two machines, or Y = $20,000; but at production levels beyond 10,000 units a new budget equation would be necessary such as Y = $30,000 for three machines.

Step-Variable Costs

Step-variable costs are those that increase not by increases in ***one*** unit of output, but by multiple units. For example, a college or university may hire one new faculty member when twenty-five additional students are enrolled. Lesser increases of students would not be sufficient to warrant a new professor. In a factory, multiple units such as 1,000 units of output may be necessary before new equipment or new personnel are budgeted. Step-variable costs are no different from proportionally variable costs if we merely assume that the unit, which is the basis of variability, is a multiple unit rather than a single unit.

Mixed or Semivariable Costs

Our discussion of cost variability has been confined to proportionally variable or total fixed costs and expenses. The fact is that costs do not behave so obediently that we end up with all purebreds. As with our pets, we have more mongrels around than purebreds, and with costs we have more ***mixed costs*** (also referred to as semivariable) than purely variable or fixed costs.

Mixed costs have both variable and fixed components. For example, indirect labor may include both clerks whose wages vary directly in response to production and a supervisor whose salary is fixed regardless of variations in production. Power and light includes the cost of electricity for production machines, which varies proportionally with output, but also includes the cost of illuminating the plant, which does not vary proportionally with output.

In this section, we examine the characteristics of mixed costs and how to isolate the variable and fixed components. Previously, in describing proportionally variable costs, it was assumed that fixed costs, a = $0, and variable costs, b = $10. In the discussion of purely fixed costs, it was assumed that fixed costs, a = $20, and variable costs, b = $0. For the purpose of discussing mixed costs it is assumed that

a = fixed costs = $20
b = variable costs per unit = $10

For X values 1 through 10, the total production costs are determined by the linear cost formula, $Y = a + b(X)$

Cost Formula	Units of Output X	Total Production Costs Y
Y = $20 + $10 (1)	1	$30
	2	40
	3	50
	4	60
Y = $20 + $10 (5)	5	70
	6	80
	7	90
	8	100
	9	110
Y = $20 + $10 (10)	10	120

Note that the total production costs increase less than in proportion with each increase in units of *X*. The increase from one to two units of *X* is a 100 percent increase, whereas the total costs increase $30 to $40, an increase of only 33⅓ percent. By assuming values for *a* (total fixed costs) and *b* (variable costs per unit), we have solved for its values of *Y* at each level of *X*, which is shown in the preceding table. The data below include variable, fixed and mixed costs.

Units Produced	1,000	2,000	3,000
Direct materials	$ 20,000	$ 40,000	$ 60,000
Direct labor	$ 25,000	$ 50,000	$ 75,000
Factory overhead			
Depreciation of building	$ 12,000	$ 12,000	$ 12,000
Power and light	$ 4,000	$ 5,600	$ 7,200
Indirect labor	$ 9,000	$ 11,400	$ 13,800

These figures show that the costs of direct materials for 2,000 units is proportionally variable with that at the 1,000 unit level. That is, the ratio of $40,000 to 2,000 units is equal to the ratio of $20,000 to 1,000 units. Furthermore, the same proportionality prevails at the 3,000 unit level. We thus observe a *proportionally variable cost*, which for expediency is referred to as a *variable cost*. Direct labor, like direct material, is usually assumed to be a variable cost because it varies proportionally with the units produced under normal production conditions.

Depreciation of building remains at $12,000 at all levels of output. It is appropriately categorized as a purely *fixed cost*. Power and light is neither a variable nor a fixed cost, according to the observations just made. That is, the ratio of $5,600 to 2,000 units is not equal to the ratio of $4,000 to 1,000 units. Nor does the cost of power and light remain constant or fixed at all levels of output. Power and light is a *mixed cost* containing both variable and fixed elements.

COST BEHAVIOR METHODS

In mixed costs, the variable portion is expressed as a *rate per unit* of output, whereas the fixed portion is expressed as a *total* dollar amount. The three methods used to separate these two cost elements are the high-low method, the least-squares method, and the scattergraph method.

High-Low Method

Step 1--Determining the variable costs per unit

Based on the number of units, the highest level, 3,000, and lowest level, 1,000, are selected. Next, the corresponding dollar amounts are selected, $7,200 and $4,000, respectively. The value of *b*, the variable rate per unit of output, is calculated by subtracting the lowest from the highest dollar amount and dividing the difference by the corresponding difference in the units. The result is the rate of change in total dollars of cost per unit of output.

In the high-low method the linear equation is $Y = a = b(X)$. In step 1, we are calculating the value of *b*, the variable cost per unit for power and light, which is also the slope of the total cost line.

$b = \frac{(\$7{,}200 - \$4{,}000)}{(3{,}000 - 1{,}000)}$	$= \frac{\$3{,}200}{2{,}000}$	$=$ $1.60 per unit

Step 2 --Determining the total fixed costs

In the equation $Y = a + b(X)$, *Y* is the dollar amount, selected at *either* the high or low point, *X* is the corresponding units, and *b* is the value determined in step 1. Solve for *a*.

$Y = a + \$1.60(X)$

Substitute for Y and X

$$\$4{,}000 = a + \$1.60(1{,}000)$$
$$a = \$4{,}000 - \$1{,}600$$
$$a = \$2{,}400$$

Step 3--Determining the cost formula

The formula $Y = a + b(X)$ is determined by substituting the values of a and b from steps 1 and 2.

$Y = \$2{,}400 + \$1.60(X)$ is the cost formula for power and light.

The cost formula represents the equation that can be used to estimate total costs of power and light (Y) at any given level of output (X).

Step 4--Applying the Cost Formula

After the cost formula for power and light, $Y = \$2{,}400 + \$1.60(X)$, is calculated, it can be used for predicting future levels of power and light costs at other levels of output. For example, the output for the month of October is expected to be 2,200 units. What is the estimated power and light costs where $X = 2{,}200$ units?

$$Y = \$2{,}400 + \$1.60\ (2{,}200)$$
$$Y = \$2{,}400 + \$3{,}520$$
$$Y = \$5{,}920$$

Thus, at an output of 2,200 units the *expected* cost of power and light is $5,920.

Illustration of Indirect Labor

Indirect labor is another mixed cost. The dollar amount for indirect labor is $13,800 at the highest output level of 3,000 units. At the lowest level, 1,000 units, the cost is $9,000. The four-step method is used to determine the cost of indirect labor at an output of 2,400 units.

Step 1

$b = \dfrac{(\$13{,}800 - \$9{,}000)}{(3{,}000 - 1{,}000)}$	$= \dfrac{\$4{,}800}{2{,}000}$	= $2.40 per unit

Step 2

The cost formula is $Y = a + b(X)$. Select the ***high*** level at 3,000 units (either the high or the low will yield the same answer):

$$\$13{,}800 = a + \$2.40\ (3{,}000)$$
$$\$13{,}800 = a + \$7{,}200$$
$$a = \$6{,}600$$

Step 3

The cost formula is $Y = \$6{,}600 + \$2.40(X)$

Step 4

Determine the cost of indirect labor at an output level of 2,400 units.

$$Y = \$6{,}600 + \$2.40\ (2{,}400)$$
$$Y = \$6{,}600 + \$5{,}760$$
$$Y = \$12{,}360$$

Least-Squares Method

The least-squares method of calculating the variable and fixed portions of mixed costs is mathematically superior to the high-low and scattergraph methods. It calculates the straight line from which the squares of the deviations of the actual data from that line are least in absolute amount. The formula for the straight-line is as previously shown:

$$Y = a + b\ (X)$$

This formula can be adapted to any two variables and is also called a linear or simple line of regression. In the least-squares method, the data for time periods, such as years, quarters, or months, can be analyzed. The number of periods, such as January through May in the demonstration problem, is the value of n.

In the problem, for example, $n = 5$.

The X value represents the independent variable, such as machine hours, volume in units, or sales dollars.

The Y value represents the dependent variable, such as cost in dollars of the indirect materials or a work cell activity. As in the high-low method, a represents the total fixed costs and b represents the variable cost per unit. The procedure requires two simultaneous equations and a step method as follows

	X	Y	XY	X^2
January	10	$ 440	$ 4,400	$ 100
February	20	460	9,200	400
March	50	490	24,500	2,500
April	40	470	18,800	1,600
May	60	500	30,000	3,600
Total	180	$2,360	$86,900	$8,200

Two simultaneous equations are used to solve for the values of a and b in the formula $Y = a + b(X)$:

Line (1) $\Sigma Y = na + \Sigma Xb$
Line (2) $\Sigma XY = \Sigma Xa + \Sigma X^2 b$

Where: $n = 5$ $\quad \Sigma XY = 86{,}900$
$\Sigma X = 180$ $\quad \Sigma X^2 = 8{,}200$
$\Sigma Y = 2{,}360$

Line (1) $2{,}360 = 5a + 180b$
Line (2) $86{,}900 = 180a + 8{,}200b$

Step 1

Multiply line (1) by 36 to obtain:
Line (1a) $84{,}960 = 180a + 6{,}480b$

Step 2

Subtract line (1a) from line (2):

$$
\begin{array}{lrcl}
 & 86{,}900 & = & 180a + 8{,}200b \\
\text{Subtract} & \underline{84{,}960} & = & \underline{180a} + \underline{6{,}480b} \\
 & 1{,}940 & = & 0 + 1{,}720b \\
 & b & = & \$1.1279
\end{array}
$$

Step 3

Substitute b in line (1)
$2{,}360 = 5a + 180\,(1.13)$
$2{,}360 = 5a + 203$
$5a = 2{,}157$
$a = \$431$

Step 4

State cost formula in terms of least-square values:

$Y = a + b(X)$

$Y = \$431 + \$1.13(X)$

Step 5

Plot on graph using any two points, for example,
$X = 10$, and $X = 40$

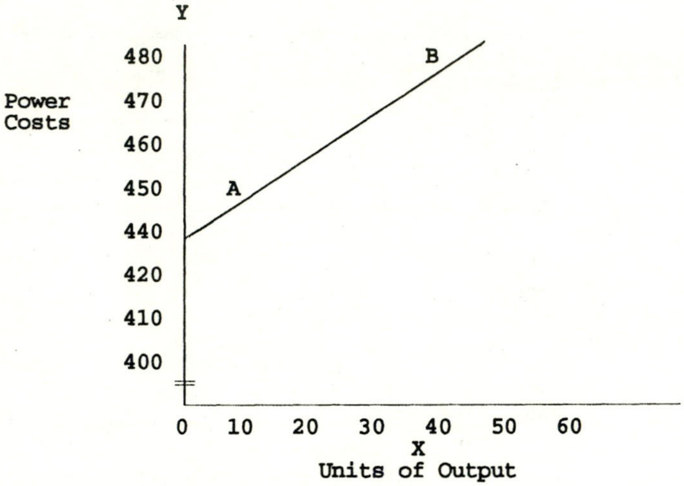

Point *A* is

$Y = \$431 + \$1.13\ (10)$
$Y = \$442.30$

Point *B* is

$Y = \$431 + \$1.13\ (40)$
$Y = \$476.20$

Step 6

Plot the actual data on the least-squares graph to show the relationship between the actual points and the least-squares line of regression.

The Scattergraph and the Freehand Method

The scattergraph is a graph on which the points representing actual *X* and *Y* values are plotted. The freehand method is the act of drawing a straight line, by visual observation, through the actual plotted data. This is a line that will fit the formula $Y = a + b(X)$, where a is the amount on the *Y* axis which is intersected by the freehand straight line and b is the slope of $\Delta Y/\Delta X$. The freehand method exposes any drastic changes or shifts in the direction of the line that can be obscured by mathematical averages.

SUMMARY

This chapter explains the variability of costs, referred to as cost behavior. Costs cannot actually behave, but their response to stimuli is analogous to what we call behavior in human beings. Costs are either proportionally variable, not variable at all, or some combination of the two extremes. Variability can be defined only in regard to another variable called the activity base. The nature of the response to a change of one unit of the activity base determines whether the cost is variable or not. The most frequently used activity base for manufacturing companies is units of output.

Once the behavior of costs has been determined, a cost formula for the prediction of future costs can be formulated. The high-low method, the least-squares method, and the scattergraph method, are the three most frequently used methods to determine the variability of costs and to formulate a cost formula. This and the preceding chapters provide us with the basic concepts of traditional and activity-based costing and with the salient terms used throughout the book. The remaining chapters describe the most important and useful techniques for the control and analysis of costs. Every marketing and manufacturing manager must understand these concepts and techniques thoroughly in order to survive in a competitive marketplace.

13

Breakeven and Contribution Margin Analysis

COST-VOLUME-PROFIT ANALYSIS

Cost-volume-profit (C-V-P) analysis, commonly referred to as *breakeven analysis*, refers to the revenue and cost relationships that exist at various levels of volume. It considers the various levels of output or revenue that will yield operating profits, breakeven, or operating losses. Cost-volume-profit analysis provides for the consideration of a target operating profit before taxes, it provides for the consideration of income taxes, and it is adaptable to sensitivity analysis, which is a change in the variables.

The three terms, cost, volume, and profit all require clarification. Each term has more than one interpretation depending on the specific adjective used with it or the situation involved. Following is an explanation of each term to clarify its use in C-V-P analysis.

Cost

The word cost in cost-volume-profit analysis, refers to operating costs and expenses, which include costs of production, administrative expenses, and marketing expenses. In the determination of the contribution margin, only variable costs and expenses are included. In the determination of profit, all costs and expenses, both variable and fixed, are included. The separation of costs and expenses into variable and fixed is required in C-V-P analysis. It provides the mathematical ratios used in breakeven analysis and operating leverage computations.

Volume

Volume is the measurement of either physical units or dollars of sales revenue. Physical units may be units of output or units sold. It is implied that units sold, not produced, are used in the C-V-P analysis.

Where there is more than one line of products, the use of physical units may be awkward or impossible. Large corporations produce and market heterogeneous product lines, whose physical units cannot be summed together. Sales revenue in dollars serves as a common denominator for any product line. Volume is most commonly expressed in sales revenue for this reason. The use of dollars enables the company to estimate the level of sales revenue that will yield a given operating profit.

Profit

In C-V-P analysis, profit means income. Income, much like the term cost, has several meanings. In determining the solution to any specific problem there must be a clarification of what is meant by profit (or income). For the C-V-P analysis described in this text, the following two definitions of income are used:

1. Operating income is defined as operating revenue less all costs and expenses other than interest and income taxes.
2. Net income is defined as total revenue less all costs and expenses.

In C-V-P analysis, the use of operating income rather than net income is of greater significance in decision making. Both income taxes and interest may be influential in decision making, however, their significance in a C-V-P analysis depends on the assumptions or circumstances. Decisions regarding the segments or divisions of large firms can be made without regard to income taxes. The effect of income taxes in C-V-P analysis is demonstrated in this chapter.

Assumptions of Cost-Volume-Profit Analysis

C-V-P analysis is based on certain assumptions that preclude the application of the conceptual approaches and the mathematical techniques. These assumptions are

1. The availability of cost behavior data separating variable costs and expenses from fixed is required in order to use the contribution margin approach.
2. Linearity of revenue and cost behavior is assumed in all C-V-P methods.
3. The relevant range of activity assumption is also applicable to C-V-P analysis.
4. All inventories are assumed to remain at a constant level so that the current costs of production are identical with the cost of goods manufactured and cost of goods sold. Cost of goods sold is made up of product costs, but is called an expense when matched to the revenues of the current period. Both production costs and organizational expenses are included in C-V-P analysis.

CONTRIBUTION MARGIN AND BREAKEVEN ANALYSIS

The *contribution margin* (CM) is the residual amount of total sales minus total variable costs and expenses. Variable costs and expenses include direct materials, direct labor, variable overhead, variable administrative expenses, and variable marketing expenses.

The *contribution margin per unit* (CM_{Unit}) is the selling price minus the variable costs on a per unit basis, that is, the total variable costs divided by the number of units. Variable costs per unit are most frequently calculated on the basis of budget estimates. The *contribution margin percentage* (CM%) is the contribution margin per unit divided by the selling price. It is also called the *contribution margin ratio.*

The *breakeven point* is defined as either the number of units or the amount of sales revenue where total sales revenue less total variable and total fixed costs is equal to zero (no profit). The breakeven point may be determined in two ways, (1) as *total sales dollars*, or (2) as *total units of sales*. Each of the two methods has a specific formula, the assumptions for which are shown here. Exhibit 13-1 illustrates the numerical relationships at the breakeven point. For demonstration purposes, let

X	=	number of units
SP	=	selling price (per unit)
SP(X)	=	total sales revenue
VC	=	variable costs (and expenses) per unit
VC(X)	=	total variable costs
FC	=	total fixed costs
CM	=	total contribution margin
CM_{Unit}	=	contribution margin per unit
$CM_{\%}$	=	contribution margin percent (or ratio)

Assume the following amounts:

SP = \$15, VC = \$10, and FC = \$20

Breakeven Point in Units (BE_{Units})

$$BE_{Units} = \frac{\text{Total Fixed Costs}}{(SP - VC)} = \frac{FC}{CM_{Unit}}$$

$$BE_{Units} = \frac{\$20}{\$15 - \$10} = \frac{\$20}{\$5} = 4 \text{ Units}$$

Breakeven Point in Sales Dollars ($BE_\$$)

$$BE_\$ = \frac{\text{Total Fixed Costs}}{(SP - VC) \div SP} = \frac{FC}{CM_\%}$$

$$BE_\$ = \frac{\$20}{(\$15-10) \div \$15} = \frac{\$20}{\$0.3333} = \$60$$

Exhibit 13-1
Contribution Margin Analysis

Sales ($15 times 1 unit)		$ 15
Less: Variable production costs	$ 6	
Variable expenses	4	10
Contribution margin		$ 5
Less: Fixed production costs	$12	
Fixed expenses	8	20
Net income (loss)		$ (15)

		Total	Per Unit	Percentage
Sales ($15 × 4 units)		$ 60	$ 15	100 %
Less: Variable production costs ($6 × 4)	$ 24			
Variable expenses ($4 × 4)	16	40	10	66 2/3 %
Contribution margin		$ 20	$ 5	33 1/3 %
Less: Fixed production costs	$ 12			
Fixed expenses	8	20		
Net income (loss)		$ 0		

Traditional Accounting Statement Format

The accounting income statement is prepared mainly for external users such as investors, creditors and banks. It must be prepared and presented in accordance with generally accepted accounting principles (GAAP). The traditional format presented in Exhibit 13-2 shows the sales revenue, the cost of goods sold (finished goods inventory is assumed to remain at a constant level) and a gross profit (margin). Administrative and marketing expenses are subtracted from gross profit to equal net income. This format is compatible with the *full (absorption) costing system*.

Contribution Margin Format

The contribution margin format, used mainly for internal decision-making purposes, separates variable and fixed expenses. The contribution margin is the residual derived by subtracting all variable production costs and other variable expenses from sales revenue. Net income, which is the same as in the traditional format, is the residual derived by subtracting total fixed expenses from the contribution margin. This format is compatible with the *direct (variable) costing system*.

Exhibit 13-2
Traditional and Contribution Margin
Income Statement Formats Compared

Traditional Format Income Statement		
Sales revenue		$ 90,000
Beginning inventory	$ 10,000	
Add: Cost of goods manufactured	48,000	
Subt: Ending inventory	(10,000)	
Cost of goods sold		48,000
Gross Margin		$ 42,000
Administrative expense	$ 12,000	
Marketing expense	20,000	
Total expenses		32,000
Net income		$ 10,000

Contribution Margin Format Income Statement		
Sales revenue		$ 90,000
Less: Variable production costs	$36,000	
Variable administrative expenses	6,000	
Variable marketing expenses	18,000	
Total variable expenses		60,000
Contribution margin		$ 30,000
Less: Fixed production costs	$12.000	
Fixed administrative expenses	6,000	
Fixed marketing expenses	2,000	
Total fixed costs and expenses		20,000
Net income		$ 10,000

SENSITIVITY ANALYSIS

Sensitivity analysis, in regard to C-V-P relationships, refers to the response to a change in any single C-V-P variable. A summary of these variables and their effect on the breakeven point follows:

Change in a C-V-P Variable	Effect on the Breakeven Point		
	Increase	Decrease	No Effect
Increase in volume (units)			✓
Decrease in volume (units)			✓
Increase in fixed expenses	✓		
Decrease in fixed expenses		✓	
Increase in per unit variable exp.	✓		
Decrease in per unit variable exp.		✓	
Increase in selling price		✓	
Decrease in selling price	✓		

As shown in the table, a change in volume, increase or decrease, has no effect on the breakeven point. Volume is not a variable in the computation of a breakeven point, it is the result of the computation. Fixed expenses, selling price, and variable expenses per unit are the variables. A change in any of these variables will have an effect on the breakeven point.

Change in Fixed Expenses

Sales revenue	(8,000 × \$8.00)	\$ 64,000
Variable expenses	(8,000 × \$3.00)	24,000
Contribution margin		\$ 40,000
Fixed expenses		40,000
Net income (loss)		\$ 0

The breakeven (BE) point is 8,000 units, where total fixed costs are \$40,000 and the CM_{Unit} is \$5. Now assume that fixed costs *increase to \$45,000*. The breakeven point in units will change to

$$\frac{\text{Fixed expenses}}{CM_{Unit}} = \frac{\$45{,}000}{\$5.00} = 9{,}000 \text{ units}$$

Assume instead, that fixed expenses *decrease from \$40,000 to \$35,000* the breakeven point will decrease to

$$\frac{\text{Fixed expenses}}{CM_{Unit}} = \frac{\$35{,}000}{\$5.00} = 7{,}000 \text{ units}$$

Change in Selling Price

A change in the selling price will have a direct effect on the contribution margin per unit and the CM percentage. For example, if the *selling price is increased to \$11 from \$8*, the CM_{Unit} will increase by \$3, and the breakeven point will decrease from 8,000 units to

$$\frac{\text{Fixed expenses}}{CM_{Unit}} = \frac{\$40{,}000}{\$8.00} = 5{,}000 \text{ units}$$

Stated in sales revenue the *BE point in dollars* is:

$$\frac{\text{Fixed expenses}}{CM_{\%}} = \frac{\$40{,}000}{0.72727} = \$55{,}000$$

Conversely, a \$3 *decrease* in the selling price, from \$8 to \$5, will result in an *increase* in the BE point from 8,000 units to

$$\frac{\text{Fixed expenses}}{CM_{unit}} = \frac{\$40{,}000}{\$2} = 20{,}000 \text{ units}$$

Stated in sales revenue the *BE point in dollars* is

$$\frac{\text{Fixed expenses}}{CM_{\%}} = \frac{\$40{,}000}{0.40} = \$100{,}000$$

Change in Variable Expenses per Unit

The breakeven point is also sensitive to changes in the unit variable expense. Assume that *variable expenses increase by \$1 per unit.* The contribution margin will decrease by \$1; the breakeven point increases to

$$\frac{\text{Fixed expenses}}{CM_{unit}} = \frac{\$40{,}000}{\$4} = 10{,}000 \text{ units}$$

Stated in sales revenue the *BE point in dollars* is

$$\frac{\text{Fixed expenses}}{CM_{\%}} = \frac{\$40{,}000}{0.50} = \$80{,}000$$

Conversely, a decrease of \$1 in variable expenses per unit will result in an increase of \$1 in the CM per unit and a decrease in the breakeven point. The breakeven in units is

$$\frac{\text{Fixed expenses}}{CM_{unit}} = \frac{\$40{,}000}{\$6} = 6{,}667 \text{ units}$$

Stated in sales revenue the *BE point in dollars* is

$$\frac{\text{Fixed expenses}}{CM_{\%}} = \frac{\$40{,}000}{0.75} = \$53{,}333$$

COST-VOLUME-PROFIT ANALYSIS AND INCOME TAXES

Target Net Income before Taxes

At the breakeven point, there is no net income. The C-V-P analysis can be used to determine the number of units and sales revenue necessary to attain a target net income. The formula is

Target Units =	$\dfrac{\text{Fixed expenses + Target net income before taxes}}{CM_{unit}}$

Assume the following data

Fixed expenses	$25,000
Contribution margin	$8 per unit
Target net income before taxes	$15,000

$$\text{Target Units} = \frac{\$25{,}000 + \$15{,}000}{\$8} = \frac{\$40{,}000}{\$8} = 5{,}000 \text{ units}$$

Target Net Income after Taxes

The target net income in the C-V-P formula is before taxes; income after taxes must be converted to before tax income by dividing by 1 minus the tax rate. For example, assume the data in the following table.

	Total	Per Unit
Sales revenue	$100,000	$ 20
Variable expenses	60,000	12
Contribution margin	$ 40,000	$ 8
Fixed expenses	25,000	
Target net income before taxes	$ 15,000	
Income tax at 40 percent	6,000	
Target net income after taxes	$ 9,000	

$$\text{Target units} = \frac{\text{Fixed expenses} + \dfrac{\text{Target net income after taxes}}{1 - \text{Tax rate}}}{CM_{Unit}}$$

$$\text{Target units} = \frac{\$25{,}000 + \dfrac{\$9{,}000}{0.60}}{\$8} = \frac{\$25{,}000 + \$15{,}000}{\$8} = 5{,}000 \text{ Units}$$

SALES MIX AND THE C-V-P ANALYSIS

The preceding examples of C-V-P and breakeven analysis have assumed that a single product or a single category of products is involved. Many companies produce and sell a variety of products with different selling prices and cost structures. The Estee Company produces and sells two products, S and T. Forty percent of Estee total sales revenue is generated by product S and 60 percent by product T. The contribution margin of product S is 25 percent and that of product T is 40 percent, as shown in the table.

Estee Company

Data for 19X3	Product S		Product T		Estee Company	
	Amount	Mix	Amount	Mix	Amount	Mix
Sales revenue	$80,000	40%	$120,000	60%	$200,000	100%
Variable expenses	60,000		72,000		132,000	
Contribution margin	20,000		$ 48,000		$ 68,000	
CM percentage	25%		40%		34%	

The total company experiences a 34 percent contribution margin, which is a weighted average of the two products. Shown next is a shortcut computation of the weighted average CM%.

19X3	Sales Mix % × CM%	Weighted Average CM%
Product S	40% × 25%	= 10%
Product T	60% × 40%	= 24%
Total company		= 34%

Change in Sales Mix

A change in the sales mix will result in a change in the contribution margin for the total company as long as the two products do not have identical CM ratios. Assume that Estee total sales revenue for 19X4 remains at $200,000 and that product S generates 70 percent of the total revenue, leaving 30 percent for product T. The contribution margin for product S remains at 25 percent and for product T at 40 percent.

Estee Company

Data for 19X4	Product S		Product T		Estee Company	
	Amount	Mix	Amount	Mix	Amount	Mix
Sales revenue	$140,000	70 %	$60,000	30 %	$200,000	100 %
Variable expenses	105,000		36,000		141,000	
CM	$ 35,000		$24,000		$ 59,000	
CM%	25 %		40 %		29.5 %	

Observe that the total company's weighted average contribution margin ($CM_{wtd\%}$) has declined from 34 percent to 29.5 percent. The shortcut computation of the $CM_{wtd\%}$ is shown next.

19X4	Sales Mix % × CM%	Wtd. Ave. CM
Product S	70% × 25%	= 17.5 %
Product T	30% × 40%	= 12.0 %
Total company		$CM_{wtd\%}$ = 29.5 %

The decline in the Estee Company's $CM_{wtd\%}$ is attributed directly to the increase in the proportion of product S with a 25 percent CM ratio and a decrease in product T, with a higher (40 percent) CM ratio.

Sales Mix and the Breakeven Point

In 19X3 and 19X4, Estee Company had fixed expenses of $40,120. For 19X3, Estee's overall company $CM_{wtd\%}$ was 34 percent. The *breakeven sales revenue* for 19X3 is calculated as

$$BE_{\$} = \frac{\text{Fixed expenses}}{CM_{wtd\%}} = \frac{\$40{,}120}{0.34} = \$118{,}000$$

In 19X4, Estee Company's $CM_{wtd\%}$ was 29.5 percent, the *breakeven sales dollars* are

$$BE_{\$} = \frac{\text{Fixed expenses}}{CM_{wtd\%}} = \frac{\$40{,}120}{0.295} = \$136{,}000$$

As we observe that the overall company's CM percentage has declined, due to the adverse sales mix, we must also observe that it takes a greater amount of sales dollars to break even under the 19X4 sales mix. The breakeven analysis is a practical gauge to measure the relative profitability of sales mixes.

Sales Mix on a Per Unit Basis

The preceding calculations of the sales mix are based on dollars of revenue. The sales mix of products S and T can be reported in terms of units rather than dollars. Assume that in 19X5, Estee Company sells 15,000 units of product S at $6, with variable expenses of $4 per unit, and that it sells 10,000 units of product T at $10 each, with $4 in unit variable expenses. A total of $72,000 fixed expenses are attributed to administrative and marketing activities.

Estee Company

Data for 19X5	Product S		Product T		Estee Company	
	Amount	Per Unit	Amount	Per Unit	Amount	Per Unit
Sales revenue	$ 90,000	$ 6.00	$ 100,000	$10.00	$190,000	$ 7.60

Variable expenses	60,000	4.00	40,000	4.00	100,000	4.00
Contrib. margin	$ 30,000	$ 2.00	$ 60,000	$ 6.00	$ 90,000	$ 3.60
Fixed expenses					72,000	
Net income					$ 18,000	
Units sold	15,000		10,000		25,000	
Pct. of units sold	60%		40%		100%	

The total company sells 25,000 units at a weighted average contribution margin of $3.60 per unit ($CM_{WtdUnit}$). Because of an intensive advertising campaign during 19X6, costing $24,000, Estee's sales mix in units shifts to 30 percent for product S and 70 percent for product T. The selling price and the $CM_{WtdUnit}$ for both products remained constant. Total fixed expenses increased from $72,000 to $96,000 due to the advertising campaign.

Estee Company

Data for 19X6	Product S		Product T		Estee Company	
	Amount	Per Unit	Amount	Per Unit	Amount	Per Unit
Sales revenue	$45,000	$ 6.00	$175,000	$10.00	$220,000	$ 8.80
Variable expenses	30,000	4.00	70,000	4.00	100,000	4.00
CM	$15,000	$ 2.00	$105,000	$ 6.00	$120,000	$ 4.80
Fixed exp.					96,000	
Net income					$ 24,000	
Units sold	7,500		17,500		25,000	
Percent of units sold	30%		70%		100%	

The shortcut computation of the $CM_{WtdUnit}$ for 19X5 and 19X6 is shown next.

19X5	Sales Mix % × CM_{Unit}	Wtd. Ave. CM_{Unit}
Product S	60% × $2.00	= $1.20
Product T	40% × $6.00	= $2.40
Total company		$CM_{WtdUnit}$ = $3.60

19X6	Sales Mix % × CM_{Unit}	Wtd. Ave. CM_{Unit}
Product S	30% × $2.00	= $0.60
Product T	70% × $6.00	= $4.20
Total company		$CM_{WtdUnit}$ = $4.80

Applying the breakeven formula for units, the breakeven units for 19X5 are

$$BE_{Units} = \frac{\$72,000}{\$3.60} = 20,000 \text{ units}$$

Consisting of

Product S = 60% × 20,000 = 12,000 units
Product T = 40% × 20,000 = 8,000 units

19X6

$$BE_{Units} = \frac{\$96,000}{\$4.80} = 20,000 \text{ units}$$

Consisting of

Product S = 30% × 20,000 = 6,000 units
Product T = 70% × 20,000 = 14,000 units

The breakeven points in units remained the same for 19X5 and 19X6, however it is the sales mix between products S and T that changed in favor of year 19X6.

	19X5		19X6	
	Units × CM_{Unit}	Total CM	Units × CM_{Unit}	Total CM
Product S	12,000 × $2 =	$24,000	6,000 × $2 =	$12,000
Product T	8,000 × $6 =	48,000	14,000 × $6 =	84,000
Total company		$72,000		$96,000

At any total company sales volume above 20,000 units, the 19X6 sales mix will be more profitable than the 19X5 mix.

OPERATING LEVERAGE

Operating leverage is the multiplier effect of the contribution margin on operating income. *Operating income* is defined as net income before taxes and interest. Hilev Company and Lolev Company have the cost structure shown in the table.

Hilev Company		Lolev Company	
Sales revenue	$100,000	Sales revenue	$100,000
Variable expenses	20,000	Variable expenses	80,000
Contribution margin	$ 80,000	Contribution margin	$ 20,000
Fixed expenses	70,000	Fixed expenses	10,000
Operating income	$ 10,000	Operating income	$ 10,000

The formula for operating leverage is

$$\text{Operating Leverage} = \frac{\text{Contribution margin}}{\text{Operating income}}$$

For Hilev Company the operating leverage (OL) is:

$$\text{OL} = \frac{\$80{,}000}{\$10{,}000} = 8$$

For Lolev Company the operating leverage is:

$$OL = \frac{\$20{,}000}{\$10{,}000} = 2$$

The importance to management of the operating leverage factor is its effect on operating income as a result of increases or decreases in sales volume. The percentage increase (decrease) in sales volume times the OL factor equals the percentage increase (decrease) in operating income. Assume a 20 percent increase in sales volume. For Hilev Company net income will increase by 20 percent times 8 = 160 percent. Thus, operating income will increase to $26,000. For Lolev Company operating income will increase by 20 percent times 2 = 40 percent. Operating income will increase to $14,000. For verification the cost structures are reconstructed in the table.

Hilev Company		Lolev Company	
Sales revenue ($100,000 × 1.20)	$120,000	Sales revenue ($100,000 × 1.20)	$120,000
Variable expenses ($20,000 × 1.20)	24,000	Variable expenses ($80,000 × 1.20)	96,000
Contribution margin	$96,000	Contribution margin	$ 24,000
Fixed expenses	70,000	Fixed expenses	10,000
Operating income	$ 26,000	Operating income	$ 14,000

Decreases in sales volume cause a multiple downward effect on operating income. By assuming a 10 percent decrease in sales volume, Hilev Company will experience an 80 percent drop in operating income (10 percent times 8) and Lolev Company will experience a 20 percent decrease in profits (10 percent times 2).

Hilev Company		Lolev Company	
Sales revenue ($100,000 × 0.90)	$90,000	Sales revenue ($100,000 × 0.90)	$90,000
Variable expenses ($20,000 × 0.90)	18,000	Variable expenses ($80,000 × 0.90)	72,000
Contribution margin	$ 72,000	Contribution margin	$ 18,000
Fixed expenses	70,000	Fixed expenses	10,000
Operating income	$ 2,000	Operating income	$ 8,000

The comparative statements show that Hilev's operating income decreased 80 percent, from $10,000 to $2,000, whereas, Lolev's operating income decreased only 20 percent, from $10,000 to $8,000. These observations lead us to conclude that, (1) assuming that the trend of sales volume is upward, it is more profitable to have a higher ratio of fixed expenses to variable expenses, and (2) conversely, with expectations of declining sales volume, it would be more profitable to have a higher ratio of variable to fixed expenses.

These observations have profound implications for management. The long-range trend of production and sales has inexorably been upward since World War II. Machinery, which is a fixed production cost (depreciation), would be preferable to direct labor, which is a variable production cost, during periods of increasing sales volume. Thus, the trend toward automation, robotics, or other nonhuman production devices is based on the fundamental observations of the effect of operating leverage on profits. As long as we expect the long-term trend of sales to increase, as it has since the history of our nation (except during the Depression, which was a cyclical downturn, not a long term trend), we can expect to observe a decrease in human labor in the production of physical products.

SUMMARY

This chapter introduced the important concept of the contribution margin. The contribution margin approach is so ubiquitous as a tool of management accounting that it reappears directly or indirectly in almost all of the succeeding chapters.

Cost-volume-profit analysis and breakeven point calculations are used prevalently in business decision-making. They are easy to understand and easy to apply to both simple and complex situations. This chapter shows how to calculate the breakeven point in both units and dollars of revenue.

The introduction of sensitivity analysis, which is merely a change in one or more of the variables, and the consideration of income taxes added new dimensions to the straight-forward breakeven analysis. At the breakeven point, there is no profit, so there are no taxes. In C-V-P analysis, the introduction of a target profit leads us to also include, for the sake of realism, income taxes. The various computational techniques for solving complex problems with changes in the variables and with a target net income both before and after taxes were demonstrated in this chapter.

This chapter also included a discussion of the operating leverage concept, which is useful in projecting future earning potential. A company whose management is aware of the operating leverage multiplier effect on operating income can predict its future earnings with more certainty and thus make better business decisions.

Finally, the chapter explored the effects of variations in the sales mix on operating income. Companies that have more than one product attempt to maximize the weighted average of the contribution margins of their sales mix. In later chapters, the consideration of scarce resources adds yet another dimension to the use of the contribution margin approach.

14

Relevant Costs and Revenues

All decisions in business, government, and in personal matters require common sense. Relevance is an academic synonym for common sense used in selecting which factors should be or should not be included in a business decision. A *relevant cost or revenue* is a future, avoidable cost that will have a differential effect on a specific decision. Relevant costs and revenues are those that should be considered in arriving at a decision involving the economic resources of the firm. Several of the terms defined and discussed in Chapter 1 are used in this chapter, such as variable and fixed costs, sunk costs, and differential, avoidable, and opportunity costs.

Avoidable costs and revenues are those future costs and revenues that are not committed. The decision maker has the option of selecting alternative projects with differing costs and/or revenues. The costs or revenues may be avoided by

Exhibit 14-1
Differental Costs and Revenues

	Old Machine	Proposed New Machine
Proposed purchase price		$ 20,000
Acquisition (historical) cost	$ 10,000	
Accumulated depreciation	$ 6,000	
Production units per year	10,000	12,000
Revenue per unit	$ 2.00	$ 2.00
Variable costs per unit	$ 1.50	$ 1.00
Fixed costs per year	$ 3,000	$ 4,000
Remaining economic life	4 years	4 years
Salvage value now	$ 1,000	$ 0

not selecting a particular alternative. ***Differential costs and revenues*** are those that differ among alternatives. Differential costs can be either variable or fixed. Exhibit 14-1 demonstrates the decisions to be considered in the purchase of a new production machine to replace an old machine.

Should the new machine be purchased? It is assumed that the old machine could be used for four more years if a new machine is not purchased. An analysis of the differential revenues and costs in favor of purchasing the proposed new machine is shown in Exhibit 14-2. Positive differential amounts are in favor of the new purchase.

Exhibit 14-2
Differential Cost Analysis

	Keep Old Machine	Purchase Proposed Machine	Differential Revenues and Costs
Revenue (1)	$ 80,000	$ 96,000	$ 16,000
Variable costs (2)	$(60,000)	$(48,000)	$ 12,000
Contribution margin	$ 20,000	$ 48,000	$ 28,000
Fixed costs (3)	$(12,000)	$(16,000)	$ (4,000)
Salvage value now	$ 0	$ 1,000	$ 1,000
Salvage value in 4 years	$ 0	$ 0	$ 0
Cost of new machine (4)		$(20,000)	$(20,000)
Total four year income	$ 8,000	$ 13,000	$ 5,000

Calculations:
1. 10,000 units × $2 × 4 years and 12,000 units × $2 × 4 years.
2. 10,000 units × $1.50 × 4 years and 12,000 × $1 × 4 years.
3. $3,000 × 4 years and $4,000 × 4 years.
4. Whether the cost of the new machine is treated as a cash outlay now or whether it is considered as depreciation over the four-year period does not change the analysis.

NONRELEVANT COSTS (SUNK COSTS)

A cost that has already been incurred is a *sunk cost*. The cost of a machine that was purchased in a prior period is a sunk cost, but the labor and material used in operating the machine are not. Sunk costs are almost always past costs. In rare instances, a future cost may be sunk. The future costs of finishing the construction of a building are not sunk costs because there is a possibility that the construction could be discontinued. However, after NASA launches a space shuttle, the future costs of returning it to earth or attempting to return it are, in a humanitarian sense, sunk costs. Unavoidable costs, past or future, are considered as sunk costs.

PROPERTY, EMPLOYMENT, AND INCOME TAXES

Income taxes are levied on businesses that earn a profit. Government agencies and bona fide not-for-profit institutions are specifically exempted from income taxes. More than one level of government may levy an income tax. In several states, there are a city (or county) income tax, a state income tax, and a federal income tax. In other states, there is only one income tax, the federal income tax. The federal income tax laws are complicated and changeable. Since 1980, there have been three major federal income tax laws passed: the Economic Recovery Tax Act (ERTA) of 1981, which adopted the accelerated cost recovery system (ACRS), the Tax Equity Fiscal Reform Act (TEFRA) of 1982 and the current Tax Reform Act (TRA) enacted in 1986, which adopted the modified accelerated cost recovery system (MACRS).

In the chapters that discuss relevant costing and capital budgeting, the federal income taxes are considered. Profit organizations must consider income taxes in their decisions. In most of the examples and problems only the federal income tax is included. State income taxes are relatively small in comparison with federal income taxes. For example, in Michigan prior to the 1986 Federal Tax Reform Act large corporations paid a maximum of 46 percent in federal and about 2 percent in state income taxes. Because some accounting income may be nontaxable or deferred the average tax rates will vary from the statutory rates in the tax law. Under the 1986 Tax Reform Act the maximum corporate tax rate is 34 percent. For purposes of illustration an average corporate tax rate of 30 percent will be used.

All business organizations, both for profit and not-for-profit, are liable for employment taxes, such as unemployment compensation and social security (FICA) taxes, unless specifically exempted by law. Some exemptions are given to very small proprietorships, charitable organizations, and governmental agencies. Profit businesses are liable for property taxes, but government agencies and most not-for-profit institutions, such as colleges, hospitals, and churches, are not.

Property and employment taxes are classified as factory costs or administrative expenses depending on the function served by the property or employees. In the discussion of relevant costing, both property and employment taxes are treated as ordinary expenses of the business.

DEPRECIATION AND INCOME TAXES

The proposed new machine is assumed to be purchased for cash. The relevant cost for the total estimated economic life of the new purchase is the total cash outlay. A machine purchased for $20,000 with a four-year depreciable life has a straight-line annual depreciation of $5,000. The use of the cash basis for analyzing the relevance of revenues and costs avoids the confusion of how to treat depreciation on the new purchase. In Exhibit 14-2, the cash outlay of $20,000 for the new machine was counted, but not the depreciation, which would be double counting. The effect of income taxes must also be considered in the depreciation of both the old and new machines in a cash flow approach. The foregoing example is re-evaluated taking federal income taxes into consideration.

Tax Effects on Depreciation and on Losses and Gains

The consideration of federal income taxes changes the four-year operating income from $5,000 (see Exhibit 14-2) before taxes to $3,500 after taxes, as illustrated in Exhibit 14-3. It also introduces the tax effect on non-cash items previously ignored. The tax effect on a loss or gain from the sale or trade-in of the old machine and the tax effect on the depreciation on the old machine are relevant. The depreciation on the old machine may be a sunk cost, but the tax savings from the four years of depreciation will be lost if the old machine is sold or traded.

Exhibit 14-3
Tax Effect on Depreciation and Gains and Losses

	Differential	Tax Effect	Differential After Taxes
Cost of new machine	$(20,000)		$(20,000)
Operating income	24,000	× 70%	16,800
Salvage value now	1,000		1,000
Loss on old machine	3,000	× 30%	900
Deprec. on new machine	20,000	× 30%	6,000
Deprec. on old machine	(4,000)	× 30%	(1,200)
After tax operating income			$ 3,500

ADDING OR DROPPING A PRODUCT LINE OR DIVISION

A recent study indicated that the introduction of a new product that is a major commitment of the company's resources, present and future, is more frequently done by the intuition and whim of a few key individuals than by circumspect market studies. Seldom are the key financial managers asked to prepare a detailed revenue-cost analysis. Perhaps members of the controller's office staff have the reputation of being conservative, negative rather than positive, thinkers in regard to the sales forecasts of the marketing analysts.

Adding a new product line is a major step that requires a realistic estimate of potential sales. If the sales estimate is inaccurate, then the total costs will also be inaccurate. The effect on other product lines must also be considered. It may be reasonable to expect that a new product line will not be instantly profitable. Marketing costs and production costs will be higher during the introduction stage.

Dropping a product line is also a major management decision. There are more objective factors for the cost analyst to consider in dropping than in adding a product line. There is an historical cost pattern already established in an existing product line. The variability of costs incurred may be known and the avoidability of specific costs can be ascertained. There are potential miscalculations in the analysis of dropping a product line that are demonstrated in the following example. Ada Company has three product lines, separated into divisions, Cosmetics, Hair Care, and Cleaning with the cost structures shown in Exhibit 14-4.

Exhibit 14-4
Estimated Income by Product Line

	Cosmetics Division	Hair Care Division	Cleaning Division	Total Company
Sales revenue	$200,000	$500,000	$300,000	$1,000,000
Variable costs and expenses	80,000	400,000	180,000	660,000
Contribution margin	$120,000	$100,000	$120,000	$340,000
Less fixed costs:				
Salaries	40,000	50,000	30,000	120,000
Utilities	10,000	20,000	10,000	40,000
Depreciation	40,000	10,000	35,000	85,000
Allocated company expenses	20,000	50,000	30,000	100,000
Total fixed costs and expenses	$110,000	$130,000	$105,000	$345,000
Net income (loss)	$ 10,000	$ (30,000)	$ 15,000	$ (5,000)

The Hair Care product line is unprofitable, which is the obvious reason that the company is operating at a loss, or is it? An analysis of the costs and expenses is found to be necessary to support a decision to drop the Hair Care line of products. The analysis shows that all variable costs and expenses are avoidable, but several important observations affect the relevance of the fixed expenses. These observations are noted as follows.

Note 1. In the salaries and wages category, it is found that 30 percent of the division's costs will not be avoided by dropping the product line.

Note 2. Utilities are paid by the total company and are allocated to the divisions. By dropping the Hair Care Division, it is estimated that only 20 percent of the total company's utilities costs would be avoided (20 percent × $40,000 = $8,000).

Note 3. Depreciation is charged to the Hair Care Division on equipment that is not usable for any other purpose. It is a sunk cost and unavoidable.

Note 4. The allocated company expense is based on sales revenue. None of this expense would be eliminated by dropping one product line. If a line is dropped the total company expense will be allocated to the remaining divisions based on sales revenue.

Note 5. All costs and expenses that are not avoided by dropping the Hair Care Division are to be added to the allocated company expense before allocation and then reallocated on the basis of sales revenue.

THE DIFFERENTIAL APPROACH

The differential approach applied to dropping a product line is illustrated in Exhibit 14-5. This approach is simpler and shorter and shows the savings or losses by dropping the product line (or division). The revenues are a loss of income to the total company, and the avoidable costs and expenses are equivalent to an increase in income. In the Ada Company example, all variable costs and expenses are assumed to be avoidable. Of the Hair Care Division's salaries, $35,000, or 70 percent could be avoided. Also, by dropping this division, $8,000, which is 20 percent of the company's total utilities of $40,000, can be avoided, but none of the depreciation nor the allocated total company expenses could be avoided. The net differential loss of $57,000 represents the incremental loss to the total company if the division is dropped. Added to the $5,000 loss, the company would suffer a total loss of $62,000 if the Hair Care Division and product line is dropped. Exhibit 14-5 uses the differential approach to explain the effect that dropping the Hair Care Division has on the operating income of Ada Company.

THE RESIDUAL APPROACH

The residual approach shows the effect of dropping the Hair Care Division and product line on the remaining divisions and the total company. The total revenues decrease to $500,000 and the contribution margin drops to $240,000. The two remaining divisions incur the same salaries, utilities, and depreciation regardless of whether or not the Hair Care Division is dropped. The unavoidable costs of the dropped division must, however, be absorbed by the remaining divisions. The method of reallocating these costs has been specified in the assumptions shown in the notes and is summarized in Exhibit 14-6, followed by Exhibit 14-7, which uses the residual approach to show the effect of dropping the Hair Care Division on the operating profit of Ada Company.

Exhibit 14-5
Effect of Dropping a Division

Accounts	Effect on Operating Income
Sales revenue	$(500,000)
Variable costs and expenses	400,000
Salaries (see note 1)	35,000
Utilities (see note 2)	8,000
Depreciation (see note 3)	0
Allocated company expenses (see note 4)	0
Net savings (loss)	$(57,000)

Exhibit 14-6
Reallocation of Costs

Salaries and wages (30% × $50,000)	= $ 15,000
Utilities ($20,000 - $8,000)	= 12,000
Depreciation	= 10,000
Total additions	$ 37,000
Company costs and expenses unadjusted	100,000
Total adjusted costs and expenses	$137,000
Allocated to divisions (based on sales):	
Cosmetics 40%	$ 54,800
Cleaning 60%	82,200
Total allocations	$137,000

Exhibit 14-7
Residual Approach

	Cosmetics Division	Cleaning Division	Total Company
Sales revenue	$200,000	$300,000	$500,000
Variable costs and expenses	80,000	180,000	260,000
Contribution margin	$120,000	$120,000	$240,000
Less fixed costs and expenses:			
Salaries	40,000	30,000	70,000
Utilities	10,000	10,000	20,000
Depreciation	40,000	35,000	75,000
Allocated company expenses	54,800	82,200	137,000
Total fixed costs and expenses	$144,800	$157,200	$302,000
Net income (loss)	$ 200	$ (37,200)	$ (62,000)

The residual method illustrated in Exhibit 14-7 not only shows the total effect of dropping the product line but also shows the effect on the income of each remaining division. The income of both divisions suffers from the absorption of the unavoidable costs from the dropped division. In fact, the Cleaning Division now shows a net loss instead of a profit after dropping the Hair Care Division. Should the Cleaning Division be dropped? If so, the Cosmetics Division would then show a net loss. Dropping one division or product line can cause a domino effect on the remaining divisions. Care must be exercised to ascertain the avoidability of both variable and fixed costs and expenses. The existence of a loss on the accounting records is no indication that a division or product line is losing money for the total company. The foregoing analysis shows how dropping a product line that shows a book loss would only lead to further losses for the company. Exhibit 14-8 shows a comparison of total company income if the division is dropped as compared to keeping the division.

Exhibit 14-8
Differential Effect of Dropping a Division

	Keep Division	Differential Effect	Drop Division
Sales revenue	$1,000,000	$(500,000)	$500,000
Variable costs and expenses	660,000	400,000	260,000
Contribution margin	$340,000	$(100,000)	$240,000
Less fixed costs and expenses:			
Salaries	120,000	35,000	85,000
Utilities	40,000	8,000	32,000
Depreciation	85,000	0	85,000
Allocated company expenses	100,000	0	100,000
Total fixed costs and expenses	$345,000	$43,000	$302,000
Net income (loss)	$ (5,000)	$ (57,000)	$ (62,000)

There is little doubt that the division should be kept, even though the accounting records show a book loss of $5,000. The problem is in the allocation of the unavoidable fixed costs incurred in the factory and in the functional areas of the company. The allocation of unavoidable costs should not be considered in decision making.

MAKE OR BUY DECISIONS

Large manufacturing companies that have one or more high-unit cost product lines must either manufacture the individual parts and subassemblies in their own plants or purchase them outside. Vertical integration refers to the situation where a company supplies itself with many of its own materials and semi-assembled parts rather than purchasing them outside. A company in an industry driven by brisk competition will not commit itself to a policy of either extreme.

An automobile has from 4,000 to 8,000 individual parts, depending on the size and options ordered. Many of these parts make up subassemblies such as the power steering unit, the battery, radio, tires, spark plugs, and windshields. Any of these could be manufactured by the automobile company or purchased from an outside supplier. General Motors has had its own power steering, battery, and spark plug divisions at one time or another. Ford Motor Company's Rouge Plant in Dearborn, Michigan, was the only automobile plant that was vertically integrated from the making of steel. At one end of the Rouge Plant, iron ore was shipped in from the Great Lakes, and at the other end finished cars were driven away.

Relevant Costs in the Make or Buy Decision

Make or buy decisions may affect entire divisions, individual plants, whole departments, or just costs within a department. Assume that the Krone Company makes a materials handling machine which requires a specialized lifting device. The lifting device is presently made in one of the company's plants with the following average cost structure for the production of 1,000 units as shown in the table. Krone Company requires 1,000 units per year.

	Cost Per Unit	Total Amount
Direct material	$ 42	$ 42,000
Direct labor	36	36,000
Indirect material	10	10,000
Indirect labor	15	15,000
Supervision	24	24,000
Allocated factory costs	83	83,000
Total costs	$ 210	$ 210,000

Make			Buy
Avoidable Costs	Units × Unit Cost	Total Amount	
Direct material	1,000 × $ 42	= $ 42,000	1,000
Direct labor	1,000 × 36	= 36,000	Units
Indirect material	1,000 × 10	= 10,000	@
Indirect labor	1,000 × 15	= 15,000	$130
Supervision	1,000 × 24	= 24,000	
Total costs	$ 127	$ 127,000	$ 130,000

The cost to make 1,000 units of the lifting device is actually $127 per unit not $210, as shown in the company data. The company will incur only the variable costs of production, which are $103 per unit plus the fixed supervision costs of $24,000. The company should continue to make the lifting device because it cost $3,000 (1,000 × $3) more to buy it from the outside supplier. Care must be taken in treating the fixed costs on a per unit basis. The per unit fixed costs of $24 per unit were based on 1,000 units. Any other level of output would alter the per unit fixed cost.

Assume that Krone Company increases its production of material handling machines to 2,000 units per year and the production of lifting devices at the company plant is increased with no increase in fixed costs. The outside supplier because of the increased demand, lowers its price to $120. Krone Company management prepares a relevant cost analysis illustrating that the fixed costs per unit decreased from $24 to $12 because of the increased production. Even though the outside supplier reduced its price to $120, the relevant cost to make the device is only $115 per unit on the basis of 2,000 units. The company should make the lifting device rather than buy it from the outside source, saving a total of $10,000 (2,000 × $5).

	Make		Buy
Avoidable Costs	Units ×Unit Cost	Total Amount	2,000
Direct material	2,000 × $ 42	= $ 84,000	Units
Direct labor	2,000 × 36	= 72,000	@
Indirect material	2,000 × 10	= 20,000	$120
Indirect labor	2,000 × 15	= 30,000	
Supervision	2,000 × 12	= 24,000	
Total costs	$ 115	$ 230,000	$ 240,000

SPECIAL ORDERS

Manufacturing companies may have special opportunities to sell certain product lines at a price lower than the normal market price. A one-time order, at less than the normal market price, from a potential customer, overseas or outside the regular domestic market area, is called a *special order*. Overseas markets or regions outside the local market area may not disrupt the regular pricing structure. The producer with excess capacity may find it profitable to sell at less than full cost as long as the incremental costs and expenses of the special order are covered. The incremental costs of a special order include (1) variable production costs of the order and (2) variable expenses, marketing, and administrative, pertaining directly to the order. Fixed production costs and expenses are assumed not to increase with the special order.

Illustration

Zollner Piston Company sells pistons to Midwestern auto manufacturers for $84 each, based on 120 percent of the full cost of $70.

Variable production costs	$ 30.00
Fixed production costs	20.00
Variable administrative and marketing expense	12.00
Fixed administrative and marketing expenses	8.00
Full cost	$ 70.00
Add profit @ 20%	14.00
Selling price	$ 84.00

A special order is received from a Finnish auto company for 10,000 pistons at a price of $60 each. Special modifications will require production changes that will add $4 to the variable production costs. Selling commissions of $2.00 per unit will be avoided, but shipping and customs duties will add $3.00 to each piston. Zollner Company has a capacity of 80,000 units and now sells only 60,000 units per year. The relevant costs associated with the special order are

Variable production costs ($30 + $4)	$34
Variable administrative and marketing expenses ($12 - $2)	10
Shipping and customs duties	3
Incremental order costs	$ 47

Zollner Piston Company will increase its overall profits by $130,000 ($60 - $47) = $13 × 10,000) if it accepts the special order from Finnish Motor Company. The producer must be aware of the federal laws pertaining to price discrimination and exporting and must protect its regular domestic market pricing structure. With these considerations satisfactorily taken into account, the Zollner Company may proceed to accept the overseas order and increase its profits.

RELEVANT COSTS AND LIMITATIONS ON RESOURCES

Manufacturers and merchandising businesses accumulate economic resources in order to make profit. Direct material and overhead items are acquired and converted by direct labor into finished products by manufacturers. Some resources such as machine hours, labor or space are limited. The firm must make the right decisions on the utilization of all resources to maximize profits.

Unlimited Input Resources

If the main inputs, such as direct material, direct labor hours, or machine hours are unlimited, the company will maximize profits by maximizing the contribution margin on the output of finished products. If there is more than one product line, the line with the highest contribution margin per unit should be produced until the output can no longer be sold. Exhibit 14-9 shows contribution margin data for the three product lines of the Bates Company.

Exhibit 14-9
Contribution Margin Data for Product Lines

Bates Company	Product Line A	Product Line B	Product Line C
Selling price	$ 20	$ 15	$ 8
Variable costs per unit	16	6	2
Contribution margin	$ 4	$ 9	$ 6
$CM_{\%}$	20%	60%	75%

Assume that there is an unlimited demand for all three products. The manufacturer should produce only product B. Product B will yield a $9 contribution margin per unit on all it produces and sells as compared with $6 for product C and only $4 for product A. The probability of both unlimited markets and resources is not high. Almost all complex firms have constraints such as limitations on markets for products or limits on the production inputs.

Limitations on Product Markets

Last month the company chose to produce and sell a total of 5,000 units of product B with the following contribution margin:

Total Contribution Margin ($9 × 5,000) = $45,000

This month the company also sells a total of 5,000 units, however, Bates Company's market for product B is limited to 1,000 units, and sales of product C are limited to 2,000 units per month. The product mix is as shown in the table.

Product	Units	CM_{Unit}	Contribution Margin
B	1,000	$ 9	$ 9,000
C	2,000	6	12,000
A	2,000	4	8,000
Total Contribution Margin			$ 29,000

A limitation on the sale of the product which has the highest contribution margin per unit results in a reduction in the total company profit assuming that the same total number of units is produced and sold.

Limitations on Inputs

Placing constraints on production inputs, such as labor or machine hours, requires the calculation of the contribution margin per the input that is constrained. Exhibit 14-10 expands the contribution margin data provided in Exhibit 14-9.

Exhibit 14-10
Constraints on Inputs

Product Line	A	B	C
CM_{Unit}	$ 4.00	$ 9.00	$ 6.00
$CM_{\%}$	20%	60%	75%
Machine hours to produce 1 unit	1	4	2
CM per machine hour	$ 4.00	$ 2.25	$ 3.00

The Bates Company has a limit of 12,000 machine hours available for the next month. The contribution margin per machine hour is calculated in Exhibit 14-10. The CM per machine hour is greatest for product A, which has the lowest CM per unit of product. The firm will produce product A until the 12,000 machine hours are used up.

Total contribution margin = 12,000 MH × $4 = $48,000

Market and Input Constraints

Assume that only 2,000 units of product A can be sold. The 2,000 units of product A will require 2,000 machine hours. The remaining 10,000 machine hours should be used to produce product C, which has a CM of $3 per machine hour.

Product B has a lower CM per MH and will not be produced unless there is a constraint on the sales of product C. The results are summarized in the table.

	Machine Hours	CM per Machine Hour	Contribution Margin
Product A	2,000	× $ 4	= $ 8,000
Product C	10,000	× $ 3	= 30,000
Total	12,000		$ 38,000

Multiple Constraints of Inputs

In large corporations that manufacture many product lines and have worldwide operations, there are complexities that may require the application of multiple constraints and linear programming. These topics require advanced mathematical techniques and are most easily solved by computer applications.

DECISIONS TO SELL OR PROCESS FURTHER

Manufacturing companies like Kellogg have products that can be sold as is or processed further. If the further processing is profitable common sense would tell us to continue. But, how is profitability measured?

Assume that Kellogg can produce 100 lb of corn flakes for $80 and sell the 100 lb for $100. It can add $30 in a sugar coating and sell the 100 lb for $120. Should Kellogg sell the corn flakes as is or process the 100 lb of corn flakes into sugar coated corn flakes? The division between selling as is or processing further is called the *split-off point*.

Exhibit 14-11
Sell or Process Further

Alternative	Revenue at Split-off	Production Costs	Increm. Revenue	Increm. Costs	Profit (Loss)
Sell at split-off	$ 100	$(80)	$ 0	$ 0	$ 20
Process further	$ 100	$(80)	$ 20	$(30)	$ 10

If the incremental sales revenue exceeds the incremental costs, the product should be processed further. Exhibit 14-11 shows that further processing would decrease revenue by $10. Kellogg should sell the corn flakes as is. Any costs incurred prior to the split-off point are sunk costs. They are not relevant to the decision to sell as is or process further.

Contribution Margin Approach to Inventory and Product Costing

The management accountant provides information and professional judgment to company executives for three primary purposes: (1) for making short-run and recurring decisions regarding costing products and pricing products, (2) for evaluating the performance of managers and supervisors, and (3) for long-run capital budgeting and other special decisions that are nonrecurring and that require large commitments of resources.

The contribution margin approach to decision making is useful in making short-run decisions, but must be used with caution in situations that require long-range commitments. In the long run, all costs and expenses must be accounted for, plus a markup or profit in order to continue in business. The contribution margin or marginal costing approach cannot be applied indiscriminately to all situations.

DIRECT COSTING VERSUS ABSORPTION COSTING

The contribution margin approach to inventory valuation and products costing is called *direct* or *variable costing*. The total cost approach is called *absorption* or *full costing*. A controversy has persisted for several decades over the use of the direct costing method for inventory costing and its effect on income reported for the first period.

The advocates of direct costing argue that the fixed factory overhead should be charged to the period as are organizational expenses, not to the product. The fixed overhead does not vary with output and is committed for periods of time, not units of output.

The advocates of full absorption costing argue that product costs include direct material, direct labor and all factory overhead, variable and fixed. They contend that all completed units of product must contain the full costs of production in order to realistically value the ending inventory and to determine the costs of goods sold. If production exceeds sales, resulting in inventory (assets), the fixed production costs are attached to the product units and have future service potential just as much as do the variable production costs.

The controversy over the use of the two methods continues to separate some concerned academic and practicing accountants. In financial accounting the issue has been resolved. Direct costing is not allowed for costing inventories and income determination in certified financial statements. This ruling does not prohibit the use of direct costing for internal decision-making purposes, but it does discourage a broader use of the method.

15

Capital Budgeting

All companies must select their investments in capital projects judiciously in order to maintain long-run profitability and growth. Businesses of all sizes, whether in manufacturing, merchandising, or service industries, must purchase or lease machines, equipment, buildings, and vehicles in order to provide a product or a service to the customers.

Capital budgeting is the process of planning for the investment in and financing of capital projects. It includes the application of analytical techniques in the review and selection of individual investment proposals. The *capital budget* is the financial plan for the current year (or for any desired time period) that provides authority to purchase and limitations on the purchase of capital items. It may itemize specifications in detail for each individual project, or it may just specify dollar limits for each major category of projects. Each company establishes its own policy for the capital budgeting process.

Manufacturing companies, as opposed to service and merchandising firms, have a greater need for long-term capital goods, such as factory buildings, heavy machinery, equipment, and vehicles, that require a materially significant sacrifice of resources and that have a future benefit to the firm. Corporations also engage in entire projects, such as a complete system of information processing hardware and software, or a complete factory complex including all of the buildings, machinery, and equipment such as the General Motors Saturn Project.

CAPITAL BUDGETING METHODS

The capital budgeting chapter describes four methods of determining the profitability of capital investments by the firm:

1. Net present value (NPV)
2. Internal rate of return (IRR)
3. Modified internal rate of return method (MIRR)
4. Payback

A fifth method, the *accounting rate of return method*, should be mentioned, but is not recommended for application to capital budgeting problems. Each of the four methods has characteristics that influence its applicability to specific capital budgeting problems. The NPV, IRR, and the MIRR methods are analytically superior to the payback method, which does not consider the time value of money. The payback method has the advantage of measuring the return as a time period rather than as a percentage. For projects with a short payback time, that is, two years or less, the payback method is satisfactory, because the time value of money effect is negligible. The table summarizes the salient characteristics of the three methods.

Method	Incremental Cash Flows	Discounted Cash Flows	After Tax Effect	Assumed Cost of Capital Rate
Net present value (NPV)	Yes	Yes	Yes	Yes
Internal rate of return (IRR)	Yes	Yes	Yes	No
Modified internal rate of return (MIRR)	Yes	Yes	Yes	Yes
Payback	Yes	No	Yes	No

Assumptions in Capital Budgeting Methods

Time Period

Projects that are analyzed using discounted present cash flow methods, such as NPV or IRR must be compared over the same time period. For example, consider the same annual cash savings over two time periods at an assumed rate of 10%.

	Annual Cash Flow	Economic Life	PV Table Value		Present Value (PV)	
Project A	$ 10,000	10 years	×	6.145	=	$ 6,145
Project B	$ 10,000	5 years	×	3.791	=	$ 3,791

The project with the longer life will inherently yield a larger present value (PV) amount. This bias can be avoided by comparing projects over the same time-period. Beyond that period there are differences in the assumptions regarding the reinvestment of cash flows.

Reinvestment of Cash Flows

Inherent in the discounted cash flow process is the assumption that the cash flows that are generated by the project are reinvested at the assumed rate.

End of Year Table Values

The table values are accurate only if it is assumed that all cash flows occur at the end of each year. The table values are given only for annual periods. In practice, the cash flows occur throughout the year, but the difference caused by this assumption is negligible.

NET PRESENT VALUE METHOD

The *net present value method* is a preferable and highly recommended method for evaluating capital budgeting projects. It considers the time value of money and uses after-tax cash flows. The NPV method requires an assumed rate that is given several different names including the cost of capital, the hurdle rate and the cut off rate. The assumed rate is determined by each company and a single company may have different rates for different purposes. The assumed rate must be given for each NPV problem.

The *net present value* is the sum of the positive and negative cash flows that are incurred or generated from a given project or investment discounted to the present time period at the assumed rate. The cash flows must be incremental, that is, they must be caused by the project, not by projects that already exist.

The financial arrangements regarding the investment are not relevant. Whether the company borrows or uses its own funds does not enter into the analysis. If a building costing $50,000 is purchased with a $10,000 down payment and a mortgage is given for $40,000, the investment is still considered to be $50,000. The financial arrangements including the interest rate and payment are not to be considered in the NPV method. Incremental cash flow refers to (1) increases in cash receipts, (2) decreases in cash expenditures, and (3) combination of increases or decreases in cash receipts and increases or decreases in cash expenditures.

Investment

The *investment* is a cash outlay necessary to acquire a capital good, such as a machine or building. An investment can be tangible or intangible, such as a patent. It can be one item, such as one machine, or an entire project, such as purchasing a hockey team or purchasing a chain of hotels. It can also be a change in a system already in use, such as changing the system of distribution by increasing the number and location of warehouses. In all cases there must always be incremental or decremental cash flows caused by the investment. Some typical investment situations are described in the table to demonstrate how capital budgeting methods can be applied.

Type of Investment Situation	Analysis
Investment in a new asset; no old asset involved	Cash inflow from purchase of proposed equipment is compared with cash outflow for proposed equipment
Investment in a choice of one or more alternative assets; no old asset involved	Incremental cash flow of proposed equipment A is compared with that of proposed equipment B.
Investment in a new asset, while trading in or selling an old asset	Incremental cash flow of proposed equipment is compared with that of old equipment.
Investment in a choice of one or more alternative assets, while trading in or selling an old asset.	Incremental cash flow of proposed equipment A is compared with that of proposed equipment B and with that of old equipment.

The net present value can be used with or without federal and state income tax considerations. Profit-seeking businesses must consider income taxes in their calculations, but nonprofit institutions and government agencies do not. The NPV method is illustrated with and without income taxes. The less complex NPV method, without taxes, is demonstrated first, followed by a demonstration of the method with income taxes.

Net Present Value Method without Income Taxes

Nonprofit institutions such as churches, hospitals, universities, state, local, and federal agencies, and foundations are exempt from federal and state income taxes. When they purchase equipment, machinery, vehicles and buildings there are no tax effects to be considered, which simplifies the calculations of capital budgeting techniques.

The *net present value method without income taxes* is an invaluable tool for the nonprofit sector. It is probably not applied as commonly as it should be. One problem is the assumed rate. In determining the cost of capital, a business takes into account the normal profit margin. The nonprofit institution should therefore have a lower assumed rate of return to reflect the balancing of revenues and expenses or a balanced budget. Their assumed rate should approximate the average or marginal cost of borrowing, or even less, considering that funds may be donated at no interest cost. The assumption that there is no cost of borrowing has led some charitable institutions to incur frivolous debt based on future donations.

The illustration of the net present value method, without income taxes, proceeds in steps. Each factor to be considered in the analysis is examined separately. Factors are then combined to form a complete solution at the end.

The step-by-step illustration of a nonprofit community hospital is followed by an illustration of a private university.

Hospitals generate revenues by offering services to patients. They have revenue-generating departments that are profit centers and other departments that are cost centers. Community Hospital is a nonprofit, community hospital in a small town. The new administrator has determined that the purchase of a new X-ray machine will double the speed of processing patients. There is an embarrassing backlog of patients who must wait for the X-ray machine.

The new administrator is told by the hospital controller that the old X-ray machine was purchased two years ago for $80,000. There is no resale market for obsolete X-ray machines, so that only $6,000 can be received now for scrap value. The controller points out that the hospital will lose $74,000 by scrapping the old machine. The revenue per day from the X-ray machine now averages $300 per day; there are 250 days per year in which X-rays are scheduled. The new machine will cost $180,000 with installation costs of $20,000. The estimated scrap value at the end of its economic life will be $5,000. The new machine will double the revenue at no additional operating costs. However, the use of X-ray supplies will double. The X-ray supplies now average $140 per day. The economic life of the new X-ray machine is eight years, but the old machine, which can be used for eight more years, will have no scrap value, and must be overhauled at the mid-point in its economic life at a cost of $10,000.

The hospital is exempt from federal and state income taxes. The controller states that the 10 percent average cost of borrowing will serve as a hurdle rate for evaluating the proposed purchase of the new X-ray machine. The controller adds that there is no way to justify the loss from scrapping the two-year-old machine, which can be used for eight more years.

Procedure for Analyzing Net Present Value Problems

A procedure and format for analyzing and solving all net present value problems without income taxes is demonstrated first. The format for NPV problems with income taxes requires the addition of one column, for tax effects, and is demonstrated later in the chapter. A differential approach is followed in the procedure. The differential method includes the incremental differences of cash flows that occur in the same time period. A demonstration of the total-cost approach follows.

Step 1.

Prepare the format for the net present value method without taxes. This format is adaptable to most NPV problems. Dollar signs are omitted in the table except for the final NPV total.

Item	Amount	*n* =	*i* = % TV =	Present Value

Step 2.

The cost of the investment and the installation costs are a negative cash flow at time period zero. The table value for n = 0 is always 1.000. If the amount is negative in the amount column it must remain negative in subsequent columns.

Item	Amount	n =	i=10% TV =	Present Value
Investment	(180,000)	0	1.000	(180,000)
Installation costs	(20,000)	0	1.000	(20,000)

Step 3.

Relevant incremental or decremental revenues and expenses must be calculated. The difference is that between purchasing or not purchasing the new machine. The revenue and expense differential is

New Machine		
Revenues (250 days × $600)	$150,000	
Less expenses (250 days × $280)	70,000	
Net revenue of new machine		$ 80,000

Old Machine		
Revenues (250 days × $300)	$75,000	
Less expenses (250 days × $140)	35,000	
Net revenue of new machine		$ 40,000

Differential net revenue of new machine	$ 40,000

Item	Amount	n =	i = 10% TV =	Present Value
Annual cash savings	40,000	1 - 8	5.335	213,400

Step 4.

The scrap value of the old machine is $6,000, which will be received at time period 0. The scrap value of the new machine will be received at the end of eight years.The cash received for both machines is a positive cash flow.

Item	Amount	n =	i = 10% TV =	Present Value
Scrap value of old	6,000	0	1.000	6,000
Scrap value of new	5,000	8	0.467	2,335

Step 5.

The old machine would have required an overhaul at the midpoint of its life, which would be at the end of year three. An avoided expense is a positive cash flow.

Economic Life	T_{-1}	T_0	T_1	T_2	T_3	T_4	T_5	T_6	T_7	T_8
New machine			1	2	3	4	5	6	7	8
Old Machine	1	2	3	4	5	6	7	8	9	10

The total economic life of the old machine is estimated at ten years; the mid-point is five years, which is at the end of year 3.

Item	Amount	n =	i = 10% TV =	Present Value
Overhaul avoided on old machine	10,000	3	0 .751	7,510

Step 6.

Combine all of the foregoing items into one format, as shown in Exhibit 15-1.

Exhibit 15-1
Net Present Value Method

Item	Amount	*n* =	*i* = 10% TV =	Present Value
Investment	(180,000)	0	1.000	(180,000)
Installation costs	(20,000)	0	1.000	(20,000)
Annual cash savings	40,000	1-8	5.335	213,400
Scrap value - old	6,000	0	1.000	6,000
Scrap value - new	5,000	8	0.467	2,335
Overhaul avoided-old	10,000	3	0.751	7,510
		Net present value	=	$ 29,245

Observations

The net present value is positive, which means that the present value of the positive cash flows exceeds the PV of the negative cash flows by $29,245. Only three possibilities can occur; a conclusion can be reached from one of these three possibilities:

1. If the net present value is positive, then the internal rate of return of the investment is greater than the assumed interest rate, *i*, that is, the IRR is greater than 10 percent.
2. If the NPV is zero (0), then the IRR is equal to the assumed rate, that is, the IRR is exactly 10 percent.
3. If the NPV is negative, then the IRR is less than the assumed rate, that is, the IRR is less than 10 percent.

The exact internal rate of return cannot be ascertained without using a trial and error process, or by modifying the data for input into a programmed calculator or computer software program.

Total-Cost Approach

The total-cost approach to discounted cash flow problems presents the total incremental amounts pertaining to each of two alternatives, rather than the incremental differences between them. The total-cost approach is demonstrated using the information gathered from a nonprofit private university.

North State University's Aeronautical Engineering Department uses its wind tunnel for instruction and for private research by aircraft manufacturers. It receives $36,000 per year in revenue with $16,000 in related expenses per year for the private research. The Aeronautical Engineering Department has included in its annual budget a request to replace the old wind tunnel with a new one costing $75,000 and requiring $28,000 in installation costs. The revenues from private industry are expected to increase to $60,000 with expenses of $20,000 per year. The new wind tunnel will have a salvage value of $10,000 at the end of ten years, which is its economic life. The new wind tunnel will require an overhaul estimated at $5,000 after five years of use. The old wind tunnel could be maintained in operation for another ten years with a major overhaul costing $3,000 at the end of the fourth year. It has a scrap value now of $8,000, and if kept would be worth $4,000 in scrap value at the end of ten years. Assume that the cost of capital is 14 percent.

Exhibit 15-2 presents the solution to the wind tunnel problem using the total-cost approach. In this approach, the alternative that produces the greatest positive net present value is preferable. The difference between the two alternatives is $10,121, in favor of purchasing the new wind tunnel over keeping the old.

Exhibit 15-2
Total Cost Approach

Alternative 1: Purchase New Wind Tunnel

Item	Amount	*n* =	*i* = 14% TV =	Present Value
Investment	(75,000)	0	1.000	(75,000)
Installation costs	(28,000)	0	1.000	(28,000)
Net annual cash inflow	40,000	1-10	5.216	208,640
Salvage value--new	10,000	10	0.270	2,700
Salvage value--old	8,000	0	1.000	8,000
Overhaul--new	(5,000)	5	0.519	(2,595)
		Net present value	=	$113,745

Alternative 2: Keep Old Wind Tunnel

Item	Amount	*n* =	*i* = 14% TV =	Present Value
Net annual cash inflow	20,000	1-10	5.216	104,320

Overhaul--old	(3,000)	4	0.592	(1,776)
Salvage value--old	4,000	10	0.270	1,080
		Net present value	=	$ 103,624

Difference in favor of purchasing new wind tunnel = $ 10,121

- **Differential Approach**

The results from the total cost approach in Exhibit 15-2 are the same as those using the differential approach, shown in Exhibit 15-3. In the differential approach, it is *assumed* that the alternative considered to be best, such as purchasing the new wind tunnel, is selected. Then, only the *differences* between the two alternatives are included in the analysis. The following items are treated differently in the two methods.

1. The net annual cash inflows of $40,000 for the new wind tunnel, less $20,000 for the old wind tunnel, represent the differential of $20,000.
2. The overhaul--old of $3,000, at period 4, is added.
3. The salvage values of $10,000 for the new wind tunnel, and $4,000 for the old, occurring at period 10, are netted to $6,000.

Exhibit 15-3
Comparison with Differential Approach

Alternative: Purchase New Wind Tunnel

Item	Amount	*n* =	*i* = 14% TV =	Present Value
Investment	(75,000)	0	1.000	(75,000)
Installation costs	(28,000)	0	1.000	(28,000)
Net annual cash inflow	20,000	1-10	5.216	104,320
Salvage value - old	8,000	0	1.000	8,000
Salvage value-differ.	6,000	10	0.270	1,620
Overhaul--old	3,000	4	0.592	1,776
Overhaul --new	(5,000)	5	0.519	(2,595)
		Net present value	=	$ 10,121

The Net Present Value Method with Taxes

The Welch Company manufactures semi-conductors. The production manager proposes purchasing a new machine to replace one purchased two years ago, and provides information to justify the purchase. The Welch Company's investment policy is to accept only proposals that exceed 16 percent after-tax rate of return using the net present value of cash flows method. The cost of the new machine is $100,000 and the old machine is traded in. The cash flow of the investment occurs at time period 0, which is the first day of year 1. The format that is shown in Exhibit 15-4 is used to demonstrate the NPV method.

Exhibit 15-4
Net Present Value Format

Item	Amount	*n* =	*i* = 16% TV =	Present Value
Investment	(100,000)	0	1.000	(100,000)

Observations

As illustrated in Exhibit 15-4 the machine was purchased for $100,000. The item column describes the nature of the cash flow. The next column indicated the amount of the purchase before tax and before present value adjustments. It is a negative cash flow indicated by brackets. The next column will show any tax effect on the cash flow. There is no tax effect on the purchase of a capital investment. The time period column will indicate a single sum, such as n = 1, or a repeated payment such as *n* = 1-4.

Revenues and Expenses

Assume further that the new machine will both increase revenues by producing faster than the present machine and will decrease the operating expenses. The net savings is $35,000 for each year. The new machine has an economic life of six years. Assume that the average corporate income tax rate is 30 percent Note in Exhibit 15-5 that the $35,000 is a positive cash flow and that there is a tax effect of 100 percent minus the tax rate, or 70 percent. The time period is *n* = 1-6 to indicate that the amount is the same for each of six years so that the present value of an annuity of $1 table is used rather than the present value of $1 table. The table value is then multiplied by the after-tax amount of $24,500 to find the present value of the incremental cash savings.

Exhibit 15-5
Incremental Cash Inflows

Item	Amount	Tax Effect	n =	i = 16% TV =	Present Value
Incremental cash inflows	35,000	× 70% = 24,500	1-6	3.685	90,283

Trade-in or Sale of Old Asset with Gains and Losses

Assume further that the old machine, which has a book value of $14,500, is traded in for $12,000. The old machine was purchased three years ago for $50,000 and was depreciated using the MACRS five-year statutory rate for tax purposes. The trade-in is shown in Exhibit 15-6.

Exhibit 15-6
Trade-Ins

Item	Amount	Tax Effect	n =	i = 16% TV =	Present Value
Cash trade-in	12,000	none	0	1.000	12,000
Loss on trade	2,500	× 30% = 750	0	1.000	750

Observations

In Exhibit 15-6, the cash trade-in of $12,000 is a positive cash flow that occurs at period 0. It is realized at the time of the purchase of the new machine regardless of whether the old machine is traded in or sold outright. The $12,000 is a return of capital and not taxable. The *loss* on trade of $2,500 is a noncash flow that is not counted, but the tax savings ($2,500 × 30 percent) is a positive cash flow, that is, it is deducted from the federal income taxes that are paid on the total income of the company. In contrast, a *gain* on trade would result in a negative cash flow, due to the tax effect.

Overhauls and Major Repairs

Any major nonrecurring expense such as an overhaul of a machine must be considered in the estimated year of occurrence. Overhauls to the new machine are negative cash flows, but an overhaul that would have been given to the old machine results in a positive cash flow. It is estimated that the new machine will require an overhaul in year 3 costing $5,000, and that an overhaul of the old machine costing $4,000 would be necessary at the end of year 1 if the machine were still in use.

Exhibit 15-7
Overhauls

Item	Amount	Tax Effect	n =	i = 16% TV =	Present Value
Overhaul-new	(5,000)	× 70% = (3,500)	3	0.641	(2,244)
Overhaul--old	4,000	× 70% = 2,800	1	0.862	2,414

Observations

Exhibit 15-7 shows the tax effect on the overhauls. Overhauls and major repairs to machinery and equipment are expenses, not capitalized. They are deducted in arriving at taxable income. The after-tax cost of the overhaul of the new machine is $3,500 and the after-tax cash savings by not having to overhaul the old machine is only $2,800. The importance of the present value concept is illustrated in this example. The actual cash outlay for overhauling the new machine is greater than that of the old machine, yet the present value of the cash flow of the old machine is greater than that of the new machine because it occurs two years earlier.

Working Capital

Working capital (WC) is defined in accounting terminology as current assets minus current liabilities. The emphasis used by managers and by cost analysts in the finance department of large corporations is on the current asset side. Inventories of finished goods, work-in-process, materials, maintenance parts and supplies are major items of working capital. The purchase of a complex machine may require the addition of working capital items such as repair and maintenance parts and supplies. For example, when a passenger jetliner is purchased by an airline company, two additional jet engines may be purchased to replace the original engines when being overhauled. Federal regulations require that the engines be overhauled on the basis of hours of use. Without the spare engines, the aircraft, which is the production line of the airline company, would be out of operation. Exhibit 15-8 will illustrate how working capital is treated in the net present value method. Assume that an increase of $2,000 in working capital is needed.

Exhibit 15-8
Working Capital

Item	Amount	Tax Effect	*n* =	*i* = 16% TV =	Present Value
Working capital	(2,000)	none	0	1.000	(2,000)
WC returned	2,000	none	6	0.410	820

Observations

Working capital is always assumed to be returned at the end of the economic life of the investment. It is increased (or decreased) at time period 0 and returned at the end, time period 6, for present value computations. There is no tax effect, it is neither revenue nor expense; it is a capital investment for tax purposes. An increase in working capital is a negative cash flow and the return is a positive cash flow.

Estimated Salvage Value

Salvage value at the end of the life of the new machine must be estimated. The salvage value of the old machine at time period 0 is known, it is the trade-in value. If the old machine could be used until the end of the estimated economic life of the new machine, then it too, must be estimated. Assume that the estimated salvage value of the new machine to be purchased by Welch Company at the end of year 6 is $15,000 and that the estimated salvage value of the old machine at the end of year 6 is $6,000. Exhibit 15-9 demonstrates how to analyze the salvage value information.

Exhibit 15-9
Salvage Value

Item	Amount	Tax Effect	*n* =	*i* = 16% TV =	Present Value
Salvage difference	9,000	× 70% = 6,300	6	0.410	2,583

Observations

The difference of $9,000 is used because of the time period. If two like items occur at the same time period, it is more expedient to use the net amount. The cash flow of the new machine is positive, and that of the old machine is negative, thus the difference is positive. The MACRS depreciation regulations in the Tax Reform Act of 1986 do not allow the salvage value to be subtracted from the acquisition cost; therefore, the estimated salvage value is considered taxable. The proceeds will be 100 percent minus the tax rate, or 70 percent, multiplied by the difference of $9,000.

Depreciation

The Tax Reform Act of 1986 (modified in 1991) made significant changes in the previous tax laws of the early 1980s, ERTA and TEFRA. The accelerated cost recovery systems, which was adopted by ERTA in 1981, is still in effect, but both the depreciable time periods and the depreciation rates have been modified by the 1986 law, which accounts for the term, modified accelerated cost recovery system.

Depreciation is not relevant because it is not a cash flow, however, the tax effect on depreciation is a positive cash flow because it reduces the cash that would otherwise be paid in taxes. Assume that Welch Company had purchased the old machine three years earlier, at the beginning of 1990, and that it is now the beginning of 1993.

The new machine will be depreciated under the 1986 Tax Reform Act provisions, and is classified as five-year property. Under the 1986 law, still in effect in regard to these provisions, the statutory rates for five-year property use a modified 200 percent declining balance, half-year convention method over six years instead of five. The old machine has been depreciated under the MACRS five year statutory tax rates of 20, 32, and 19 percent, for the first three years. The remaining rates for the old machine are 12, 11, and 6 percent.

Analysis Procedure for Depreciation

The procedure to follow in calculating the depreciation for present value analysis is as follows

Step 1. Prepare a time frame for reference

Period	T_{-2}	T_{-1}	T_0	T_1	T_2	T_3	T_4	T_5	T_6
End of yr	1990	1991	1992	1993	1994	1995	1996	1997	1998
New mach				1	2	3	4	5	6
Old Mach	1	2	3	4	5	6			

Step 2. Prepare a depreciation schedule for the new machine.

Period	Year	Acquisition Cost	Depreciation Rate	Tax Depreciation
T_1	1993	100,000	× 0.20	20,000
T_2	1994	100,000	× 0.32	32,000
T_3	1995	100,000	× 0.19	19,000
T_4	1996	100,000	× 0.12	12,000
T_5	1997	100,000	× 0.11	11,000
T_6	1998	100,000	× 0.06	6,000

Step 3. Prepare a depreciation schedule for the old machine starting at T_1.

Year	Cost	Rate	Tax Depreciation
1993	50,000	× 0.12	= 6,000
1994	50,000	× 0.11	= 5,500
1995	50,000	× 0.06	= 3,000

Step 4. Prepare a differential depreciation schedule.

Period	Year	New Machine	Less Old Machine	Differential Tax Depreciation
T_1	1993	20,000	- 6,000	14,000
T_2	1994	32,000	- 5,500	26,500
T_3	1995	19,000	- 3,000	16,000
T_4	1996	12,000		12,000
T_5	1997	11,000		11,000
T_6	1998	6,000		6,000

Step 5. Enter the differential depreciation into the present value formula.

Item	Amount	Tax Effect	$n =$	i = 16% TV =	Present Value
1993	14,000	× 0.30 = 4,200	1	0.862	3,620
1994	26,500	× 0.30 = 7,950	2	0.743	5,907
1995	16,000	× 0.30 = 4,800	3	0.641	3,077
1996	12,000	× 0.30 = 3,600	4	0.552	1,987
1997	11,000	× 0.30 = 3,300	5	0.476	1,571
1998	6,000	× 0.30 = 1,800	6	0.410	738

Exhibit 15-10 consolidates all of the present value calculations. The net present value represents the sum of the positive and negative cash flows.

Exhibit 15-10
Summary of Net Present Value Method

Item	Amount	Tax Effect	$n =$	i = 16% TV =	Present Value
Investment	(100,000)	none	0	1.000	(100,000)
Incremental cash savings	30,000	× 70% = 21,000	1-6	3.685	77,385
Cash trade-in	12,000	none	0	1.000	12,000
Loss on trade	2,500	× 30% = 750	0	1.000	750
Overhaul--new	(5,000)	× 70% = (3,500)	3	0.641	(2,244)
Overhaul--old	4,000	× 70% = 2,800	1	0.862	2,414
Work. capital	(2,000)	none	0	1.000	(2,000)
WC returned	2,000	none	6	0.410	820
Salvage diff.	9,000	× 70% = 6,300	6	0.410	2,583
Depreciation:					
1993	14,000	× 30% = 4,200	1	0.862	3,620
1994	26,500	× 30% = 7,950	2	0.743	5,907

1995	16,000	× 30% = 4,800	3	0.641	3,077
1996	12,000	× 30% = 3,600	4	0.552	1,987
1997	11,000	× 30% = 3,300	5	0.476	1,571
1998	6,000	× 30% = 1,800	6	0.410	738
			Net Present Value	=	$8,608

Observations

First, the net present value is positive. This means that the IRR is greater than 16 percent, and second, the production manager's proposal to purchase the new machine should be approved by the Welch Company. Even though the machine to be replaced is only two years old the new machine meets the minimum rate of return specified by the company.

INTERNAL RATE OF RETURN METHOD

The internal rate of return method of determining the acceptance or rejection of a capital project is a sophisticated analytical tool, widely used and accepted by industrial and financial managers. The method calculates the *actual rate of return of a project,* which is measured against the individual company's cost of capital *(i)*. If the project's IRR exceeds the company's hurdle rate, the project is accepted. The method uses after-tax discounted cash flows, and requires the same analysis as in the net present value method. A major difference is that the reinvestment of future cash flows in the IRR method is assumed to be at the IRR rate. The NPV method assumes that the reinvestment of future cash flows is at the assumed cost of capital rate.

The necessity of using iteration (trial and error) in arriving at a precise solution makes it impractical to calculate the internal rate of return manually. With the widespread use of microcomputers and the almost universal access to electronic spreadsheet software it is more important to learn how to adapt the data from the net present value method for the computer. In Exhibit 15-10, the net present value method showed that the project was acceptable. The data from Exhibit 15-10 must be rearranged to conform to the format shown in Exhibit 15-11 in order to load the calculator or spreadsheet. The use of a programmed calculator, or an electronic spreadsheet with the IRR function can provide the exact answer, which for this data is 19.6 percent.

Exhibit 15-11
IRR Method

Period	T_0	T_1	T_2	T_3	T_4	T_5	T_6
Investment	(100,000)						
Incremental cash savings		21,000	21,000	21,000	21,000	21,000	21,000
Cash trade-in	12,000						
Loss on trade	750						
Work. capital	(2,000)						2,000
Overhauls		2,800		(3,500)			
Salvage diff.							6,300
Depreciation		4,200	7,950	4,800	3,600	3,300	1,800
Totals	(89,250)	28,000	28,950	22,300	24,600	24,300	31,100

MODIFIED INTERNAL RATE of RETURN METHOD

The modified internal rate of return method (MIRR) calculates the internal rate of return, assuming that the reinvestment of future cash flows are at the cost of capital rate instead of at the IRR. This modification provides a more realistic rate of return than the IRR. It is more likely that actual future cash flows will be reinvested at the company's cost of capital than at the IRR. The MIRR will be a better indicator of the investment or project's actual profitability than the IRR. By following the same assumptions about future reinvestment of cash flows the MIRR is also more likely to be in agreement with the NPV method.

The MIRR calculates the rate of return that equates the present value of the sum of the future values of all cash inflows (from T_1 to T_n) at the end of period *n*, the last period in the economic life of the investment, with the present value of the cash outflows, (the net costs of the investment at $T_{0)}$. Exhibit 15-12 illustrates how the MIRR is calculated using the data in Exhibit 15-11, which assumes a cost of capital rate of 16%.

The future value of the T_1 value, $28,000, is calculated at the cost of capital rate, i = 16%, and the time period, n = 5. The future value of the T_2 value is calculated at n = 4. The future value of the T_3 value is calculated at n = 3, etc. Finally, the future value of the T_6 value, $31,100, is calculated at n = 0. This adds up to a total future value, at time period T_6, of $238,436, which is present valued back to period T_0 at a rate, the MIRR, that equals $89,500, the PV of the net cash outflow.

Exhibit 15-12
MIRR Method

T_0	T_1	T_2	T_3	T_4	T_5	T_6
(89,500)	28,000	28,950	22,300	24,600	24,300	31,100
FV of T_1	28,000 ⇒					58,810
FV of T_2		28,950 ⇒				52,418
FV of T_3			22,300 ⇒			34,808
FV of T_4				24,600 ⇒		33,102
FV of T_5					24,300 ⇒	28,188
FV of T_6						31,100
(89,500)				Total Future Value of cash inflows	=	$238,426

The MIRR is calculated on a financial calculator by entering

PV = 89,500	$n = 6$
FV = 238,426	CPT (compute key) = %i = the MIRR = 17.8%
PMT (payment key) = 0	

The MIRR of 17.8 percent is the rate at which the present value (PV) of $238,426, the sum of the future values of the cash inflows, is equal to $89,500, the present value (PV) of the net cash outflows. The MIRR is greater than the 16 percent cost of capital rate, but lower than the IRR of 19.6 %.

PAYBACK METHOD

The payback method is commonly used in determining the time period required to receive the cost of the investment back. It is measured in a time period, years and months. It is in after-tax cash flow method preferable for projects with a short life. Its simplicity and ease of application makes it a popular method. The time value of money is not taken into consideration in the payment method.

$$\frac{\text{Cost of investment (less trade or sale value of old machine)}}{\text{Annual after-tax cash flow}} = \text{Payback Period}$$

Example 1: Investment in Asset (New Equipment)

A nonprofit laundry in a military base considers the purchase of new commercial coin-operated washing machine for $1,600 that is estimated to produce revenue of $1,200 less $400 in related expenses for a net cash flow of $800 per year. The tax rate is irrelevant and there is no trade-in. The payback period is

$$\frac{\text{Investment}}{\text{Annual cash flow}} = \frac{\$1,600}{800}$$

Example 2: Trade-In or Sale of Old Investment

The following year the nonprofit laundry considers trading in a machine purchased two years ago for a $200 trade-in allowance off the purchase price of a new coin-operated commercial machine. The new commercial washing machine will cost $1,600 and the net cash flow is $800. The payback period in years is

$$\frac{\text{Investment less Trade-in}}{\text{Annual net cash inflow}} = \frac{\$1,600 - \$200}{\$800} = \frac{\$1,400}{\$800} = 1.75 \text{ yrs}$$

Example 3: Tax Effect on Payback Method

The following year, the military base allows a private owner to operate the laundry inside the base property. An additional washing machine is being considered for purchase (with no trade-in) at a cost of $1,600. The net cash inflow is estimated at $800 per year. The private company will pay an income tax of 30 percent. Tax depreciation of the new machine is assumed to be straight-line over five years for demonstration purposes. The payback period is

Investment	=	$1,600	= 2.44 yrs
Annual after-tax cash inflow*		$ 656	

*Tax Effect Calculations: Annual cash inflow		= $800 × 0.70	$560
Depreciation	($1600 ÷ 5)	= $320 × 0.30	96
			$656

Observations

The payback period was shortened by the trade-in in Example 2, which is treated as a reduction in cost. The tax effect in Example 3 reduces the realized cash inflow, which lengthens the payback period.

Example 4: Payback Method with Uneven Cash Inflows

The Tax Reform Act of 1986 does not provide for even cash flows that occur under the straight-line method. The same information from Example 3 is used now, except that the MACRS rates of 20, 32, 19, 12, 11 and 6 percent will be used for five-year property. Because of uneven cash flows a procedure, such as that demonstrated below, must be followed.

	1	2	3
Balance at beginning of year	$(1,600)	$(944)	$(230)
Annual after-tax cash inflow	560	560	560
Depreciation tax savings:			
Year 1--1,600 × 0.20 = 320 × 0.30 =	96		
Year 2--1,600 × 0.32 = 512 × 0.30 =		154	
Year 3--1,600 × 0.19 = 304 × 0.30 =			91
Total cash inflows	$656	$714	$651
Balance at end of year	$(944)	$(230)	$421

Payback Period = 2.35 years

The fraction is determined by dividing the balance at the beginning of the year by the total cash inflows, for example, 230 ÷ 651 = 0.35.

Example 5: Payback Method Using Discounted Cash Flow

The payback method can be used with present values, but it would not be consistent with its main advantage of being easy to understand and to apply. Using the data from Examples 3 and 4 a procedure, such as that shown in the table, can be followed in order to calculate the payback period. A discount rate of 12 percent is assumed.

	1	2	3
Balance at beginning of year	$(1,600)	$ (1,014)	$ (445)
Annual after-tax cash inflow	560	560	560
Depreciation tax savings:			
Year 1--1,600 × 0.20 = 320 × 0.30 =	96		
Year 2--1,600 × 0.32 = 512 × 0.30 =		154	
Year 3--1,600 × 0.19 = 304 × 0.30 =			91
Total cash inflows	656	714	651
Present value factor @ 12%	0.893	0.797	0.712
PV of cash flows	586	569	464
Balance at end of year	$ (1,014)	$ (445)	$ 19

Payback Period = 2.96 or 3.0 years

Observations

1. The introduction of the present value concept lengthens the payback period from 2.35 years to almost three years.
2. The advantage of using present values is that the results are more realistic.
3. The disadvantages are that using present values makes the payback method more complicated and always results in longer payback periods. Both factors may have negative psychological effects on managers who use the payback method without present values.

APPENDIX

Discounted Cash Flow: The Time Value of Money Concept

The "time value of money" refers to the effect of time on the value of money. The passage of time has a price tag in regard to the use of money. The price of using someone else's money over time is called *interest*. The price of using our own money over time is called *imputed interest*. Thus, money in the present has a greater value than money in the future.

For example, assume that we place $1,000 in a money market fund which yields 10 percent interest per annum.

T_0 = January 1 19X1
T_1 = December 31 19X1
T_2 = December 31 19X2
T_3 = December 31 19X3

Period	T_0	T_1	T_2	T_3
Investment at beginning of period	$1,000			
Interest @ 10%		100	110	121
Balance at end of period		$ 1,100	$ 1,210	$ 1,331

This is the basis for the *future value table* for $1 shown at the end of the chapter. The table shows 1.100, 1.210 and 1.331 for years 1, 2, and 3. Multiplying the table values by the initial investment yields the three balances shown in the table.

Future Value of an Annuity of $1

Assume that instead one lump sum of $1,000 being placed in a fund yielding exactly 10 percent, that $1,000 is placed in the fund at the end of each year for three years. The future value of the annuity at the end of each period will be as shown in the table.

Period	T_1	T_2	T_3
Investment at end of period	$ 1,000	$ 1,000	$ 1,000
Interest @ 10%	0	100	210
Balance at end of period	$ 1,000	$ 2,100	$ 3,310

The table for the future value of an annuity of $1 shows 1.000, 2.100, and 3.310 for years 1, 2, and 3, respectively. Multiplying the amount of the periodic payment of $1,000 by the table value yields the balances shown here. At the end of year 3 a total amount of $3,310 will accrue from the three $1,000 payments at a 10 percent interest rate.

Present Value of $1

The present value of $1 concept is most useful in evaluating investment projects. Amounts received in the future are not rationally considered at face value because of the time value of money. Tables that show present values are predicated on the following procedure. Assume an interest rate of 10 percent. An amount of $1,000 is required at the end of period T_3.

End of Period	T_0	T_1	T_2	T_3
Future amount @ 10%				$ 1,000
PV end of T_2			$ 909	
PV end of T_1		$ 826		
PV end of T_0	$ 751			

The present value of $1,000 received at the end of year 3 is $751. Another way of stating this relationship is that the amount of $751 invested at T0 (the beginning of year 1) will yield $1,000 at the end of year 3.

Present Value of an Annuity of $1

The example in the table assumes that a given amount, $1,000, is placed in a fund at a 10 percent interest rate, at the end of each of three years. The present value of the annuity is the sum of the present value of each $1,000 payment. The table values shown will yield the same present value below when multiplied by $1,000.

Present Value at T_0	Investment at end of T_1	Investment at end of T_2	Investment at end of T_3
$ 909	$ 1,000		
826		$ 1,000	
751			$ 1,000
$ 2,486			

The present value concept should be applied to certain situations, for example, the lottery, a gambling device adopted in many states. The state lottery advertises that a sum, such as $1 million, will be paid to the winner or winners. The actual payments are $50,000 per year for twenty years. Using the present value of an annuity of $1 table and assuming a reasonable interest rate of 10 percent we can calculate the present value. It is not $1 million, but $425,700 ($50,000 × 8.514). Perhaps because the winners never complain there is no outcry of deception. The state is nevertheless deceiving the public, as long as the interest rate or the rate of return on investments is positive.

Table A15.1
Present Value of $1

Period	6%	8%	10%	12%	14%	16%	18%
1	0.943	0.926	0.909	0.893	0.877	0.862	0.847
2	0.890	0.857	0.826	0.797	0.769	0.743	0.718
3	0.840	0.794	0.751	0.712	0.675	0.641	0.609
4	0.792	0.735	0.683	0.636	0.592	0.552	0.516
5	0.747	0.681	0.621	0.567	0.519	0.476	0.437
6	0.705	0.630	0.564	0.507	0.456	0.410	0.370
7	0.665	0.583	0.513	0.452	0.400	0.354	0.314
8	0.627	0.540	0.467	0.404	0.351	0.305	0.266
9	0.592	0.500	0.424	0.361	0.308	0.263	0.225
10	0.558	0.463	0.386	0.322	0.270	0.227	0.191
11	0.527	0.429	0.350	0.287	0.237	0.195	0.162
12	0.497	0.397	0.319	0.257	0.208	0.168	0.137
13	0.469	0.368	0.290	0.229	0.182	0.145	0.116
14	0.442	0.340	0.263	0.205	0.160	0.125	0.099
15	0.417	0.315	0.239	0.183	0.140	0.108	0.084
16	0.394	0.292	0.218	0.163	0.123	0.093	0.071
18	0.350	0.250	0.180	0.130	0.095	0.069	0.051
20	0.312	0.215	0.149	0.104	0.073	0.051	0.037
22	0.278	0.184	0.123	0.083	0.056	0.038	0.026
24	0.247	0.158	0.102	0.066	0.043	0.028	0.019

Table A15.2
Present Value of an Ordinary Annuity of $1

Period	6%	8%	10%	12%	14%	16%	18%
1	0.943	0.926	0.909	0.893	0.877	0.862	0.847
2	1.833	1.783	1.736	1.690	1.647	1.605	1.566
3	2.673	2.577	2.487	2.402	2.322	2.246	2.174
4	3.465	3.312	3.170	3.037	2.914	2.798	2.690
5	4.212	3.993	3.791	3.605	3.433	3.274	3.127
6	4.917	4.623	4.355	4.111	3.889	3.685	3.498
7	5.582	5.206	4.868	4.564	4.288	4.039	3.812
8	6.210	5.747	5.335	4.968	4.639	4.344	4.078
9	6.802	6.247	5.759	5.328	4.946	4.607	4.303
10	7.360	6.710	6.145	5.650	5.216	4.833	4.494
11	7.887	7.139	6.495	5.938	5.453	5.029	4.256
12	8.384	7.536	6.814	6.194	5.660	5.197	4.793
13	8.853	7.904	7.103	6.424	5.842	5.342	4.910
14	9.295	8.244	7.367	6.628	6.002	5.468	5.008
15	9.712	8.559	7.606	6.811	6.142	5.575	5.092
16	10.106	8.851	7.824	6.974	6.265	5.668	5.162
18	10.828	9.372	8.201	7.250	6.467	5.818	5.273
20	11.470	9.818	8.514	7.469	6.623	5.929	5.353
22	12.042	10.201	8.772	7.645	6.743	6.011	5.410
24	12.550	10.529	8.985	7.784	6.835	6.073	5.451

Table A15.3
Future Value of $1

Period	6%	8%	10%	12%	14%	16%	18%
1	1.060	1.080	1.100	1.120	1.140	1.160	1.180
2	1.124	1.166	1.210	1.254	1.300	1.346	1.392
3	1.191	1.260	1.331	1.405	1.482	1.561	1.643
4	1.262	1.360	1.464	1.574	1.689	1.811	1.939
5	1.338	1.469	1.611	1.762	1.925	2.100	2.288
6	1.419	1.587	1.772	1.974	2.195	2.436	2.700
7	1.504	1.714	1.949	2.211	2.502	2.826	3.185
8	1.594	1.851	2.144	2.476	2.853	3.278	3.759
9	1.689	1.999	2.358	2.773	3.252	3.803	4.435
10	1.791	2.159	2.594	3.106	3.707	4.411	5.234
11	1.898	2.332	2.853	3.479	4.226	5.117	6.176
12	2.012	2.518	3.138	3.896	4.818	5.936	7.288
13	2.133	2.720	3.452	4.363	5.492	6.886	8.599
14	2.261	2.973	3.797	4.887	6.261	7.988	10.147
15	2.397	3.172	4.177	5.474	7.138	9.266	11.974
16	2.540	3.426	4.595	6.130	8.137	10.748	14.129
18	2.854	3.996	5.560	7.690	10.575	14.463	19.673
20	3.207	4.661	6.727	9.646	13.743	19.461	27.393
22	3.604	5.437	8.140	12.100	17.861	26.186	38.142
24	4.049	6.341	9.850	15.179	23.212	35.236	53.109

Table A15.4
Future Value of an Ordinary Annuity of $1

Period	6%	8%	10%	12%	14%	16%	18%
1	1.000	1.000	1.000	1.000	1.000	1.000	1.000
2	2.060	2.080	2.100	2.120	2.140	2.160	2.180
3	3.184	3.246	3.310	3.374	3.440	3.506	3.572
4	4.375	4.506	4.641	4.779	4.921	5.066	5.215
5	5.637	5.867	6.105	6.353	6.610	6.877	7.154
6	6.975	7.336	7.716	8.115	8.536	8.977	9.442
7	8.394	8.923	9.487	10.089	10.730	11.414	12.142
8	9.897	10.637	11.436	12.300	13.233	14.240	15.327
9	11.491	12.488	13.579	14.776	16.085	17.519	19.086
10	13.181	14.487	15.937	17.549	19.337	21.321	23.521
11	14.972	16.645	18.531	20.655	23.045	25.733	28.755
12	16.870	18.977	21.384	24.133	27.271	30.850	34.931
13	18.882	21.495	24.523	28.029	32.089	36.786	42.219
14	21.015	24.215	27.975	32.393	37.581	43.672	50.818
15	23.276	27.152	31.772	37.280	43.842	51.660	60.965
16	25.673	30.324	35.950	42.753	50.980	60.925	72.939

16

Return on Investment and Transfer Pricing

In a corporation, authority is delegated to corporate officers by the board of directors who derive their authority from the stockholders. The authority trickles down to the divisions, departments, and eventually to all organizational units (cost centers) of the company. With the authority to command the resources of the corporation goes a specified, or sometimes an implicit, responsibility to accomplish the goals of the organizational unit.

Traditional costing systems and organizational patterns are assumed for the following discussion. Activity-based concepts and methods are applicable except where organizational structures are involved. The formal organization chart determines the flow of authority and responsibility.

SCOPE OF RESPONSIBILITY

The organization must define the boundaries of authority, and thus responsibility, of each manager. The existence of ambiguous, overlapping or excluded areas of authority will result in confusion and friction. The scope of authority and responsibility must include

1. Organizational boundaries
2. Budgetary commitments
3. Goals and objectives

DECENTRALIZATION

The emergence of mergers of already large corporations into giant, complex organizations with diverse product lines has fostered the decentralization movement in world industries. *Decentralization* is the delegation of authority to layers of management emanating from the top downward. A *decentralized organization* is one in which autonomous decision-making authority has been given to the managers of organizational budget units. The scope of authority is effectively and efficiently limited by the budget authority. The decentralized organization is too large and divergent to depend on personal observations of management performance by top management. A systematic approach to performance evaluation is required.

Advantages of Decentralization

Decision Making

Decentralization provides the opportunity for decisions to be made closer to the operations. Managers who are directly involved in operations are better informed about the details and also about the consequences of their decisions.

Motivation

Managers who are given an unrestricted and well-defined area of authority have a vested interest in consequences of their decisions. They know that the responsibility for the success or failure in their area is visible to top management. Nothing can be a more powerful motivating force to managers than the recognition of a job well done, or conversely, the stigma of being responsible for a failure.

PERFORMANCE MEASUREMENT

Each manager is responsible for accomplishing the goals and objectives of the department. It is necessary for the management hierarchy to evaluate the performance of all managers. The company must establish a practical, equitable and effective system of evaluating its managers. Motivation, which is a key factor in high achievement, depends on recognition and fairness in evaluating performance. Several methods and techniques of evaluating management performance are examined.

CONTROLLABLE COSTS

Controllable costs are those that are (1) directly traceable to a responsibility center, (2) incurred within the budgetary authority of the responsibility center, and (3) avoidable at the option of the manager. The costs must be traceable so it can be known if they are controllable. The costs must be within the budgetary control of the manager in charge, which requires that the budget system give complete autonomy to the manager up to the budget limits. There can be no control if the budget places arbitrary restrictions on the spending authority of the manager.

RESPONSIBILITY CENTER

A *responsibility center* is an organizational budget unit in which controllable costs are present, and in which revenues or investment decisions may be present. This includes departments, divisions, groups, functions, processes, and other organizational units, including the entire company. It does not include activity centers or business processes as defined in ABC/ABM systems unless they replace traditional organizational units.

COST CENTER

A *cost center* is a responsibility center that has control over costs only. A cost center may have costs allocated to it over which it has no control. It has no jurisdiction over revenues or investment funds. All budgetary units from the smallest to the overall company are cost centers.

PROFIT CENTER

A *profit center* is a responsibility center that has control over both costs and revenues. An example of a profit center is a product line division of a multiproduct company. The product line division generates revenue and incurs costs most of which are controllable, however, the division does not issue capital stock separate from corporate headquarters. Investment decisions such as new plants, major changes in product lines, and stock issues are made at the corporate level, not at the division level.

INVESTMENT CENTER

An *investment center* is the corporate headquarters or any segment of the corporation that has control over costs, revenues and investment funds. Operating divisions that are given autonomy in making investment decisions, such as expansion of physical plant and changes in product lines, are investment centers. Operating divisions that are given autonomy in making operating decisions, but not in the use of investment funds are profit centers. The authority over investment funds remains with the corporate headquarters.

The spread of decentralization has been augmented by the increase in mergers and takeovers. A purchased company may continue to operate as a semiautonomous investment center. The parent corporation may have little or no experience in the purchased company's product lines. One U.S. conglomerate has absorbed separate companies that produce cheese products, luggage, and Chinese foods. Such a diversity of product lines places a greater dependence on the managers of the former companies, which may be reorganized as divisions of the parent corporation.

MEASURING MANAGEMENT PERFORMANCE

The *Statement on Management Accounting* (SMA) Number 4A, which defines and describes the uses of the cost of capital in making capital investment decisions, in managing working capital, and in evaluating performance. It states that the cost of capital is a composite of the cost of various sources of funds comprising a firm's capital structure. It is the minimum rate of return that must be earned on new investments that will not dilute the interests of the stockholder.

Management often makes decisions that affect the firm's capital structure. Sources of financing may be different, costs may vary, or the proportion of each source in relation to the entire capital structure may change. Each of these variations affects the firm's cost of capital. The cost of capital is found by determining the costs of the individual types of capital and multiplying the cost of each by its proportion in the firm's total capital structure. The cost of capital is therefore a weighted average.

The cost of capital may be employed as a benchmark for the evaluation of performance. The reported return on capital or return on net assets may be compared with the cost of capital for this purpose.

RETURN ON INVESTMENT

The large corporation raises additional investment funds by issuing more capital stock or by issuing bonds and other long-term debt instruments. The investment centers, whether they are divisions or acquired companies, compete for the funds raised by the corporate headquarters. A reliable and efficient system is needed to determine (1) which segments should receive funds and (2) how well funds already received have been managed.

Return on Investment (*ROI*) is the ratio of operating income to operating assets employed in the division or other investment center of the company.

$$\text{ROI} = \frac{\text{Operating Income}}{\text{Operating Assets}}$$

Operating Income

The measurement of divisional income may vary in actual practice. The measurement of net income for formal presentation in the corporation's financial statements is subject to numerous promulgations by both the accounting profession and the legal system. The measurement of income for internal use, on the other hand, is at the discretion of each corporation.

Operating income is net income before interest and income taxes. The divisional managers do not control the raising of invested funds nor do they have any responsibility for the income taxes levied on the corporation.

For the purpose of measuring the performance of an operation division the concept of operating income is preferable to the net income as presented in the formal financial statement. The use of operating income holds the divisional managers responsible for only those elements of income that are under their direct control.

Operating Assets

The division receives from the corporation investment funds that are used to purchase inventories, supplies, physical plants, equipment, machinery, and numerous other resources necessary to generate revenue. These are the *operating assets* of the division or other investment center. Not included in operating assets are those assets, such as property held for the recreational use of employees, that do not generate operating revenue.

If operating assets are subject to wide differences in a given time period, such as one year, it may be preferable to use an average of the beginning and end of the period. Otherwise, the amount of operating assets at the end of the period is the amount used in the ROI formula. Erie Corporation has a division that manufactures carburetors. Operating data for the Carburetor Division is shown in the table.

Carburetor Division Operating Data for 19X3

Operating revenue (OR)	$ 800,000
Operating income (OI)	$ 100,000
Operating assets (OA)	$ 400,000

The Carburetor Division has a return on investment of

$$\text{ROI} = \frac{\$100{,}000}{\$400{,}000} = 25\%$$

The relationship between operating income and revenue is also a common measurement of profitability. The *margin* is defined as

$$\text{Margin} = \frac{\text{Operating income (OI)}}{\text{Operating revenue (OR)}}$$

For the Carburetor Division of the Erie Corporation the margin is:

$$M = \frac{\$100{,}000}{\$800{,}000} = 12.5\%$$

The margin of 12.5 percent is the return on operating revenue (or sales) that measures profitability in regard to sales but not to the investment. The invested assets are used by the division to generate sales revenue. The more sales revenue the more profitable are the invested funds. The ratio of the operating revenue to the operation assets is a measure of *turnover* (*T*). The turnover multiplied by the margin is equal to the ROI.

$$\text{Turnover} = \frac{\text{Operating revenue (OR)}}{\text{Operating assets (OA)}}$$

For the Carburetor Division of the Erie Corporation,

$$T = \frac{\$800{,}000}{\$400{,}000} = 2 \text{ times}$$

$$M \times T = \text{ROI}$$

$$12.5\% \times 2 = 25\%$$

$$\text{ROI} = 25\%$$

The relationships among the three equations are arranged below to show the mathematical proof of the formulas as presented.

$$M = \frac{\text{OI}}{\text{OR}}$$

$$T = \frac{\text{OR}}{\text{OA}}$$

$$\text{ROI} = \frac{\text{OI}}{\text{OA}}$$

$$\text{ROI} = \frac{\text{OI}}{\text{OR}} \times \frac{\text{OR}}{\text{OA}} = \frac{\text{OI}}{\text{OA}}$$

The ROI measurement is much more than a set of academic equations. Major U.S. corporations now use the ROI concept in performance measurement. It is a widely accepted and respected criterion for evaluating the use of invested funds and the performance of those managers responsible for the funds.

CONTROL FACTORS

The divisional managers have direct control over the operating revenues and costs of the division, and over the use of invested funds assuming that the division is an investment center. The ROI may be increased by

1. Increasing the operating revenue by
   a. a price increase
   b. a volume increase
2. A decrease in operating costs
3. A decrease in the operating assets

Increasing Operating Revenue (Sales)

Increasing operating revenue may be achieved by a price increase or by an increase in volume. First, the effects of a price increase on the ROI will be demonstrated. Assume that the Carburetor Division has the following cost structure.

Operating revenue		$800,000
Variable costs	$400,000	
Fixed costs	300,000	700,000
Operating income		$100,000

If operating revenue is increased by a price increase, the variable and fixed costs will not change. An increase of 25 percent in *price* will result in an increase in operating revenue of $200,000 and an increase in operating income of $200,000. The results are

Operating revenue	$1,000,000
Operating income	$ 300,000
Operating assets	$ 400,000

These changes affect the margin, the turnover, and the ROI.

$$M = \frac{\$\ 300{,}000}{\$1{,}000{,}000} = 30\%$$

Also affected is the ROI, which originally was:

$$ROI = \frac{OI}{OA} = \frac{\$100{,}000}{\$400{,}000} = 25\%$$

The increase in operating revenue increases the ROI to:

$$ROI = \frac{\$300{,}000}{\$400{,}000} = 75\%$$

Or, using the $M \times T = ROI$ formula:

$$M = 30\%$$

$$T = \frac{\$1{,}000{,}000}{\$\ 400{,}000} = 2.5 \text{ times}$$

$$ROI = 30\% \times 2.5 = 75\%$$

Increase in Operating Revenue by an Increase in Volume

An increase of 25 percent in *volume* affects the Carburetor Division's revenue and variable costs but not their fixed costs.

Operating revenue		$1,000,000
Variable costs	$500,000	
Fixed costs	300,000	800,000
Operating income		$200,000

The effect on the three ratios is

$$\text{Margin} = \frac{OI}{OR} = \frac{\$\ 200{,}000}{\$1{,}000{,}000} = 20\%$$

$$\text{Turnover} = \frac{OR}{OA} = \frac{\$1{,}000{,}000}{\$\ 400{,}000} = 2.5 \text{ times}$$

$$ROI = \frac{OI}{OA} = \frac{\$200{,}000}{\$400{,}000} = 50\%$$

Decreasing Operating Costs

The Carburetor Division has operating revenue of $800,000 and operating income of $100,000. A reduction of operating costs of $100,000, with no other charges, will increase operating income to $200,000. Operating revenue remains at $800,000, and operating assets remain at $400,000.

$$\text{ROI} = \frac{\text{OI}}{\text{OA}} = \frac{\$200{,}000}{\$400{,}000} = 50\%$$

or, using $M \times T = \text{ROI}$

$$M = \frac{\text{OI}}{\text{OR}} = \frac{\$200{,}000}{\$800{,}000} = 25\%$$

$$T = \frac{\text{OR}}{\text{OA}} = \frac{\$800{,}000}{\$400{,}000} = 2 \text{ times}$$

$$M \times T = 25\% \times 2 = 50\%$$

The ROI increased from 25 percent to 50 percent by decreasing the operating costs by $100,000.

Reducing Operating Assets

The reduction of operating assets is theoretically possible, but in practice it is difficult. The division may already have an efficient combination of resources and an imbalance caused by indiscriminate reductions may be disastrous. In contrast, some company divisions have made significant reductions in inventory levels with satisfactory results.

Using the Carburetor Division as an example again, assume a reduction in operating assets from $400,000 to $300,000 with no change in the revenues or costs, the revised ROI will be

$$\text{ROI} = \frac{\text{OI}}{\text{OA}} = \frac{\$100{,}000}{\$300{,}000} = 33\tfrac{1}{3}\%$$

or, using $M \times T = \text{ROI}$

$$M = \frac{\text{OI}}{\text{OR}} = \frac{\$100{,}000}{\$800{,}000} = 12.5\%$$

$$T = \frac{\text{OR}}{\text{OA}} = \frac{\$800{,}000}{\$300{,}000} = 2\tfrac{2}{3} \text{ times}$$

$M \times T \quad = \quad 12.5\% \times 2\frac{2}{3} \quad = \quad 33\frac{1}{3}\%$

The ROI increased from 25 percent to 33⅓ percent resulting from an increase in the operating assets. The divisional manager whose performance is evaluated by the ROI measurement must develop a strategy to outperform the other divisions. Without the knowledge of how increases in the ROI are achieved, the manager may pursue the wrong strategy or one that is filled with obstacles. For example, an increase in the price may yield more revenue in the very short run, but may result in a loss of customers who seek other sources. The loss of revenue may not occur for several months, which hides the longer-range negative effect of the new strategy. All of the control factors that result in increases in the ROI must be explored to find the combination that yields positive and lasting effects.

RESIDUAL INCOME

Several criteria are used to evaluate the performance of divisional managers. Return on investment emphasizes short-run rather than long-run performance and does not use the cash-flow or present value techniques.

Residual income measures the positive excess of operating income over a minimum rate of return on operating assets. The division or other investment center is expected to exceed the rate of return established by the company. The result is measured in dollars of income rather than a percentage rate. The Erie Corporation has a 20 percent minimum rate of return for measuring the residual income of its divisions. Carburetor Division's operating data and residual income for 19X3 is calculated in the table.

Operating Income	$100,000
Operating Assets	$400,000
Calculation of residual income:	
Actual operating income	$100,000
Expected operating income (20% x 400,000)	80,000
Residual income	$ 20,000

The division attempts to maximize residual income rather than ROI. Increases in dollar amounts of residual income represents improved performance. The residual income method is limited by the use of absolute dollar amounts. Comparisons between divisions of different sizes are not realistic. Consider the data of two divisions of a company that expects a 20 percent return on operating assets. Division A has a 25 percent ROI and Division B a 30 percent ROI.

	Division A	Division B
Operating assets	$ 500,000	$ 200,000
Operating income	125,000	60,000
Expected operating income	100,000	40,000
Residual income	$ 25,000	$ 20,000

The residual income of Division A is greater than that of Division B even though the return on the operating assets of Division B is greater. The residual income method should be used along with other measurements of performance, such as the ROI, in order to reach comparative conclusions.

TRANSFER PRICING

Producers of complex products such as automobiles, airliners, computers, and major appliances have a choice of either making or buying the individual parts. Automobile companies purchase tires and radios from outside suppliers, but may manufacture their own clutches, brakes, carburetors, fuel pumps, and even steel in vertically integrated divisions or other responsibility centers within the company.

These divisions may sell their products to an outside or intermediate market as well as to other divisions within the same company. If there is an outside market for the product the market price may be used as a factor in determining what price should be charged by the selling division. If there is no outside market or if there is not enough outside activity to determine a market price, then only cost considerations are relevant.

A *transfer price* is the price charged by one responsibility center to another responsibility center in the same company. Both responsibility centers must be profit or investment centers that are held accountable for both revenues and costs by upper-level management.

For a transfer pricing decision to exist there must be an outside market for selling division's product. If there is no outside intermediate market for the selling a division's product, then the division is not a profit center, but a cost center. The costs transferred from cost centers to profit centers, investment centers, or other cost centers include both direct and indirect costs.

With the existence of an outside market, the selling division has the option of selling to outsiders or to the buyer division in the same company. A transfer price should be set that will not decrease the operating income of the overall company. That transfer price will fall within a range of prices and will depend on factors such as the capacity of the selling division and the presence of alternate suppliers of the product to the buying division.

Relevant Costs

Costs that are relevant in transfer price decisions are those production, marketing, or administrative costs and expenses that will increase as units of production increase. Fixed production costs and fixed expenses are not relevant unless they are specifically designated to be incremental. A transfer price is usually included in one of four categories.

Variable Costs

Variable costs of the selling division include the variable production, marketing, and administrative costs. Variable costs may be actual or standard costs. They should exclude any savings that may occur by selling to the in-house division. In transfer pricing problems, variable costs are equivalent to incremental costs. The use of variable costs as a transfer price is appropriate under certain circumstances. The incorrect use of a transfer price will result in understated operating income to the selling division and overstated operating income to the buying division.

However, the variable costs of the selling division should be used as the transfer price in situations in which their use will result in an increase the operating income of the overall company. Where there is an outside market for the product, and the selling division has idle capacity, the variable costs will normally be the appropriate transfer price.

Full Costs

Full costs include all production, marketing, and administrative costs. The use of standard costs would be preferable to actual cost in order to avoid passing on inefficiencies of the selling division. If the buying division purchases a large proportion of the selling division's output, the selling division may show heavy losses if a transfer price equal to full cost plus a markup is not charged.

Market Price

The market price is the price the buying division must pay for the product in the outside market. The market price is frequently the upper limit in the transfer price range. The buying division will not pay more for the products of its own company's selling division than the market price. The market price of the buying division may be different from that of the selling division. A competitive supplier may charge less to the buying division than the selling division can charge in its markets. However, in a freely competitive market situation there is only one market price.

Negotiated Price

The negotiated price is a price within the minimum and maximum limits in the transfer price range. The minimum is the variable costs (less any adjustments) of the selling division and the maximum is the intermediate market price. The overall company neither gains nor loses income if the negotiated price is within this range, so it behooves top management to allow the division managers to negotiate a fair transfer price.

A negotiated price is appropriate when there is no intermediate market price to serve as a transfer price. It also serves to balance the operating incomes of the two bargaining divisions, even when there is a market price.

THE TRANSFER PRICE FORMULA

A general formula for transfer pricing is

Transfer Price = Variable Costs + Lost Contribution Margin

The variable costs are those of the selling division less any savings in selling to an intracompany division. The contribution margin lost is the difference between the selling division's market price and its variable costs in selling to outside customers. The formula results in the ***minimum*** transfer price, but not the only satisfactory price. A higher price may be negotiated, which, up to a limit, will have no negative effect on total profits.

The ***transfer price range*** is the price range within which two divisions of the same company can exchange goods or services without gain or loss to the overall company.

The ***minimum*** price in the transfer price range is the variable costs and expenses of the selling division. The ***maximum*** price is the market price that the buying division would pay to an outside supplier. The selling division cannot charge less than its variable costs and the buying company will not pay more than the market price.

Transfers at Market Price

Intracompany transfers may take place at the market price in accordance with company policy. A market price policy will work well if certain conditions are present. One of the conditions is a well-defined intermediate market. A well-defined intermediate market is a competitive outside market in which there is one market price for the product. Consider the following situation:

BEVINS COMPANY

Restaurant Division	Transfer Price	Sausage Division
Buys from Enrich Sausage Company @ $2.00/lb	= $2.00	Sells to Bill Naps @ $2.00/lb Variable costs = $1.50/lb

Bevins Company has two segments, a Restaurant Division and a Sausage Division. The Sausage Division sells to another restaurant chain at $2.00 per lb. Company policy is that (1) the Sausage Division must supply the needs of the Restaurant Division if the Restaurant Division is willing to pay the competitive market price and (2) the Restaurant Division must buy from the Sausage Division as long as it meets the market price.

Both segments should be free, however, to seek outside customers or suppliers where the results are an increase in the operating profits of the overall company. In the situation above, with a market price of $2.00 per lb it is assured that the Sausage Division has outside customers at $2.00 per lb. The transfer price range is between $1.50 and $2.00, the minimum is the variable costs of the Sausage Division and the maximum is the market price. Any price within this range would be satisfactory from the viewpoint of the overall company. But the market price would more realistically reflect the situation as it pertains to both divisions.

Full Capacity versus Idle Capacity

The selling division will forfeit its contribution margin when the division is at full capacity. At *full capacity* the selling division can only supply the buying division's needs by giving up sales to the outside. With *idle capacity* the selling division can supply the needs of the buying division without losing any contribution margin. At full capacity the transfer price (TP) formula is

TP = Variable costs + Lost contribution margin

(Any savings in selling within the same company are subtracted from the variable costs).

At idle capacity the transfer price formula is

TP = Variable cost (less any savings in selling within the same company)

At idle capacity the selling division will not forfeit any contribution margin. The minimum transfer price represents the selling division's variable costs less any reduction in selling or any other variable costs saved by selling within the company.

Comprehensive Example

Assume that Division S is the selling division and Division B is the buying division. Marmon Corporation produces automobiles; Division S produces batteries, and Division B assembles the Marmon Pacer. An outside supplier of batteries will sell a competitive battery to Division B for $30. Division S has variable costs of $28 per battery, but will save $1 by selling to Division B instead of outsiders.

Three situations are described. The first situation is where the selling division is at full capacity. The buying division requests that Division S sell them 5,000 units, which must be withdrawn from the outside market. The second situation is where Division S has idle capacity, that is, there is no outside market for the 5,000 units. In the third situation, Division B requests 8,000 units from Division S, 5,000 of which are at full capacity and 3,000 of which are at idle capacity.

	Situation 1	Situation 2	Situation 3
Capacity in units	25,000	25,000	25,000
Sales to outside markets	25,000	20,000	20,000
Units requested by Division B	5,000	5,000	8,000
Division S selling price	$35	$35	$35
Division S variable costs	$28	$28	$28
Savings in variable costs by selling intracompany	$1	$1	$1
Supplier's price to Division B	$30	$30	$30

Situation 1--Full Capacity

Assume that Division S has a capacity to produce 25,000 batteries a year without increasing its fixed costs. It now sells 25,000 batteries to the retail auto supply market for $35, which is the competitive market price. Division B requests that Division S provide 5,000 batteries at a transfer price of $30. Should Division S sell 5,000 batteries to Division B at $30 each?

MARMON COMPANY

Division B		Division S
Can buy from outside supplier @ $30	Transfer Price = $ 34	Capacity = 25,000 Can sell to outside dealers @ $35 Variable costs = $ 28 Saves $1 in variable costs by selling to Division B

Solution: The transfer price formula is

TP = Variable costs + Lost contribution margin

The contribution margin lost is the selling price to the outside market, $35, minus the variable costs of the selling division, $28, which is $7 per battery. The variable costs are $28 less $1 if sold within the company.

TP = $28 - $1 + $7 = $34

Division S should not sell the batteries to Division B for less than $34, which is the minimum transfer price. Acceptance by Division S at a lower price will result in a loss to the Marmon Company. The savings to the overall company by not selling to Division B is ($34 - $30) times 5,000 units, or $20,000.

Situation 2--Idle Capacity

In situation 2 Division S is able to sell 5,000 units to Division B without sacrificing the contribution margin from outside sales. The transfer price is

TP = $28 - $1 = $27

The transfer price range is from $27, the variable costs of Division S less the $1 savings from selling within the same company to $30, which is the price Division B must pay to the outside supplier.

Any price negotiated between this range by the two divisions will not reduce the overall company operating profit. The refusal of Division S to sell to

Division B or by Division B to buy from Division S within the range, however, will result in a loss to the overall company. The loss is $15,000, ($30 - $27) × 5,000 units = $15,000.

Situation 3

In situation 3, Division B requires 8,000 units, 5,000 of which Division S can supply within its idle capacity, but 3,000 of which must be withdrawn from the outside market. The transfer price of the 8,000 units is calculated as shown.

5,000	× $27	=	$135,000
3,000	× $34	=	102,000
8,000			$237,000

$$\text{Transfer price} = \frac{\$237{,}000}{8{,}000} = \$29.63$$

The transfer price is below $30, the competitive supplier's price, so that all 8,000 units could be traded by the divisions at the transfer price of $29.63 per unit. The minimum loss to the overall company, however, is achieved by splitting the order, with Division S supplying the 5,000 units at a transfer price between $27 and $30, and the outside company supplying the 3,000 units at $30 per unit.

Bibliography

"Activity Based Costing Glossary: Concepts and/or Definitions." *Management Accounting,* August 1990.

Bartley, J. W. and R. L. Jenson. "Applying ABC to Product Design." *Corporate Controller*, September/October 1991.

Benke, Ralph. "Teaching Activity-Based Costing." *Management Accounting*, August 1992.

Brimson, James. *Activity Accounting* New York, John Wiley & Sons, Inc., 1992.

Campi, John P. "It's Not as Easy as ABC." *Journal of Cost Management*, Summer 1992.

Chaffman, Beth M., and John Talbott. "Activity-Based Costing in a Service Organization." *CMA Magazine (Canada)*, December 1990/January 1991.

Cokins, Gary, et. al. *An ABC Manager's Primer*. Montvale, N. J., Institute of Management Accountants, 1993.

Cooper, Robin. "A Structured Approach to Implementing ABC." Accountancy, June 1991.

Cooper, Robin. "Five Steps to ABC System Design (Activity Based Costing)." *Accountancy*, November 1990.

Cooper, Robin. "ABC: A Need, Not an Option." *Accountancy*, September 1990.

Cooper, Robin, and R. Kaplan. "Activity-Based Systems: Measuring the Costs of Resource Usage." *Accounting Horizons*, September 1992.

Cooper, Robin, and R. Kaplan. "Measure Costs Right: Make the Right Decision (Activity-Based Costing)." *The CPA Journal*, Feb. 1990.

Cooper, Robin, et al. *Implementing Activity-Based Cost Management: Moving from Analysis to Action* Montvale, N. J., Institute of Management Accountants, 1992.

Drury, Colin. "Product Costing in the 1990's." *Accountancy (UK)*, May 1990.

Ferrara, William. "The New Cost\Management Accounting: More Questions Than Answers." *Management Accounting*, October 1990.

Gilligan, Brian P. "Traditional Cost Accounting Needs Some Adjustments . . . As Easy As ABC." *Industrial Engineering*, April 1990.

Heskett, J. L., Ivie, R. M., and Glaskowsky, N. A., Jr. *Business Logistics Management of Physical Supply and Distribution* New York: The Ronald Press Company, 1964.

Johnson, H. Thomas. "It's Time to Stop Overselling Activity-Based Concepts." *Management Accounting*, September 1992.

Johnson, H. T., and R. Kaplan. "The Rise and Fall of Management Accounting." *Management Accounting*, January 1987.

Kaplan, Robert S. "The Four-Step Model of Cost Systems Design." *Management Accounting*, February 1990.

Koehler, Robert W. "Triple-Threat Strategy." *Management Accounting*, October 1991.

Lee, John Y. "Activity-Based Costing at CAL Electronic Circuits." *Management Accounting*, October 1990.

Lewis, Ronald J. *Activity-Based Costing for Marketing and Manufacturing.* Westport, Conn., Quorum Books, Greenwood Publishing Group, Inc., 1993.

Lewis, Ronald J. "Activity-Based Costing for Marketing." *Management Accounting*, November 1991.

Lewis, Ronald J. "Strengthening Control of Physical Distribuion Costs." *Management Services (AICPA)*, January/February 1968.

Most, K., and R. Lewis. *Cost Accounting* Columbus, Ohio, Grid (Wiley) Publishing, 1982.

Noreen, Eric. "Conditions Under Which Activity-Based Cost Systems Provide Relevant Costs." *Journal of Management Accounting Research*, Fall 1991.

O'Guin, Michael. "Focus the Factory with Activity-Based Costing" *Management Accounting*, February 1990.

Ostrenga, Michael R. "Activities: The Focal Point of Total Cost Management." *Management Accounting*, February 1990.

Raffish, Norm. "How Much Does That Product Really Cost?" *Management Accounting*, March 1991.

Roth, Harold P., and A. Faye Borthick. "Are You Distorting Costs by Violating ABC Assumptions?" *Management Accounting*, November 1991.

Roth, Harold P. and Linda T. Sims. "Costing for Warehousing and Distribution." *Management Accounting*, August 1991.

Sharman, Paul. "A Practical Look at Activity-Based Costing." *CMA Magazine (Canada)*, February 1990.

Sharp, Douglas and Linda Christensen. "A New View of Activity-Based Costing." *Management Accounting*, September 1991.

Turney, Peter. "Activity-Based Management." *Management Accounting*, January 1992.

Tyson, Thomas. "Let Bar Coding Capture Indirect Costs for Activity-Based Costing." *Financial & Accounting Systems*, Fall 1991.

Warner, Paul D. "Activity-Based Costing (Easy ABC)." *The CPA Journal*, March 1992.

Index

About the Author

RONALD J. LEWIS, Professor Emeritus of Accounting at Central Michigan University, has extensive experience in industry and academia and as an international lecturer. Among his various publications are *Activity-Based Costing for Marketing and Manufacturing* (Quorum, 1993), his latest award-winning article "Activity-Based Accounting for Marketing" in *Management Accounting*, and a novel *Murder in Mackinac* (1995).

ISBN 0-89930-965-8

90000>

EAN

9 780899 309651

HARDCOVER BAR CODE